Foreign Bodies

Foreign Bodies

GENDER, LANGUAGE, AND CULTURE
IN FRENCH ORIENTALISM

MADELEINE DOBIE

STANFORD UNIVERSITY PRESS

STANFORD, CALIFORNIA

2001

Published with the support of Tulane University

Stanford University Press
Stanford, California
© 2001 by the Board of Trustees of the
Leland Stanford Junior University

Printed in the United States of America
On acid-free, archival-quality paper

Library of Congress Cataloging-in-Publication Data
Dobie, Madeleine.
    Foreign bodies : gender, language, and culture in French
orientalism / Madeleine Dobie.
        p.   cm.
Includes bibliographical references and index.
ISBN 0-8047-4104-2 (alk. paper)
        1. French literature—Oriental influences.   2. Orient—In
literature.   I. Title.
PQ143.O75 D63   2002
840.9'325—dc21   2001041079

Original Printing 2001

Last figure below indicates year of this printing:
10   09   08   07   06   05   04   03   02   01

Designed by Janet Wood
Typeset by BookMatters in 11/14 Adobe Garamond

For Wayne

Contents

List of Illustrations

Preface

This book builds on an existing critical foundation, the reflection on the relationship between literary representations of the Orient and European colonial history first examined in depth in 1978 in Edward Said's seminal study, *Orientalism*. It focuses on a single but essential component of this relationship: the figure of the "Oriental woman" and the prevalence, in Orientalist representation, of gendered metaphors of race and culture. The chapters that follow ask how the interplay between race and gender in this corpus of texts participated in France's domestic cultural history, and in its changing colonial landscape, over the period stretching from the early eighteenth century to the latter part of the nineteenth. A principal goal of this analysis is to provide a genealogy of contemporary Western, and particularly French, attitudes to Islamic culture, in which issues of sexuality and gender relations continue to occupy a privileged place. This book maintains, in fact, that the character of these Western attitudes, along with Islamic responses to them, can only properly be understood within an historical perspective.

In its first form, as a doctoral dissertation, this project sought to nuance Said's account of the Orientalist literature by demonstrating the textual complexity of this corpus and by extension its political heterogeneity. The need for this kind of revision has largely been obviated by the appearance, in the 1990s, of several studies that offer more complex accounts of Orientalism and its political ramifications. However, as I read these new studies, I came to the conclusion that in certain respects, the debate over the political status of Orientalist scholarship, art, and literature has not progressed significantly beyond the preliminary recognition that Orientalism is a facet of Western colonial power. That is to say, critical reflection on the French encounter with alterity has remained excessively abstract, attuned to theoretical questions but not to the specific ways in which Orientalist art and literature reflect, or fail to reflect, the changing circumstances of French colonial history.

Although critics writing in the wake of Edward Said consistently acknowledge the need to historicize, this book proposes that even the most recent studies of French Orientalism fail to read cultural representations against the specific contexts, domestic and colonial, in which they came into existence. In certain cases, this omission has produced significant distortions. For example, the notorious fascination of eighteenth-century France with things Oriental has typically been read as a rehearsal of the nation's expansion into the Orient at the end of the century. What such a reading does not take into account, however, is the relationship between Orientalist representation and France's *existing* colonies in the Atlantic world and Indian Ocean. I argue that we can trace in political and fictional accounts of the Orient in this period a marked displacement away from the old colonies and the slave trade that sustained them, toward the Oriental world. In the very different context of nineteenth-century French Orientalism, this book suggests that the failure to historicize has resulted in an anachronistic assimilation of colonial politics to other political ideologies, such that it is presumed, for example, that the left-wing attitudes of a writer such as Gérard de Nerval toward a number of domestic issues led him to criticize French colonial aspirations, whereas in reality, in the 1830s and 1840s, colonial expansion was primarily a project of the left-wing opposition, and one that Nerval, among other oppositional writers, fundamentally supported.

This book also tries to historicize in a second sense: by addressing the place of thinking on the Orient and the colonies within France's domestic history. For example, it considers connections between the almost obsessive representation of the enclosure of the Oriental harem in eighteenth-century France and the emergence of a gendered polarization of public and private spheres of life. Histories of colonialism and literary scholarship on Orientalist literature have tended to concentrate on Europe's impact on its "others" without engaging in substantial reflection on the reciprocal impact of the colonies on European culture. By contrast, I argue the necessity, at once historical and political, of working with a multidirectional model of influence that challenges the long-standing opposition between domestic and global, metropolitan and colonial. This study takes a small step in this direction by examining the profound penetration of words and fashions borrowed from the Orient, and of raw materials imported from the colonies, into the terrain of French intellectual and material culture.

This project began several years ago as a doctoral dissertation; I am deeply grateful to Peter Brooks for getting it off the ground and for patiently guiding it through its first awkward stages. I am indebted also to my readers at Yale University, Chris Miller, Charles Porter, and Elena Russo, for challenging observations that mapped out ways in which this study could grow, and to Kevin Newmark, whose example as a teacher and writer was an inspiration.

My views on the correlation between representations of the Oriental harem and the domestic politics of gender coalesced during a 1996 National Endowment for the Humanities summer seminar devoted to the topic of "Women's Place in Eighteenth-Century France." I would like to express my gratitude to the NEH for sponsoring this seminar, and to Carol Blum and Madelyn Gutwirth for both their exemplary leadership of it and their continuing encouragement and support.

Tulane University's provision of a sabbatical leave greatly accelerated the completion of this book. I was fortunate to spend much of this leave in the idyllic setting of the Camargo Foundation in Cassis, France, where numerous drafts were written. I am grateful to Camargo's Board of Trustees for providing me with a residential fellowship and to director Michael Pretina for his hospitality and support. The fellows in residence in spring 1998 became valuable interlocutors; Tip Ragan and Dennis McInnerney in particular listened patiently to my ideas and contributed their own in return.

In its final form, this book owes much to the insightful observations and suggestions of colleagues and friends who read part or all of the manuscript. For generously taking time to do so, I offer my sincerest thanks to Carol Blum, Hope Glidden, Dena Goodman, Felicia McCarren, Vaheed Ramazani, Rebecca Saunders, Dick Terdiman, Georges Van den Abbeele, and to an anonymous reader for Stanford University Press. My greatest debt in this regard is to Wayne Klein, harshest critic and strongest advocate.

At Tulane University, it has been my privilege to share my ideas with many stimulating students; the energetic engagement of Katherine Gracki, Michele Heintz, Scott Powers, and Karen Reichard, in particular, has always made my research feel worthwhile. To my colleague Connie Balides I owe thanks for warm intellectual companionship—and for seeing *The Mummy* with me.

E.I.E.D. and M.R.K., my mothers, passed away before this project came to fruition, but in their different ways, both provided inspiration and support for my writing; their spirit lives on this book.

Finally, I wish to express gratitude to Helen Tartar at Stanford University Press for supporting this project and for making its publication possible, and to the editorial staff at SUP for their able assistance.

Foreign Bodies

Introduction

> Neither you nor I nor anyone, no ancient and no modern can know
> Oriental woman for the reason that it is impossible to visit her.
>
> GUSTAVE FLAUBERT Letter to C. A. Sainte-Beuve, 1862

> Literature, it seems to me, is the discourse most preoccupied with
> the unknown, but not in the sense in which such a statement is usually
> understood. The "unknown" is not what lies beyond the limits of
> knowledge.
>
> BARBARA JOHNSON *The Critical Difference*

By 1862, when Gustave Flaubert wrote the letter to Sainte-Beuve that is
cited above, the expression "Oriental woman" held a particular meaning for
French readers. Like the word "Orient" itself, it did not simply designate a
concrete social or geographic reality—women from North Africa or the
Middle East—but rather triggered a series of associations involving harems
and veils, polygamy, eunuchs and political despotism, and perhaps above all,
desire intensified by the obstacles placed in its way. These connotations
began to coalesce in the travel literature of the late 1600s, and by the early
nineteenth century, the expression "la femme orientale" had become
idiomatic, a figure of speech denoting a determinate set of characteristics, a
mystery, an enigma, a promise. Judged from a more politicized perspective,
it was an all-encompassing cultural label that emphasized only certain features of Oriental life while erasing numerous differences between women of
different Eastern nations, cultures, and religions.

Although the expression "Oriental woman" no longer trips off the tongue,
more contemporary labels such as "Third World woman" or "Middle Eastern

woman," widely used in contemporary sociology and political theory, have not only absorbed many of its cultural connotations but also retained its problematic generality.[1] Given this genealogy, and the continuing polarization of relations between East and West, Islam and Christianity, I have felt it worthwhile to look back to the literary and visual culture of the eighteenth and nineteenth centuries to perform a genealogy of this figure in which issues of race and gender, politics and sexuality, are intertwined. What this genealogy uncovers is not simply the central role that the idea of the "Oriental woman" has played in defining France's relation to the Maghreb, Egypt, and the Levant, but also the important place that ideas about gender relations in the Orient have occupied in the history of domestic cultural politics.

It is, I have found, possible to draw a clear analogy between these two vectors because Western representations have not only "feminized" the Orient but also "Orientalized" the feminine; that is to say, the foreignness ascribed to Oriental woman can be read as a displaced representation of all of the forms of "otherness" ascribed to women in Western culture—criminality, perversion, homosexuality, and neurosis, to cite but a few.[2] In this regard, Orientalist representation constitutes an exemplary illustration of the fact that race and gender are, in Anne McClintock's terms, "articulated categories"—modalities of difference that are constructed in relation to each other and that therefore need to be examined together as overlapping dimensions of an integrated cultural perspective.[3]

The necessity of this kind of perspective is political and wholly current. With remarkable uniformity, cultures have attempted to control the experience of difference by subsuming it under a monolithic category of "the Other." However diverse the field of cultural difference may be—and certainly differences in race, class, gender, sexual orientation, or religious affiliation have been experienced in a wide variety of ways by members of the dominant cultural group and by members of the oppressed group or cultural minority—historical investigation testifies to the existence of a seemingly universal drive to reduce all differences to the congealed sameness of "the Other." One of the principal means by which this reduction or containment of difference takes place is precisely the articulation of categories of difference, the process by which different modes of difference are made to interpenetrate and define each other.

Thus, in the case of Oriental woman, race and gender operate as categories of difference whose apparent parallelism neatly confirms the existence of an alterity or foreignness that lies beyond the bounds of identity. The product of this kind of erasure of the specificity of "the Other" has predominantly been identity politics and particularism: the current wave of anti-Western sentiment traversing the Islamic world, for example, is clearly in some measure a reaction to the reductive "othering" of Moslems that has taken place in Europe and North America over the last two centuries. In retracing this process of social abstraction, I want to propose that rather than simply heralding the cries of "death to America" currently resonating in the Sudan or Iraq as confirmation of the intrinsic religious fanaticism of Islamic culture—as our foreign policy institutions and the mainstream media generally invite us to do—it behooves us to consider the roots of these attitudes of resentment and condemnation that lie in the dominant Western representations of Islam.

Representations of Oriental women are extraordinarily abundant in the art and literature of the eighteenth and nineteenth centuries. Indeed, they constitute a key dimension of what Edward Said has described as the "citational" repertory of Orientalism: the practice of intertextual borrowing and repetition from which Western representations of the Orient derive their authority (Said, *Orientalism*, 20). They occur in genres as varied as travel narratives, ethnography and the novel, lyric poetry and opera-ballet, painting, postcards, and film, and across epistemologies and aesthetic movements as diverse as empiricism, romanticism and symbolism, the neoclassical realism of Jean-Dominique Ingres and Jean-Léon Gérôme, and the formalisms of Stéphane Mallarmé and Henri Matisse. Although in the wake of the publication of Said's seminal study *Orientalism*, a number of critics have turned their attention to the politics of the Orientalist tradition,[4] none has examined the figure of the Oriental woman as a central category of Orientalist representation or asked why over the last three centuries Oriental sexuality has occupied such an important place in the European imaginary.[5]

This book attempts to fill this void by situating representations of the Oriental woman within the history of European colonialism; by examining the centrality of the figure of Oriental woman to the consolidation of aesthetic movements, notably artistic and literary modernism; and by exploring the array of functions it has fulfilled in the field of domestic cultural politics. It has for some time been acknowledged that "the Orient" has functioned in European thought as, in Lisa Lowe's terms, a "critical terrain," a dense representational field on which political ideologies, aesthetic ideals, and critical models have been distilled and bodied forth. The time is now ripe to take a closer look at this appropriation of the Orient and to explore the specific, historically changing agendas—both domestic and global—that Orientalist representation has fulfilled.

It seems to me that although the studies of Orientalist literature published in the wake of *Orientalism* invariably promise to deliver a historical interpretation of this cultural production, they just as consistently fail to follow through, privileging the theorization of the literary construction of alterity over the analysis of the historical evolution of French colonial policy and the changing interplay between this policy and the literary sphere. This book, by contrast, explores ways in which the changing realities of French colonialism are paralleled by shifts in the mode of literary representation. It also attempts to do something further, going beyond the mere elucidation of the relationship between Orientalist literature and colonial ideology by asking about the range of functions that representations of Oriental others have fulfilled within the domestic social and political economy. In my view, this shift in emphasis constitutes an important first step toward dismantling the opposition between metropole and colony, center and margin, that has underpinned most thinking on colonialism, whether by historians or by literary scholars.

The chapters that follow cover the period roughly from the beginning of the eighteenth century to the middle of the nineteenth. It is my view that insofar as European representations of the Orient are concerned, this time frame manifests a strong internal coherence. This is to say, unlike other recent theorists, I do not approach French Orientalism before the last quarter of the nineteenth century as a properly "colonial" discourse. This is not because I think that literary representations of the Orient have no relation to or affinity with colonial history—they clearly do—but because I want to argue that to conflate the two is to overlook and even to mask a subtle process of displacement by which, for over two centuries, French literature managed to distance itself from the central concerns of colonialism. If we focus closely on historical context, rather than applying to the Orientalist corpus a set of transhistorical theoretical postulates, we observe that the cultural sphere has consistently aestheticized colonial experience, devoting its energy and attention to relatively peripheral matters, while saying almost nothing about the nuts and bolts process of colonial expansion. The ubiquitous figure of the Oriental woman exemplifies this tendency because it embodies a core of idealized longing for an "other," even when in strictly material terms this "other" was already conquered and possessed.

The pattern of aestheticization and displacement that I will describe also had its own history. During the eighteenth century, the "sublimation" of the colonial to which I am alluding involved the displacement of French *interests* in the New World onto a veritable *fascination* with things Oriental; in the nineteenth century, after incursions into the Egypt and Algeria in 1798 and 1830, when Orientalist representation and colonial politics became more closely intertwined, it involved the consecration of an idea of the "timeless" Orient that obscured changes occurring in the region as a result of the European presence. All of this began to change when, as a preliminary to the "Scramble for Africa," the acute phase of colonial expansion that began around 1870, a coherent national policy of colonial expansion was elaborated for the first time in France. In this period of overt expansionism, the colonies enjoyed unprecedented prominence in the national consciousness, a heightened level of awareness that in the literary sphere generated representations of the Orient that departed from the patterns of displacement and aestheticization characteristic of the earlier period.

Perhaps in reaction to this political shift, in the latter part of the nineteenth century, Orientalist representation also began to change in a different, indeed almost diametrically opposed, fashion. Beginning around midcentury, a number of avant-garde artists, including most prominently Théophile Gautier, Gustave Flaubert, Stéphane Mallarmé, Gustave Moreau, Oscar Wilde, and Henri Matisse, created images of Oriental women that abandoned the ethnographic concerns of earlier representations. Anecdote has it, for example, that when Matisse was told that his images of odalisques did not really resemble women, he replied that they were not women, but paintings. His response (a paraphrase of Mallarmé's famous statement that a dancer is not a woman who dances because she is not a woman, but a metaphor resuming the elementary aspects of form, and because she doesn't dance, but rather writes with her body; "Ballets," 304) illustrates the fact that for many avant-garde artists, including Mallarmé and Matisse, the Oriental woman was such a common figure of artistic representation that it no longer referred to anything beyond art itself and could therefore be marshaled to represent representation: Matisse himself used the odalisque as a framework for the valorization of color and form.

The final chapter of this book traces the beginnings of this shift to a modernist aesthetic in Orientalism in the work of Théophile Gautier. I do not, however, follow its evolution through the late nineteenth and early twentieth centuries, largely because this corpus of representations seems to me to exhibit a distinct formal paradigm—one that does not manifest the constant shifting between aestheticism and ethnography, or between Oriental woman as a literary figure and as an empirical referent, that characterizes literature of the earlier period.

FOREIGN BODIES

In the letter cited in the epigraph, Flaubert responds to some rather pedantic historical corrections that his friend, the writer and literary critic Charles-Augustin Sainte-Beuve, had proposed to his novel *Salammbô* (1863) with the sweeping assertion that Oriental woman can never truly be known because, hidden beneath a veil or enclosed within the walls of a harem, she cannot be visited. He emphatically declares that "neither you nor I, no ancient and no modern can know Oriental woman": Oriental woman is, by definition, inaccessible and unknowable (Flaubert, *Correspondence*, 3:277). Yet despite this categorical assertion, we know from Flaubert's travel notes, published posthumously in 1910, that during his voyage to the Orient in 1849–1851, the writer frequented several Egyptian *almées* (dancers who sometimes doubled as prostitutes), including the now famous Kuchiouk Hânem.[6] This discrepancy between rhetoric and reality suggests that in the mind of Flaubert and his reader the expression "la femme orientale" did not simply denote a woman from Egypt or the Maghreb whose sexual services might, on occasion, be bought and enjoyed, but that it also functioned as a metaphor for an unknown and unknowable other.

But if we are tempted to ascribe to this sense of transcendent otherness the ideological neutrality of a philosophical ideal, a letter that Flaubert wrote in March 1853 to his lover, the writer Louise Colet, clearly demonstrates that political forces were also at work in this construction of absolute alterity (*Correspondance*, 2:279–89). Colet had just read Flaubert's travel notes and reacted strongly to his account of his visits to Kuchiouk Hânem, expressing jealousy but also bemoaning the degrading depiction he gives of her rival. In response, Flaubert attempts to assuage her jealousy by claiming that the courtesan felt nothing, either emotionally or (because of her circumcision) physically; indeed, he goes so far as to state that "Oriental woman is a machine, nothing more": the interests of Oriental women are restricted to going to the baths, smoking, and drinking coffee. Seemingly inspired by this idea, he goes on to observe that what makes this woman poetic is the fact that she is "thoroughly natural" ("elle rentre absolument dans la nature"): she is like the Oriental dancer whose eyes express tranquillity and emptiness because they are unmoved by passion.

What these remarks show is that if the Oriental woman has functioned in European art and literature as a figure for radical alterity, it is in large part because women of the Orient are deemed to exist in a mechanical state of self-absorption, experiencing no desire for anything beyond themselves. Implied in the ascription of absolute alterity is thus the secondary assumption that male, European identity constitutes the unique locus of desire, subjectivity, and knowledge. Yet as we will see, in the fragile economy of Orientalist writing, *knowledge of "the other,"* which participates in the erasure of the other's subjectivity and in the corresponding assertion of European superiority, is in many instances counterbalanced by a discovery of *the other in knowledge.*[7]

In delineating what he describes as the "heterological" tradition in European thought, Michel de Certeau observes that the ethnographic production of "the other" has historically been a means of constructing a discourse authorized by "the other"; that is to say, there is typically a circularity between the social construction of categories of alterity and the claim that discourse is authorized by something beyond itself, an inaccessible exterior or *hors texte* (*Heterologies*, 68). De Certeau is certainly right to assert that ethnographic discourse is saturated with implied assertions of textual authority that in many instances involve claims to have witnessed or experienced something extraordinary, something beyond the life experience of the reader. However, it is also possible to discern in early European ethnography a contrasting dynamic, a process by which the representation of others generates a sense of otherness *within* knowledge that undermines rather than authorizes formulations of sameness and difference.

As Barbara Johnson states in the epigraph to this Introduction, literature has always been preoccupied with the "unknown"—for instance, with the Orient as an unknown and enticing ideal. Yet as a self-conscious mode of representation its primary object has been the unknown that is "in" rather than "beyond" knowledge. For Johnson, as for a whole school of deconstructive readers, this "unknown" corresponds to the fact that knowledge is constructed in language, and language can never be thoroughly grasped or controlled by the subject who speaks or writes: as subjects of language, we cannot simply step outside of the semantic order and enjoy a commanding view of the infinite and ungraspable play of difference that makes meaning possible.

The idea that language, the very medium in which knowledge is constituted, might itself constitute an "unknown" is an important one for this study, for when I began to examine the feminine figures of Orientalist texts, I found that they are often interwoven with self-reflexive representations of language, and more specifically, with representations of language as something "foreign," an alien and resistant code. It would seem in fact that the Western meditation on the absolute alterity of Oriental woman—"other" in terms of both gender and race—has had the unintended effect of exposing alterity closer to home. This book is in part about the status of Oriental women as "veiled figures" of linguistic alterity,[8] or to put this another way, about the recurrent linkage between the figure of the Oriental woman and the textual "cognizance" that language is not simply the transparent medium of ideology, experience, and identity.

To designate this potentially disruptive core of alterity within the economy of knowledge and its categorization of identity and difference, the presence of "the other" *within* as well as *between* genders and cultures, I use the metaphor of the "foreign body," a term primarily deployed in biomedical discourse to denote the presence of a foreign entity, usually a virus or bacterium, within the confines of the body. But my use of this term is in fact more than merely metaphorical, for in this study I examine the perceived alterity of quite literal foreign bodies—the mysterious solar tattoos that adorn the body of the Javanese slave of Gérard de Nerval's *Voyage en Orient* (*Voyage to the Orient*; 1851), the "imperceptibly African" lips of Gautier's Egyptian heroines, the loquacious genitals of Denis Diderot's female protagonists—and because I show that perceptions of foreignness, and anxiety about its destabilizing impact on the self, are frequently conveyed through medical metaphors of contagion and disease with which the trope of the foreign body is aligned.[9]

Yet at this juncture I need to introduce an important caveat by emphasizing that the fact that representations of Oriental women frequently disclose the existence of radical uncertainty within the order of knowledge, and therefore within hierarchical categories of social and racial identity, does not give immediate grounds for embracing their political message. The relationship between the political agenda of a text and its epistemological instability is rather a complex one that requires slow and nuanced consideration. To begin to broach this issue, I think it will be helpful to compare my reading of the way that ethnography takes "cognizance" of its own linguistic frailty with a similar, although in several important respects divergent, perspective—the position that Roland Barthes outlines in *L'Empire des signes* (*The Empire of Signs*; 1970).

In his often-cited meditation on Japanese culture, Barthes observes that Orientalist representation has consistently erased the foreignness of the Orient by translating it into the conceptual framework of European culture. In his own writing, he struggles against the current of this history, reversing the flow of knowledge such that the unmediated foreignness of Japan floods European culture and provokes an interrogation of European cultural norms. For Barthes, the ultimate promise of this contact with unmediated otherness is to expose these cultural limits in such a way that the Western sense of what is real is undone, the subject's "topology" is displaced, and "everything occidental in us totters" (*Empire*, 6).

Like Barthes, I believe that the most far-reaching questioning of cultural identity demands recognition of the contingency of the language in which societies and selves are constructed. However, my perspective differs from his in two important ways. Although I agree that the Orientalist tradition must be viewed as the history of a missed opportunity, a failure to ponder the nature and effects of difference, I would nonetheless argue that there have been moments in this history when the signifying system of European culture has been shaken by its contact with alterity. In the critical moment of the Enlightenment, for example, awareness of other cultural norms clearly stimulated the contestation of political institutions and social practices. It is, however, equally apparent that in the case of the Enlightenment, this self-reflexive sense of alterity was rapidly reabsorbed into the postulates of Western universalism. I will therefore argue—again, contra Barthes—that even the most profound disturbances of our signifying system are inevitably reabsorbed into the structures of meaning and understanding—that we can never simply transcend these structures and enter a utopian space of pure difference.

What I will identify in the European representation of the Orient is therefore a constant *fluctuation* between the fleeting and destabilizing manifestation of the unknown within knowledge and the inexorable reconfiguration of categories of knowledge and power. In this regard, my analysis differs not only from Barthes's, but also from most previous studies of Orientalist literature. By this I mean that the debate over the political stakes of Orientalist representation has progressed through the kind of pendulum swings between politicized criticism and close textual reading that have characterized other debates over the cultural politics of literature. I would like to call a halt to this back-and-forth debate, at least insofar as Orientalism is concerned, by arguing that it is important to acknowledge *both* the geopolitical power encoded in Orientalist representation *and* the ways in which specific texts and individual writers offer resistance to this power.

The play of forces that characterizes Orientalism operates on two distinct, although interrelated, levels: the broad linguistic–epistemological plane that I have begun to outline, and a more circumscribed historical frame that I now want to delineate. Ethnographic thought, of which Orientalism can be considered a subcategory, came into existence in the early eighteenth century—which is to say, in a historical context of unequal power relations between Europe and the rest of the world. It bears the traces of this history in the sense that it offers spontaneous confirmation of the Western observer's superior ability to travel and to gather information; to the extent that it represents other cultures as "more primitive" or "less advanced"; and, finally, for the reason that the accrual of ethnographic knowledge has often served as a preliminary to conquest and occupation.

Yet despite ethnography's obvious complicity with the accretion of European power, it is nonetheless important to recognize that the geographical discoveries that furnished the basis for the primitivization of other cultures also profoundly shook existing conceptions of the globe, provoking an interrogation of Europe's systems of authority, notably in the domain of religion.[10] When we evaluate ethnography as a mode of inquiry, it is necessary to acknowledge both of these dimensions: the critical force of the representation of alterity in relation to the established order, or ancien régime, and its central contribution to the consolidation of Western dominance. What is at stake in this analysis is not simply the construction of an accurate and fair-minded historical model, but rather the chance to reflect upon the paradoxes of our modernity, to trace the origins of the contradictory relationship between our experience of political liberalism and the ongoing history of racial and sexual prejudice and injustice. We are wont to wring our hands in despair while asking how it can be that racial prejudice and sexual discrimination coexist with the tolerance and political openness of liberal democracy. The roots of this contradiction are, however, elucidated when we look back to the Enlightenment and consider the role that encounters with "others" played both in the genesis of modern liberalism and in the consolidation of exclusionary national, cultural, and racial identities.

Over the past two decades, much has been written on the subject of the cultural and political implications of Orientalist representation, and it is clearly necessary to situate any further reflection on this subject within the parameters of this debate. In the following section, I present the key terms of this discussion and situate my own approach in relation to it. Broadly stated, I propose a new reading of the relationship between Orientalist discourse and colonial history, and I extend to a broader cultural context the arguments for a double movement of reading that I have already made in relation to the figuration of the Oriental woman.

ORIENTALIST DISCOURSE AND COLONIAL HISTORY

The publication in 1978 of Edward Said's *Orientalism* marked a watershed in the scholarly discussion of European representations of the Orient. Whereas previous accounts of Oriental exoticism had isolated cultural productions from the history of European imperialism, *Orientalism* drew an irresistible connection between the two, demonstrating that no rigorous analysis could avoid at least raising the question of the relationship between Orientalism and empire.[11] Transcending disciplinary boundaries among literature, science, and political discourse, Said grouped all representations of the Orient under the rubric of Orientalism, defined as "a distribution of geopolitical awareness into aesthetic, scholarly, economic, sociological, historical and philological texts," and, more bluntly, as "a Western style for dominating" (*Orientalism*, 12, 3). He also maintained that when we consider its pervasiveness and extraordinary internal coherence, Orientalism must be seen to constitute a "discursive formation," as defined by Michel Foucault (*Orientalism*, 3). In other words, Said argues that "the Orient" is not simply something that is "there"—an "inert fact of nature" awaiting discovery by Western scholars—but rather amounts to a cultural construct propagated by a relatively homogeneous and highly organized set of representations whose historical condition of possibility has been the unequal power relationship between East and West (*Orientalism*, 4). Underpinning this analysis is Foucault's contention that knowledge is never pure or objective but always historically determined, allied with prevailing power structures and (as in the case of Orientalism) geopolitical forces.

Said's application of Foucault presents a number of methodological difficulties. One of the most substantive of these is that whereas the Foucauldian notion of a "discursive formation" entails the rejection of the view that power consists of constraint exercised from above over the lower or more vulnerable strata of society in favor of an analysis of how power is disseminated across the whole grid of social relations, how it is embedded in every act of communication,[12] Said approaches Orientalism as a pure expression of the power exercised by one group over another. By extension, whereas Foucault seeks to dismantle the accustomed belief that truth and power are opposed—arguing instead that truth, even when it presents itself as critique or resistance, is always complicit with power—Said holds that Orientalism represents Middle Eastern culture in a recognizably false or distorting way. This discrepancy is not, I think, simply the result of a failure on Said's part to grasp the full implications of Foucault's theorization of power. Rather, it is a reflection of the fact that colonialism constitutes a special and complex case for the reason that Europe's colonies were not merely sites of exploitation but also contexts in which discourses impinging on both colonial and metropolitan life emerged and were disseminated.[13]

Because Said alludes only briefly to Foucault's elaboration of the concept of discourse in *The Archaeology of Knowledge* and *Discipline and Punish*—books that were written six years apart and that represent different phases of Foucault's thinking—it is perhaps not worth dwelling on this methodological disparity. Instead, I want to focus on the two principal ways in which literary theorists have reacted to Said's characterization of Orientalism as a "discursive formation," a web of discourse and power that produces its own object. The first of these responses has been to affirm Said's contention that Orientalism is a discourse—and indeed to extend this argument by demonstrating the capacity of this discourse to absorb all attempts at critique or alternative representation. The second has been to question this seamlessness either by affirming the relative autonomy of art or the independent voice of individual artists, or by identifying structures through which texts themselves subvert their own discursive function. As may already be apparent, my own analysis of Orientalist literature falls loosely into the second category, both because it identifies tremendous gaps in the historical record in Orientalist representation and because it emphasizes the constant and inevitable fluctuation between the hegemonic transmission of power and the eruption of textual resistance.

One of the most common criticisms made of *Orientalism* is that although it focuses on a relatively circumscribed historical period—from the late eighteenth through the early twentieth centuries—it intermittently invokes a broader perspective, postulating that as a European, "One belongs to a part of the earth with a definite history of involvement in the Orient almost since the time of Homer" (Said, *Orientalism*, 11). Terminology lends some support to this claim, since the word "Orient," derived from the Latin *oriri*, to rise, was first employed to designate Asia at the time of the Roman Empire.[14] Yet it is by no means certain that in classical times the word did more than denote a geopolitical reality, or that the trajectory of the sun was at that moment interpreted in terms of a narrative of human progress.[15] When we examine the historical record, it is clearly important to look for historical breaks as well as patterns of continuity, for we otherwise risk transforming an historically limited relationship of inequality into a quasi-ontological affirmation of the differences between two opposing cultures.[16] By avoiding sites of historical complexity—such as, for example, whether Homer can be considered straightforwardly "Western"—*Orientalism* unwittingly reinforces the historiographical "myth of Westernness" whose by-product has been a conviction in the cultural inferiority of the Orient.[17]

The temptation to extend the parameters of Orientalism to encompass the whole of recorded history reflects, I believe, a wider trend within the critical reception of Foucault that has important implications for the present study. Let us consider, for example, the influential model of "discourse/counterdiscourse" developed by Richard Terdiman to describe the oppositional writing practices of the mid-nineteenth-century French avant-garde. Terdiman claims that midcentury intellectuals began to feel that in the new, mediatic age of bourgeois capitalism, social domination was becoming a seamless phenomenon capable of absorbing all would-be subversion and also to recognize that even their own contestatory counterdiscourses were being caught up in the culture's "determined and determining structures of representation and practice" (*Discourse/Counter-Discourse*, 12–13). Terdiman presents Orientalism as one element in the interlocking field of dominant discourse and illustrates the point by showing how Gustave Flaubert's attempt to produce anticonventional travel writing on the Orient ultimately participated in the very Orientalist paradigms he had sought to escape (*Discourse/ Counter-Discourse*, 227–57).

Terdiman's model has been applied to the field of colonial discourse analysis in more sustained fashion in the work of Ali Behdad, who proposes that although nineteenth-century Orientalist literature can in many instances be read as a counterdiscourse that sets out to subvert the official discourse of bourgeois liberal thought, the heterogeneity of the Orientalist corpus is ultimately a sign of its cultural dominance rather than a mark of political vulnerability, an argument that is informed not only by Terdiman's dialectical model but also by Homi K. Bhabha's postulation that discursive hybridity demonstrates not the weakness but the productivity of a system, its capacity to become, as Behdad puts it, "all-inclusive in the epistemological field" (*Belated Travelers*, 13).

This assessment of the social effects of discursive hybridity provides an important challenge to the assumption of many poststructuralist theorists that racism and ethnocentrism are always the product of nostalgia for the purity of a lost origin and, correspondingly, that all manifestations of hybridity and diversity are politically liberating.[18] It is also clear that Behdad is right to suggest that although many Orientalist texts present themselves as subversive counterdiscourses, their assumptions regarding the Orient ineluctably tend to reproduce or fall back into dominant political attitudes.

What is more problematic is the assertion that the whole political apparatus and emergent bourgeois culture of the mid–nineteenth century constituted a single dominant discourse of which Orientalism was a constituent part—and to which the literary avant-garde unanimously opposed itself. Such a claim flattens distinctions and rifts among different political discourses, overlooking fundamental questions such as whether the oppositional attitudes of avant-garde writers *in fact* extended to the arena of colonialism at all. Given that Gérard de Nerval, Gustave Flaubert, and Théophile Gautier, all commonly portrayed as oppositional or avant-garde writers, at one time or another wrote as explicit advocates of colonial expansion,[19] and given that during both the July Monarchy and the Second Empire colonial expansion was principally advocated not by supporters of the ruling regime but by left-wing opposition groups such as the Saint-Simonians, Fourierists, Freemasons, and Bonapartists, this question merits examination. (See Chapters 4 and 5.) The presumption that some form of questioning of colonialism was an integral part of a generalized resistance to the rampant commercialism and political censorship of the industrial age reflects, I think, an ahistorical projection of the agenda of contemporary liberalism—an extension that is made possible by the adoption of an all-inclusive model of discourse and counterdiscourse.

But what is problematic here is not merely the erasure of historical distinctions between different discourses and counterdiscourses, but also the suggestion that all social practices, whether verbal or nonverbal, can be analyzed in terms of discursive unities—a compression that in the case of colonialism does not withstand the test of historical analysis. Let us consider, by way of an example, Behdad's claim in *Belated Travelers* that the heterogeneity of Orientalist discourse ultimately served to perpetuate Western hegemony by problematizing, softening, and stabilizing repressive models of colonial relations. From my perspective, the deficiency of this argument is that episodes of barbarism and repression were not limited to the initial phase of French colonial expansion, but rather were a recurrent feature of colonial practice. Given this history, it is difficult to accept that the hybridity of Orientalism effected a progressive softening of colonial policy. The underlying problem is clarified when Behdad proceeds to ask "No matter how 'weak' the Orientals were, would they really have accepted the European colonizers if they were only being dominated and repressed by Colonialism?" (*Belated Travelers*, 12). His rhetorical question makes the important point that colonial rule was seductive as well as simply repressive, but it oversteps the mark by suggesting that the peoples of the Orient simply did not resist, whereas in reality, the history of French expansion was fraught with instances of resistance. In Algeria, armed resistance to the French conquest of 1830, led by the Emir Abd El-Khader, continued until 1847; neighboring Morocco resisted the encroachments of the French until, as a result of the campaign waged by General Hubert Lyautey, it became a protectorate in 1912, and one could also cite in other parts of the world the stalwart resistance of the Malagasy people and the slave revolts on the island of Saint-Domingue that led, in January 1804, to the unanticipated and remarkable independence of Haiti. The erasure of this history of resistance is the direct result of the absorption of all aspects of colonial history into the apparent seamlessness of Orientalist representation. It is, as I will later argue at more length, the product of a broad tendency of Foucauldian theory to incorporate all instances of resistance into the machinery of power.

The Marxist critic Aijaz Ahmad, who takes a skeptical view of discourse theory's exclusive focus on representations, has argued that what is needed at this juncture is a micrological account of "the determinate set of mediations which connect the cultural productions of a period with other kinds of productions and political processes" (*In Theory*, 5). Although like Foucault, Said, and Behdad I believe that culture should be approached as a field of representations, I would nonetheless second Ahmad's claim that in thinking about Orientalism's relationship to colonialism, we need to address discontinuities and processes of mediation within this field. My own work offers a preliminary contribution to this account to the extent that it draws much stronger connections between textual practice and historical context than previous studies of Orientalism.

The critical reflection on the French encounter with alterity, from Tzvetan Todorov (*Nous et les autres*) and Roland Barthes to the work of critics writing in the wake of *Orientalism*, has unfortunately remained remarkably abstract, centered on theoretical questions and largely indifferent to the ways in which art and literature reflect, or fail to reflect, the *changing* nature and focus of French colonial policy. As Linda Nochlin presciently feared in 1983 in "The Imaginary Orient," the term "Orientalism" has itself become an obfuscating umbrella concept that impedes the analysis of individual works of art and literature as documents of an evolving colonial and domestic history (187).

To advance our understanding of the relationship between colonialism and the cultural sphere, it is now necessary to move beyond the level of theoretical abstraction and to undertake more detailed investigations of the ways in which, at different historical moments, Orientalist representation has expressed or served colonial policy. In many cases, as I now want to show, this analysis involves the identification of structures of *suppression* and *displacement* as well as patterns of congruence between colonial history and Orientalist literature. In the following paragraphs, I will illustrate this claim by suggesting, first, that the almost metaleptic reversal between colonial history and Orientalist discourse that I have discerned in contemporary theory mirrors a displacement already operative in eighteenth- and nineteenth-century exoticism; and second, that the deployment of a broadly undifferentiated concept of colonial discourse has served to mask this displacement.

Theoretical studies of Orientalism have generally held that the French obsession with the Orient during the Enlightenment served as a preliminary to the expansion into North Africa and the Levant that began with the Expédition d'Égypte of 1798. Although I would not want to reject this interpretation, advanced by Edward Said in *Orientalism* (e.g., 62–67, 80–86, 96–97) and Lisa Lowe in *Critical Terrains* (52), among others, I do want to suggest that this reading of eighteenth-century Orientalism overlooks and in a sense masks the fact that this tradition took hold contemporaneously with the establishment of New World colonies that are scarcely evoked in ancien régime literature. Viewed in this light, eighteenth-century Orientalism seems to me not a properly colonial discourse, but on the contrary, the negation or displacement of a discourse on the colonies.

In marked contrast to the almost obsessive drive to represent the Persian, Turkish, and Siamese Orient, before the mid-1760s, we encounter very few attempts in canonical French literature to represent the territories that were already French colonies: the French Antilles, the slave ports of Gorée and Saint-Louis in Senegal, and the Indian Ocean possessions, the Île Bourbon and the Île de France. Even France's vast territories in Canada and Louisiana seem to have occupied a relatively small place in the literary imaginary in comparison with either the Orient or Peru.[20] This is not to suggest that there were absolutely no representations of French colonial practice,[21] but rather to state that these representations never attained either the prevalence or the systematic coherence of Oriental exoticism.

This paucity of representations seems surprising when we consider the length and extent of France's history in the *vieilles colonies* (old colonies), many of which had been French since the mid-1600s; the fact that by the 1780s well over half a million slaves labored in the French Antilles,[22] most of them brought to the New World on French *bateaux négriers*; that by mid-century these colonies were the richest in the world, producing 40 percent of the global sugar crop and 50 percent of coffee; and finally, that until 1763 Britain and France were engaged in a fierce struggle for control of North America and the Caribbean basin.

It is almost universally supposed that throughout the eighteenth century, the leading *philosophes* actively voiced their opposition to the establishment of colonies and to the Atlantic slave trade. In reality, until the 1760s, such discussions were predominantly confined either to condemnations of the cruelty of the Spanish conquistadors or to the abstract use of slavery as a metaphor for political despotism. The pattern for this avoidance of, or blindness to, what would seem to us a crucial philosophical issue was set by that father of the Enlightenment, John Locke, who, despite asserting in his *Two Treatises of Government* that slavery is opposed to the spirit of Englishmen and gentlemen, apparently did not extend this conclusion to the British

Atlantic colonies: as secretary to Lord Ashley, he transcribed the Constitution of Carolina (which stated, among other things, that church membership was to have no effect on the status of slaves), and he subsequently became an investor in the Royal Africa Company, the monopoly that supplied African slaves to the British colonies in the New World.[23] This inconsistency is repeated in the work of one of Locke's first and most influential French followers, Montesquieu. As I argue at greater length in Chapter 1, the text most often cited as the first sustained critique of both slavery and Colonialism is Montesquieu's *De l'Esprit des lois* (*Spirit of the Laws*; 1748). It is certainly accurate to say that Montesquieu presents moral and economic arguments against slavery and the establishment of colonies and that these arguments proved enormously influential later in the century. However, it should also be observed that the discussion of the colonies in the *Esprit des lois* refers almost exclusively to Spanish and Portuguese colonies, while the attendant problem of slavery is transposed onto the Oriental context. Only in one brief paragraph does Montesquieu address the *French* Antillean colonies. He deems them "admirable." There is also only a single chapter on the Atlantic slave trade.[24] In this passage, which has become famous in the annals of French anticolonialism, Montesquieu presents a biting critique of the *traite des noirs* (black slave trade). He states, ironically, that if pressed to justify the enslavement of Africans, he would argue that because they are black from head to toe, it is impossible to pity them; that God in all his wisdom would not have placed a soul in a black body; and that sugar would be prohibitively expensive were it not grown by slaves. Despite the force of this critique of the cultural prejudice and specious justifications that sustain the slave trade, the absence of any further concrete reference to slavery suggests that we should read in the ironic structure of this passage a deep-rooted ambivalence toward the place of slavery in the national economy. This interpretation is supported by the fact that the displacement of the realities of slavery and Colonialism from the New World to the Orient that I identify in the *Esprit des lois* is replicated in the work of Voltaire[25] and Rousseau,[26] and in Diderot and D'Alembert's *Encyclopédie*.[27]

The first major work to take a detailed look at the colonies was the Abbé Raynal and Denis Diderot's multivolume work, *Histoire philosophique et politique du commerce et des établissements des Européens dans les deux Indes*

(1770). Contemporaneously, a number of works of fiction, notably Saint-Lambert's *Ziméo* (1769) and Louis-Sébastien Mercier's *L'An 2441* (1771), took the colonies and slave revolts as their theme, such that for a short period, the Caribbean maroon emerged as an exotic and heroic figure. In the last quarter of the century, hostility toward slavery escalated, paving the way for the foundation, in 1788, of the abolitionist *Société des amis des noirs* and for the suppression of slavery in 1794 by the government of the Convention.[28]

The causes underlying the sudden emergence of a discourse on the colonies after a century and a half of relative silence are complex. As Reinhart Koselleck argues in *Critique and Crisis*, under the old regime, the world of politics, government, and foreign policy had been closed to the *philosophes* as to most other subjects of the crown. As a result, they "took power" by constructing their own abstract and utopian versions of social and political reality. By contrast, as individuals affiliated with the *philosophes* came to be included in the process of government, direct discussion of colonial policy at last became possible[29] (the fact that the colonies figure more extensively and more explicitly in British art and literature of the same period reflects, among many other things, the more established role of intellectuals in British government). The formulation of *economic* as well as moral arguments against slavery in the work of the physiocrats, notably Mirabeau and Turgot, also certainly played a part. Last, and perhaps most persuasively, we must consider the cultural impact of the losses that France incurred during the Seven Years' War. By the Treaty of Paris of 1763, France surrendered all of its colonial possessions with the exception of Guadeloupe, Martinique, Sainte-Lucie, Saint-Domingue, French Guyana, the island of Gorée off the coast of Senegal, five trading posts in India, and Louisiana, which was almost immediately ceded to Spain. Forced to abandon its territorial ambitions in North America, France undoubtedly began to reevaluate the strategic importance and economic value of the colonies.

Orientalist discourse and colonial history were of course more closely connected in the nineteenth century when, in the wake of Bonaparte's Expédition d'Égypte of 1798, France began its slow expansion into the Orient.[30] The availability of both commercial and official patronage for travel to the Orient—many artists and writers received sponsorship from literary journals

or newspapers; others received official "missions" from government min-
istries providing letters of introduction to French representatives and commercial agents[31]—testify to the perceived political and economic significance
of cultural Orientalism. But I would nonetheless argue that when considered
against the backdrop of colonial practice, nineteenth-century Orientalism
manifests a high level of displacement and aestheticization.

Until the final quarter of the nineteenth century, what we predominantly
encounter in Orientalist representation is not a celebration or even a record
of conquest and occupation, but a marked aestheticization of both Oriental
culture and colonial life. Just as it was only in the 1760s that Enlightenment
writers began actively to reflect on the Atlantic colonies, so it was not until
the 1870s, when France for the first time in its history developed a coherent
national policy of colonial expansion, that colonialism and its impact on the
Orient were substantively addressed in the cultural sphere. In both instances,
a traumatic military defeat at the hands of other European powers triggered
shock waves that had a profound impact on the relationship between
metropolis and colonies. In 1763, colonial expansion came to a temporary
halt, a retreat that seems to have facilitated the emergence, in metropolitan
France, of the first sustained public reflection on the function and moral
implications of the colonies. France's defeat at the hands of the Prussians in
1871 had a parallel but opposite effect. Humiliated in Europe, France looked
overseas to reinvigorate itself, embarking on a new phase of colonial expansion and revising the rhetoric of national identity to include the colonial
project, henceforth primarily characterized as the "civilizing mission."

I would not wish to suggest that the literary output of the first two-thirds
of the nineteenth century makes no reference whatsoever to Europe's military and administrative presence in the Orient. What I do want to observe
is that taken together, these references present only a fragmentary account of
colonial experience and relegate to the margins of representation the main
preoccupations of French foreign policy. For example, many of the famous
travelers of the period neglected to visit Algeria, although after the conquest
of Algiers in 1830 it constituted the primary focus of French foreign policy
and mercantile interest.[32] For Flaubert and his traveling companion Maxime
Du Camp, the term "Orient" did not even include the Maghreb, but rather

referred to Egypt, Syria, Iraq, and Persia—a de-Orientalization of North Africa that testifies to the dampening effect of colonial familiarity on Western fantasies of the exotic other.[33]

A parallel erasure of the colonial architecture can be seen in the visual arts, in which the presence of French tourists or military personnel is almost never registered. This occlusion does not, however, amount to a negation of Western power over the Orient; rather, as Linda Nochlin asserts, the gaze of the Western spectator, by virtue of its very absence, establishes itself as the controlling gaze that "brings the Oriental world into being." Paradoxically, the erasure of spectatorship also fosters the illusion that there never was any "bringing into being," that Orientalist representation mirrors rather than constructs the realities it portrays ("Imaginary Orient," 122).

Such omissions and displacements show that we must be cautious in our use of cultural productions as indexes of broader political or economic processes. They also illustrate a need to question the ostensible plenitude of discursive formations, to recognize that the apparent seamlessness of Orientalist discourse can obscure many aspects of the colonial experience. This is of course a political exigency as well as a matter of historical fact, for the lacunae within and between different discursive formations provide the essential critical standpoints from which it becomes possible to evaluate the social functions and effects of discourses. In the case at hand, for example, the selective and partial relation of Orientalist discourse to colonial practice enables us to consider how prevailing discourses may mask whole strata of historical processes, perhaps in the interests of perpetuating them.[34] Following the lead of Michel de Certeau (*Heterologies*, 190–92), critical theorists have for some time argued that Foucault's portrayal of a vast machinery of power or infinite web of discourse is an historical abstraction that, with a kind of reverse imperialism, threatens to erase the boundaries of power and with them all history of resistance. Clearly the time has now come to extend this demand for a more varied and complex account of the dynamics of power and resistance to the theorization of Orientalist discourse.

The past several years have in fact seen a number of attempts to qualify the claim that Western representations of the Orient constitute a discourse whose fundamental purpose is the assertion of Western hegemony over

Asia—although in certain cases, this attempt reflects a desire simply to dispense altogether with the idea that Orientalism serves a determinate ideological function. In this category I would include James Mackenzie's rejection of the politicization of Orientalist art[35] and French critic Alain Buisine's brusque dismissal of the ideological "Puritanism" of Said's approach.[36] Buisine's rather cavalier position is indicative of a much broader French suspicion of cultural politics in general and the politics of Orientalism in particular. Because of this critical reticence, exoticism has not lost its aura of innocence in France; novels set in ancient Egypt or the Maghrebian desert still abound on the shelves of bookstores, while works such as Buisine's often seem to reproduce the exoticism they dissect.[37] There have, however, been more thoughtful reconsiderations of the relationship between literary text and geopolitical context, and these have predominantly focused on the ways in which texts effectively block the transmission of their own hegemonic discourses.

Examining the texture of European travel literature, Dennis Porter follows Roland Barthes in approaching the literary text as a "dépouvoir" as well as a "discourse," a "powerless" language as well as a medium for ideology.[38] In a similar manner, Lisa Lowe, whose work underscores the heterogeneity of Orientalist discourse, has argued that to perceive Orientalism as a univocal tradition is to make the unjustifiable assumption that Orientalist narratives are not subject to the multivalence and indeterminacy of language; in other words, it is to reproduce the determinism that has seemed to characterize Orientalism itself (*Critical Terrains*, x).

Like both Porter and Lowe, I believe that cultural analysis must be complemented by attentiveness to the dynamics of individual texts. But I want to nuance this recognition with the observation that these two imperatives are not easily reconciled. Whereas political criticism generally ascribes determinate meanings and cultural values to literary texts, textually based analyses expose the instability of the binary oppositions on which representations of racial and sexual difference are founded and question whether politicized accounts may not confirm established categories and structures of knowledge, rather than challenging them. In the chapters that follow, I address the problematic interval between these two modes of reading by underscoring the constant, and in my view inevitable, flickering back and forth between the textual inscription of the unmasterable alterity of language and the irresistible reimposition of structures of knowledge and meaning. In this vein, I suggest that although ethnocentrism invites deconstructive readings—readings that disclose the unstable rhetorical foundations of identity and difference—this deconstruction is, in a sense, the corollary and ironic complement to ethnocentrist representation.[39]

This demonstration takes different forms in the different sections of this book. In Chapter 5, it centers on the tension between the modernist cooptation of the Oriental woman to represent the autonomy of the artistic sign, and the entirely unintended sense in which this figure actually conveys the unmasterable otherness of language. In Chapter 3, which looks at the genre of the Oriental tale, it explores the relationship between texts and their historical reception; I suggest that critical readings that emphasize the fragmentary or decentered representational economy of Orientalist narratives often fail to address the ways in which these stories have been received historically. Because literary history is replete with examples of works that, from the perspective of the specialist, have been read in ways that reflect neither the full range of authorial intentions nor the overall complexity of the text, it is, I argue, important to acknowledge the dimensions of Orientalist works that generate ethnocentric readings. This is not to imply that texts' historical reception constitutes an *hors texte* more significant or more real than the texts themselves, but simply to say that it is essential to broaden the scope of critical interpretation to address both the intricacies of texts and the different readings they engender.

To the extent that my practice of "double reading" affirms the determining influence of cultural context and admits the pertinence of the history of reception to the analysis of the text, it departs markedly from the kind of critical praxis that we have come to associate with deconstructive reading, a methodology that underscores the multivalence of textuality and its resistance to univocal meaning. I nonetheless want to argue that in a certain way, the readings that follow respect the goals of deconstructive theory. By this, I mean that they affirm—indeed, insist on—a plurality of levels and of modes of interpretation, rather than subordinating the process of "reading" to a concern with "history," or vice versa.

ORIENTAL WOMAN AND THE ICONOGRAPHY OF TRUTH

In the preface to *Beyond Good and Evil* (1886), Friedrich Nietzsche playfully invites his reader to imagine that truth is a woman. "Supposing truth to be a woman," he asks, "what then?" (1)—a provocative rhetorical question grounded in the observation that philosophers have been seduced by the prospect of uncovering the truth in much the same way that they have been enticed by the idea of undressing a woman. Although Nietzsche's rhetoric is playful, the idea it upholds is by no means incongruous, for in the Western iconographic tradition, truth *has* conventionally been represented by a veiled woman, an allegorical figure that suggests that if the veil is removed, then truth, represented by the unadorned female body, is exposed.

This iconographic convention has proved remarkably resilient, the veiled woman having represented truth across a long and complex history of epistemological change. For example, although Enlightenment philosophy is generally credited with the rejection of allegorical representation in favor of more "objective" models of truth,[40] this image retained all of its currency in the age of empiricism. Surely the most prominent illustration of this use of the veiled woman to represent empirical methodology is the frontispiece to Diderot and D'Alembert's *Encyclopédie*, shown in Figure 1. This engraving, drawn in 1764 by Charles-Nicolas Cochin, represents Reason unveiling Truth while Theology and Metaphysics stand aloof, their backs uncooperatively turned to the unfolding process of Enlightenment. A century later, the image of the veiled woman had evolved to signify scientific positivism; for example, statues in the Paris Medical Faculty and Conservatoire National des Arts et Métiers depicted Nature unveiling herself before triumphant Science.[41] Yet only a few years earlier, the figure of the veiled woman had been coopted by an epistemology diametrically opposed to both Enlightenment empiricism and the positivism of nineteenth-century science: Arthur Schopenhauer's idealist refutation of the reality of the material world. In *The World as Will and Representation* (1819), Schopenhauer drew on the Oriental scholarship of the period to represent human perception of reality as an illusion, a "veil of Maya" cast over the true essence of the world, which he identified as the eternal striving of the will.

The remarkable adaptability of this iconography testifies not only to an

Figure 1.   Frontispiece to Diderot and D'Alembert's *Encyclopédie*, drawn by Charles-Nicolas Cochin, 1764. Source: *Encyclopédie, ou dictionnaire raisonné des sciences, des arts et des métiers*, Paris: Briasson, 1751–1765, vol. 1. Courtesy of General Research Division, New York Public Library, Astor, Lenox and Tilden Foundations.

enduring paradigm of Western metaphysics (truth is held to be an ideal entity concealed by appearance or representation) but also to the important role of gender in the elaboration of epistemological models—to the fact that the subject of philosophical inquiry has consistently been gendered male, while its object has been imagined as a desirable female body. This sexualized relationship was in part what Nietzsche had in mind when he invited his readers to envisage truth as a woman, irreverently signaling the constant intrusion of gender politics and erotic desire into the purportedly objective pursuit of truth.

Nietzsche's purpose, however, was not simply to expose the material and psychological forces that shape philosophical inquiry. He was also attacking the philosophical belief that concealed beneath the veil of appearance and representation there abides some form of hidden essence or foundational truth, and the accompanying view that if we could dispense with representation we could arrive at truth. To make this point, he compared truth and woman, observing that both seduce men "from a distance," creating the illusion of a reality that exists beyond representation. This reality, he concluded, can never be attained because distance or deferral are inherent to the structure of truth, just as they are constitutive of the masculine ideal of woman. These brilliant, if fragmentary, remarks on truth later provided the foundation for the more sustained meditation undertaken by Martin Heidegger. Casting back over the history of philosophy, Heidegger drew a key distinction between the pre-Socratic conception of truth as *aletheia* and the Platonic model of truth as correspondence or *adequatio*.[42] Expressing a preference for the pre-Socratic notion (which, he argued, had been eclipsed by Platonic metaphysics), Heidegger argued that truth consists not of the correspondence between two entities—for example, between human perception and real objects in the world—but rather of an unlimited process of veiling and unveiling that occurs within the structure of experience and knowledge.

I offer this condensed (and vastly simplified) history of philosophical reflection on truth because in this book, I argue that in the late seventeenth century, the allegorical figure of truth as a veiled woman became intertwined with ethnographic representations of Oriental women. What I primarily mean by this is that a great many Orientalist representations evince the belief that to unveil the woman is to know her, and to know the woman is to render the entire culture transparent: "win over the women, and the rest will follow," as Frantz Fanon once paraphrased French colonial strategy in Algeria ("Algeria Unveiled," 37). This type of exchange operates in accordance with what Heidegger calls the "correspondence" model of truth, for it translates the conviction that with the impediments or representations removed, the culture/woman can be understood, known, penetrated. There are, however, more complex cultural productions, works of art that acknowledge a definitive unveiling to be impossible, not only because cultural differences constitute incontrovertible barriers to transparency but also because truth is not perceived as the binary opposite of representation. I argue that the figure of the Oriental woman is poised between these two contrasting visions of truth—*adequatio* and *aletheia*, the Western preoccupation with unveiling women and penetrating the Orient, and the recognition that representation is ultimately irreducible—and show that even within a single work, the balance between these two poles continuously shifts back and forth.

The veil has historically been the primary signifier by means of which Islamic women are represented,[43] and as such, it has shaped cultural perceptions in several important ways. The fact that Islamic women are veiled has often been seized on as an indication of Islamic misogyny—the outward sign of an oppressive cultural system of which women are little more than passive victims, a paradigm whose secondary effect has been to affirm the moral superiority of western liberalism. By contrast, it has also contributed strongly to the eroticization of Oriental women; as Alain Buisine observes, the veil invites unveiling—it is precisely because the Orient is a civilization in which many women are veiled that Orientalist art has seized every opportunity to represent them as nudes ("Voiles," 76). Most important, perhaps, is the fact that the philosophical model of the veil as a barrier to truth and knowledge has had important political applications within the economy of colonialism. As the most immediate and visible sign of Oriental civilization, the veiled woman has served as a metonymy, the most tangible marker of Islam's (perceived) inscrutability to the Western observer.

Images of veiled women continue in our own times to operate as conducting rods for the highly charged relations between East and West, Islam and Christianity. Let us consider by way of example the image shown in Figure 2, which appeared on the cover of the French newsmagazine *L'Express*

SEMAINE DU 17 AU 23 NOVEMBRE 1994

L'EXPRESS

FOULARD

LE COMPLOT

COMMENT LES ISLAMISTES NOUS INFILTRENT

LE PREMIER ROMAN DE GISCARD

(PAGE 141)

Figure 2. Cover of *L'Express* newsmagazine, November 17–23, 1994. Photograph by Marianne Rosenstiehl. Courtesy of *L'Express.*

(November 17–23, 1994). This was a year of tension arising from a fundamentalist bombing campaign targeting French cities; it was also a year in which France was in the grip of one of the recurrent waves of anxiety over the wearing of the Islamic veil in French public schools that have swept over the nation since the initial "Affaire du collège de Creil" first introduced this issue in 1989. In this eye-catching photograph, the veil (*foulard*) connotes the threatening alterity of Islam, and the line of rupture now being drawn *within* metropolitan France, between the openness of civil society and the closed world of theocracy. Paired with its alarmist caption, this image conveys the message that Islamic fundamentalists are "infiltrating" "us," using the veil— as metonymy for the assertion of cultural difference—to do so, while also managing to imply that women are the seductive face that the Islamic fifth column presents to the world.

In several respects, the *Express* image builds on, and competes with, one that had appeared on the cover of *Figaro Magazine*, October 26, 1985. This even more provocative cover represents Marianne, the emblem of French nationhood, draped in an Islamic veil, and browbeats the reader with the (evidently rhetorical) question, "Will we still be French in thirty years?" What makes these images work—what confers their power to shock and alarm—is, I think, the combination of a number of venerable Orientalist ideas concerning the veil as a form of gender discrimination no longer acceptable in Europe; the veil as an instrument of Islamic political duplicity; and finally, the veil as a weapon of sexual and cultural seduction.

Alarm about immigration from Islamic nations and the threat of terrorism is of course not confined to France. Images similar to this one appear in the media of many of the Western countries in which these issues have become significant social concerns. Yet in certain respects, this image is distinctively French. The use of a female figure to embody the perceived threat of Islam is the product of a long French tradition in which perceptions of the foreignness of the Orient—of its danger and its seduction—have been interwoven with perceptions of the foreignness of woman. Similarly, the targeting of the veil as the primary instrument of disguise and infiltration reflects a specifically French preoccupation with the presence of the Islamic *tchador* in metropolitan France. The intensity of this concern, which surfaced for the first time in 1989, when the Affaire du collège de Creil launched a national debate over the wearing of religious symbols in French schools, reflects the fact that the veil, like other religious insignia, is widely perceived to compromise France's secular republicanism.

To understand the significance of the veil to both sides in this debate, we must perform a cultural genealogy, looking back to France's colonial history and weighing the long-term effects of the *mission civilisatrice*'s policy of replacing indigenous religious practices—including the wearing of the veil—with "enlightened" French ones. During the struggle for Algerian independence, this policy was attacked, both symbolically and viscerally, as Algerian women freedom fighters concealed bombs and grenades beneath their veils, or, by contrast, as they shed their traditional clothing and dressed in European style in order to infiltrate French army battalions or to act as decoys. The alarm generated today by images of veiled women is certainly a legacy of this reversal of fortunes. But to attempt to understand what is at stake for France's Moslems in the wearing of the veil by means of a revisitation of their colonial history does not amount to unilaterally determining that cultural rights take primacy over the values of civil society, including women's rights, or to suggesting that the fear of Islamic-backed terrorism is irrational. Rather, it is to hold that perhaps our best hope for ameliorating the current inter- and intracultural conflicts lies in an examination of the historical roots not only of Islamic fundamentalism, but also of the particular forms espoused by French concerns over identity and difference.

Therefore, although it might legitimately be asserted that after two decades of reflection on the politics of Orientalism the time has now come to turn our attention elsewhere, I suggest that the abiding force of representations rooted in the Orientalist tradition bespeaks a need for continuing critical reflection on this topic. The continuing power to disturb of the cover image of *Express* demonstrates the particular need for a study that examines race and gender together. One of the main objectives of this book is therefore to represent the interaction between these terms in the French Orientalist tradition: to explore the variety of ways in which, at different historical moments, Western representations have produced the Orient as a compliant female body that invites penetration and possession, or in a different scenario, as an impenetrable veiled body that harbors hostility and deception; and how, in parallel fashion, Orientalist representations effectively

"Orientalized" European women, constructing them as "foreign bodies" within the domestic economy.

The chapters that follow work with texts generally considered part of the French literary canon and that, with the possible exception of Diderot's *Les Bijoux indiscrets* (*The Indiscreet Jewels*; 1748) and Crébillon-fils's *Le Sopha* (*The Sofa*; 1748), have also been viewed as key constituents of the Orientalist tradition. I must emphasize that I do not attempt to catalog all representations of Oriental women. This is in part because the task of documenting Orientalism has already been undertaken by Pierre Martino, Marie-Louise Dufrenoy, and Raymond Schwab,[44] but also because I have preferred to focus on the textual complexity of a small number of influential texts. I also make no attempt to provide a continuous history of the dialogue between Orientalism and the unfolding of French domestic and colonial history. Much could be said that is not said in this book, regarding, for example, the use of Oriental imagery in the pamphlet wars of the revolutionary period. But in my view, it is impossible to present detailed textual analyses, theoretical arguments, and historical coverage in a single study, and in lieu of this, I have opted to build an historically based theory of Orientalism around the examination of a few key texts and the cultural contexts with which they are interwoven.

This book deals exclusively with texts by male authors. This is not because it would not be of interest to consider attitudes or themes that reflect a distinctly feminine perspective, but rather because very few French women writers of the eighteenth and nineteenth centuries undertook to represent the Orient, in part because of the obstacles that faced women travelers, and perhaps also because of the erotic preoccupations of the genre. A number of women writers, including Mlle. de Scudéry, Mme. de la Calprenède, and Mme. de Villedieu in the latter half of the seventeenth century,[45] and Mme. de Gomez and Mme. de Puisieux in the eighteenth, did publish "Oriental tales," but these works are Oriental only in the loosest possible sense of the term.[46] Only in the mid–nineteenth century did a woman writing in French, Princesse Christine de Belgiojoso, produce an ethnography of the contemporary Orient.[47] Before Belgiojoso, there was no French equivalent of Lady Mary Wortley Montagu, the Englishwoman who accom-

panied her husband to Constantinople when he became ambassador to the
Sublime Porte (1717–1718) and wrote a series of highly influential travel letters published posthumously in 1763 as *The Letters of the Right Honourable
Lady Mary Wortley Montagu*. In reality, Montagu's letters show that authorial gender is never fully determining in relation to the representation of
either sexual or ethnic difference, for although they articulate a distinctly
feminine perspective in their affirmation of women's rights to travel, to
observe, and to engage in literary production (Montagu lends authority to
her account of Turkish culture by insisting on the special privileges afforded
her as a woman, notably admission into the harem and public baths), her
narrative explores many of the same themes and epistemological concerns
that are raised in male-authored works. A similar point may be made of
Belgiojoso in the sense that her attempt to debunk "masculine" erotic
stereotypes of the Orient—to represent the cracks in the harem walls and the
grime in the Turkish baths—can be located within a broader literary shift
toward what one might call "Oriental realism," a style exemplified by
another text of the same period, Gustave Flaubert's *Voyage en Égypte* (*Voyage
to Egypt*).

Each of the chapters of this book draws on a particular text or corpus of
texts to illustrate broader cultural issues and theoretical problematics in the
history of Orientalism. The first three chapters investigate how figures of
"the other" participated in the redrawing of cultural and political boundaries
in Enlightenment France. Chapter 1, which focuses on Montesquieu's *Esprit
des lois*, considers the factors—both international and domestic—that in the
early eighteenth century precipitated the transformation of a long-standing
fascination with the Orient into a coherent, quasi-scientific discourse. It
argues that the French fascination with the Orient marked a displacement of
France's colonial interests in the New World. It also considers how representations of the enclosure of the harem reflected the development in
Europe of a new, more open social and political system, the so-called bourgeois public sphere, along with the shifts in gender ideology that accompanied this political transformation. Chapter 2 builds on this reading by examining how these cultural concerns are articulated in the complex narrative
economy of a work of fiction, Montesquieu's *Lettres persanes* (*Persian Letters*;
1721). Chapter 3 turns to the Oriental tale, one of the most popular forms of

eighteenth-century writing on the Orient, but a genre rarely examined for its representation of cultural difference. Focusing on texts by Diderot and Crébillon-fils, and on the representational economy of "feminized" and "Orientalized" furniture, it considers how fascination with gender relations in the Orient expressed a redetermination of the categories of publicity and intimacy. The last two chapters examine exchanges between colonial history and aesthetic movements in nineteenth-century France. Chapter 4 explores the nineteenth-century travelogue; it traces the changing political climate in which travel narratives were produced and considers how these shifts were reflected in the representation of Oriental women. With a focus on Nerval's *Voyage en Orient*, it also explores representations of Oriental women as sites of tension between the perception of language as a medium of knowledge and authority and the countervailing sense that language constitutes a field of dispossession and barred access. The final chapter, which looks at the career of Théophile Gautier, links the emergence of a modernist aesthetic that asserts art's autonomy from social and political forces to the literary aestheticization of colonial experience in mid-nineteenth-century France.

CHAPTER ONE

Polygamy, Slavery, and the Colonies: Montesquieu's *De l'Esprit des lois*

De l'Esprit des lois (*Spirit of the Laws*; 1748), Montesquieu's monumental reflection on the cultural origins of codes of law, is the natural starting point for any reflection on the representation of Oriental women in eighteenth-century French letters, for it contains the most detailed and systematic exposition of the theory of Oriental culture that runs throughout the fiction and political literature of the period. By organizing the observations and anecdotes of seventeenth-century travelers into a coherent ethnographic theory, Montesquieu can be said to have raised a preexisting fascination with the Orient to the level of quasi-scientific discourse.[1] As the Oriental scholar Abraham-Hyacinthe Anquetil-Duperron later observed, the president of the Parliament of Bordeaux may not have invented the theory of "Oriental despotism"—the supposition that the whole of Asia, from Turkey to Japan, labored under the yoke of a uniformly oppressive mode of government, inextricably tied to the practice of polygamy and the enclosure of women in the harem—yet "the reflections of M. Montesquieu in some sense fixed our ideas about the nature of despotism; since then he has only been copied, and in fact, no one has explored this subject in greater depth than he" (Anquetil-Duperron, *Législation orientale*, 9).[2] One need only turn to Diderot and d'Alembert's *Encyclopédie*, the leading index of Enlightenment cultural attitudes, for confirmation of Anquetil-Duperron's claim, for the article "Despotism," penned by the Chevalier de Jaucourt, represents little more than a paraphrase of Montesquieu's ideas on the subject.[3]

De l'Esprit des lois constitutes a necessary starting point for the analysis of cultural constructions of alterity for the second, far more pressing reason that it is one of the first historical documents to offer a universal theory of what we now understand as "culture." Montesquieu uses the term *esprit* (spirit) to denote the interaction among political, religious, climactic, and geographic factors to shape the codes of law of any given society.[4] This approach to jurisprudence illustrates what I will call the "anthropological turn" in secular humanism, a radical paradigm shift by which, over the course of the eighteenth century, social theory was transformed by the perception that human society, like the natural world, is subject to laws, and by the apprehension that the various components of the social whole—government, education, and religious and sexual practices—are all interdependent.

The seemingly inexhaustible array of references to exotic locations in *De l'Esprit des lois* testifies to the fact that this new awareness of "culture," and the descriptive methodology that accompanied it, were to a considerable degree the product of Europeans' heightened awareness of other cultures— and, most notably, of the differences between "Oriental" civilization and European society.[5] As Homi K. Bhabha has argued, we are inclined to think that it is a preexisting sense of cultural identity that creates consciousness of difference, but in many instances it is rather the experience of difference that precipitates the attempt to isolate and define cultural boundaries ("Signs Taken for Wonders," 175).

The "anthropological turn" that may be read in *De l'Esprit des lois* manifests the polarized structure that I outline in my Introduction. That is to say, like all anthropological writings of the period, it expresses the emerging historical reality of European military and technological superiority over the rest of the world; yet at the same time, awareness of cultural difference is channeled here, as in other Enlightenment texts, into the critical examination of European institutions and values. The representation of the "Oriental feminine" in the *Esprit des lois* is also poised between these two tendencies. On the one hand, it lies at the core of the process by which difference is elucidated and defined, the *Esprit* providing one of the strongest early illustrations of the metaphor by which the Orient is made to appear feminine in relation to a more masculine European counterpart, and by which European women are "Orientalized," stamped as outsiders or "others," an alien presence within the body politic. At the same time, however, Montesquieu's account of gender relations in the Orient bears a critical dimension, functioning as a key element in the subtextual movement by which identity is problematized and the fixity of difference called into question.

This chapter establishes the foundation for my examination of the figure of Oriental woman by considering the social and political factors—both domestic and global—that in the early years of the eighteenth century precipitated a surge of investigative curiosity about the Orient, and more specifically, about gender relations in the Orient. The harem and polygamy had been objects of fascination in France at least since the time of Montaigne, but in the eighteenth century, they became key constituents, not only of literary discourse but also of political, social, and economic writing. Focusing on the *Esprit des lois*, the most extensive contemporary account of Oriental life, I argue that the *fascination* with the Orient that permeated eighteenth-century French culture was the symptom of a displacement of France's *interests* in its New World colonies, and, by extension, of a repression of France's involvement in the Atlantic slave trade.

Second, following the lead of previous scholars, I argue that like many of his contemporaries, Montesquieu used the threat of Oriental despotism to critique the perceived despotism of the Bourbon monarchy, and that this critical appraisal was accompanied by a reevaluation of the role of women in French politics and society. Although these two sets of concerns are obviously quite distinct, in the complex unfolding of Montesquieu's text, as in the wider culture, the issues of slavery and gender were intermeshed. Not only are concerns about French society projected onto the Orient, but there are also clear structural parallels between Montesquieu's account of Oriental politics and his reflection on the Atlantic colonies—or to put this another way, between his approach to questions where sexual difference is at issue and questions involving ethnicity and race. Slavery practiced in Spain's New World colonies and Oriental polygamy, both perceived to entail the inequality and subordination of "others," draw criticism from Montesquieu not only because they contradict the spirit of Enlightenment, but also—although less overtly—because both women and the colonies, with their large slave populations, are ascribed a dangerous alterity that must be cautiously neutralized rather than violently suppressed.

SLAVERY DISPLACED

Above, I discuss the surprising lack of representations of France's New World colonies in art and literature before the mid-1760s, a paucity that seems particularly surprising when one considers the enormous wealth of literature representing others from the Orient, or from the parts of the New World controlled by Spain rather than by France. Although it is generally taken for granted that throughout the eighteenth century the leading *philosophes*—Voltaire, Montesquieu, Rousseau, and Diderot—actively voiced their opposition to slavery as practiced in the European colonies, in reality, before the mid-1760s, discussions of the colonies and of the enslaved workforce that sustained them were essentially confined to critical attacks on Spanish colonialism and to the use of slavery as a metaphor for political subjugation in the domestic context.[6]

The few existing studies that address the relationship between French colonialism and the literary record in this period have approached the Enlightenment's fascination with things Oriental as a discursive prefiguration of France's expansion into the Orient at the end of the century.[7] Although I find this argument compelling and believe that there are historical grounds for embracing it—notably the fact that the "Eastern Question," the debate over the partitioning of the Ottoman Empire's Levantine territories, was indeed raised in France as early as the 1760s—I want to propose a second, somewhat different argument: that France's *fascination* with the Orient served to mask the magnitude of its *interests* in its existing New World colonies. In the Introduction, borrowing a term from psychoanalytic theory, I describe the overall reluctance of eighteenth- and nineteenth-century French writers to acknowledge the realities of colonialism as a form of "displacement." In psychoanalysis, this term denotes a mechanism of psychological control: the replacement of a disturbing object of revulsion or desire with a more anodyne substitute. I now want to look more closely at this process as a cultural mechanism and to examine how the geopolitical shift from Atlantic colonies to Oriental world occurs within a single, enormously influential Enlightenment text.[8]

Montesquieu's *De l'Esprit des lois* is frequently cited as the first French work to undertake a systematic representation of the colonies and slavery. It is credited with foreshadowing and inspiring the abolitionist discourse that emerged later in the century. This claim is not entirely misplaced: Montesquieu certainly exposes both the social and economic flaws of colonialism and advances moral and economic arguments against slavery. Yet despite a few energetic declarations against these morally questionable contemporary practices, in the *Esprit des lois*, the issue of colonialism is largely displaced onto the Spanish context, while the attendant problem of slavery is transposed onto the arena of domestic life in the Orient.

The topic of slavery is first broached in book XV, a book whose general subject is the influence of climactic conditions on codes of law. It is here that Montesquieu elaborates his notorious "climate theory," the claim that warm climates create physiological weaknesses, which in turn generate moral and political subservience and a predisposition to resign oneself to despotic rule. The discussion of slavery in this context opens with the sweeping statement that the institution is neither good in itself nor good for either the master or the slave. However, having made this universal pronouncement, Montesquieu immediately proceeds to observe that enslavement is more readily tolerated in despotic regimes in which liberty is already compromised (490). This ambiguous pattern—slavery is first condemned by reference to a general moral principle, then justified in a more limited context—is repeated later in this same book in the form of the argument that although slavery goes against the dictates of natural law, it may nonetheless have a natural cause. This cause is soon identified as the physical and moral debility of the populations of regions with warm climates (496).

Following these preliminary observations, Montesquieu turns his attention to the juridical origins of the institution of slavery, boldly dismissing the standard legal argument, which dates back to Hugo Grotius's seminal treatise *De Jure belli et pacis* (*Of the Rights of War and Peace*; 1625), that slavery arises from pity felt for debtors or prisoners of war. In *De l'Esprit des lois*, the critical thrust of the president's rejection of these widely accepted claims becomes evident in chapters III and IV, in which he argues, in the conditional tense, that he "could just as well say" ("j'aimerais autant dire") that slavery arises out of the contempt that civilized societies feel for the less civilized (he cites Spain's enslavement of the population of South America), or from religious intolerance (here he briefly cites a French example, Louis XIII's acceptance of slavery in his colonies on the grounds that it would promote the conversion of savages). The conditional voice is maintained in the next chapter, in which for the first and only time, Montesquieu directly addresses the plight of black Africans. He states with considerable irony that if pressed to justify the enslavement of these unfortunates, he would say that because Africans are black from head to toe, it is impossible to pity them; that God in all his wisdom would not have placed a soul in a black body; and that sugar would be too expensive were it not grown by slaves (494).

Although one must acknowledge the critical force of this ironic attack on the European rationalization of slavery, it is also necessary to consider the surprising way in which this attack is inscribed in the text. Having staked out in the ironic mode these cutting cultural positions, Montesquieu brusquely states that the time has now come to seek the *true* origins of slavery—implying, of course, that the preceding attacks on prejudice and intolerance were more speculative than substantive. The "true origins" that he identifies are political despotism—said to erode the individual's desire for freedom—and warm climates, in which men are physically weak and therefore lacking in courage and a desire for independence. The outcome of this analysis is that the whole issue of servitude is surreptitiously projected onto the Oriental context. This displacement is confirmed and consolidated in the next book, book XVI, in which polygamy and the enclosure of women in the harem are relabeled, without commentary, as "domestic slavery" ("esclavage domestique"). Given the absence of any further concrete reference to France's involvement in the Atlantic slave trade, it seems clear that we must read in Montesquieu's ironic tone, as well as in his use of the conditional voice, the expression of a deep-rooted national ambivalence toward the practice of slavery in the French colonies.

Louis Sala-Molins, the only critic to date to have devoted serious attention to the *philosophes'* ambivalence on the issues of slavery and the colonies, has observed that although Montesquieu, the foremost juridical thinker of his age, offers a detailed account of the laws governing the treatment of slaves in ancient Rome and the Greek republics, he never refers to the *Code Noir*, the body of laws that since 1685 had governed the treatment of slaves in the French colonies (Sala-Molins, *Code Noir ou le calvaire de Canaan*, 221–37).[9] This omission was probably not the result of ignorance. In 1742, a volume detailing the provisions of the *Code Noir* had been published by the Parisian publisher Prault, and it sold well enough to be reprinted on three occasions before 1788 (Sala-Molins, *Code Noir ou le calvaire de Canaan*, 83). Rather, Sala-Molins suggests, not implausibly, that the movement by which Montesquieu first condemns slavery outright, then justifies it by reference to "natural causes" or "particular circumstances"—he argues that "servitude should be limited to *certain particular countries*" (496; my italics)—translates a desire to create an exception in the case of the French colonies. Certainly it is worth noting that the only direct reference that Montesquieu makes to French rather than Spanish colonies is a laudatory one: he states, quite unequivocally, that "our colonies in the Antilles are *admirable*" (644).

Having addressed the origins of slavery, Montesquieu—reacting perhaps to the long history of slave revolts in both the French and British Antillean colonies—turns his attention to the dangers that can arise either from the abuse of slavery or from the accrual of an excessive number of slaves (chapters XI–XIX). The remedies that he proposes are humane treatment and a reduction in the number of slaves employed. As Sala-Molins rightly observes, these humanitarian prescriptions, like the provisions of the *Code Noir* itself, seem contrived as much for the long-term security of the institution of slavery as for the benefit of the slaves (*Code Noir ou le calvaire de Canaan*, 230–31).

What Sala-Molins fails to address, however, is the status of these prescriptions within Montesquieu's overall methodology, a form of argumentation that in the eighteenth century was new and distinctly radical. *De l'Esprit des lois* in most instances approaches legal codes not as heuristic devices, but as tools for preserving the social equilibrium or for perpetuating a particular form of government. As Jean Starobinski asserts, in this economy, "a law that appears unjust to abstract reason . . . is in reality the product of a long series of causes and effects . . . one could not change it without at the same time contradicting the overall spirit of the nation" (*Montesquieu par lui-même*, 86–87). This approach to law reflects Montesquieu's commitment to representing cultural difference empirically rather than from a moral metaperspective, a commitment that shocked the authorities of the age. When the *Esprit des lois* was placed on the papal Index of proscribed books in 1751, it was largely because theologians recognized in its refusal to condemn outright practices such as polygamy and suicide a dangerous progression toward cultural relativism. However, the surreptitious displacement of the issue of slavery from the New World onto the Oriental context that I have begun to trace alerts us to the fact that despite Montesquieu's best intentions, the empiricism thrust of the text is often (and inevitably) shaped by the presence of deep-rooted cultural investments.

The question of slavery is not, as one might perhaps suppose, neutralized by its transposition onto the Oriental context. On the contrary, slavery becomes a defining metaphor that runs throughout Montesquieu's account of Oriental culture, such that one might advance the loosely psychoanalytic hypothesis that the cultural repression of the problem leads to its reemergence in a different context. Thus Montesquieu boldly equates despotic government with "political servitude," while polygamous marriage, presented as the domestic correlate of despotism, is rendered as "domestic servitude." Although this characterization of polygamy as "domestic servitude" became a commonplace of the Enlightenment discourse on the Orient[10] largely because of the influence of Montesquieu, I think it is important to observe that it is by no means self-evident. The depiction of polygamy as a form of slavery testifies, rather, not only to the widespread and abiding conviction that Islamic cultures are uniformly misogynistic,[11] but also to the tacit displacement of the whole problem of slavery from the Western colonial arena of the Atlantic to the Eastern world.

In *De l'Esprit des lois*, the suggestion that Islamic culture simply represses women's rights and preferences is supported—as it still often is today—by the imputation that Oriental women are uniformly passive and submissive. Montesquieu argues that because in warm climates women become nubile and lose their physical charms while they are still relatively young, the period of their beauty never coincides with their intellectual maturity, with the result that they are always subordinate to their husbands (509). This portrait of the passivity of Oriental women is reinforced by the assertion that the enclosure of women in the seraglio contradicts the very spirit of slavery because harems are in reality experienced by women as "delightful places" ("lieux de délices") in which they are at liberty to indulge their natural indolence (499), a paradoxical image that paved the way for many later meditations on the passivity and indolence of Oriental women—one thinks of Flaubert's declaration that the interests of Oriental women are limited to smoking, going to the baths, and drinking coffee (see above, 7), or of his contemporary Christine de Belgiojoso's assertion (*Scènes de la vie turque*; 1858) that smoking, drinking tea, and beating their children are the unique pastimes of women in the harem—and which also confirms the fact that slavery had become an overarching metaphor for Oriental existence.

THE PERILS OF POLYGAMY

I now want to turn for a time away from the issue of slavery and colonialism to take a closer look at Montesquieu's intricate account of polygamy and the harem. The principal thing to be noted about this account is that, far from being a titillating depiction of exotic sexuality, it is essentially a cautionary meditation that gives voice to anxieties about gender relations in the European context. These concerns fall loosely into two categories. The first reflects a shift in the biomedical modeling of sexual difference that occurred between the late seventeenth and early nineteenth centuries. The second stems from conflicts arising from the unprecedented expansion of the public sphere that occurred in conjunction with the social and political forces of Enlightenment.

Montesquieu's lifelong fascination with the structure of Oriental government, expressed not only in the *Lettres persanes* (*Persian Letters*; 1721) and the *Esprit des lois* but also in a number of short Oriental tales, is conventionally interpreted in terms of his opposition to the perceived absolutism of the Bourbon monarchy. It is claimed that as a result of his class affiliation (he was a member of the *noblesse de robe*, the branch of the aristocracy involved in regional governance and oversight of the judicial system), Montesquieu deplored the abrogation of aristocratic privileges that had occurred since the revolts of the *Fronde*, and he used the menace of "Oriental despotism" to caricaturize the expansion of royal power at the expense of the nobility. On this reading, the Oriental despot corresponds to the Bourbon ruler, Louis XIV or his successor Louis XV, closeted in the seraglio of Versailles, a clandestine world of absolute power from which directives emanate that govern the fate of France.

This interpretation is persuasive, even if the precise extent to which Montesquieu's own social position shaped his perception of political forces remains open to question.[12] The drawback of this reading, however, is that the presence of domestic political undercurrents in Montesquieu's account of the Orient has been used by Montesquieu scholars as a means of dismissing its ethnographic content and of proleptically defending the president against accusations of ethnocentrism or mythography.[13] It appears to me that the breadth and complexity of Montesquieu's reflection on Oriental despotism belie the claim that his intentions were purely allegorical. Rather, they suggest that what we are presented with is a discourse in which beliefs about the Orient are articulated with a vision of French society. The deployment of despotism to attack French absolutism represents a classic case of the use of an external threat to stir up anxiety about a domestic issue—one thinks, for example, of the Cold War demonization of the Soviet Union to attack socialist movements within western Europe and the United States. However, I would submit that the fact that the representation of an other fulfills a domestic political agenda does not mean that it does not also communicate genuine beliefs about that other.

From the very beginning of *De l'Esprit des lois*, Oriental polygamy is represented not as the ultimate realization of a male fantasy, but as a vice-ridden and self-defeating practice: "it is said that the King of Morocco has in his harem white women, black women, and yellow women. Unfortunate man! he scarcely needs one color," Montesquieu laments. Yet having thus shed doubt on the amplitude of male virility, he proceeds to assert that "the possession of many women does not always eliminate the desire for those of another: lust is like avarice—the possession of many treasures only increases one's thirst." Apparently unable finally to determine whether polygamy inspires or drains desire, he circles back in the following paragraph to the claim that it culminates in satiety, disgust, and even homosexuality: "The possession of many women—who would suppose it!—leads to the love that nature disavows" (513).

This zigzagging between heterosexual excess and homosexual revulsion is not without precedent in Western writing on the Orient. In his widely read *Present State of the Ottoman Empire* (1668), for example, Sir Paul Rycaut claims that although the prophet Mohammed sanctioned polygamy with the aim to fight declining population, "this course thrives not so well among the Turks as formerly because of their accursed vice of sodomy" (153). The key to the surprising claim that polygamy leads to sodomy (i.e., homosexuality) emerges in Rycaut's allusion to the prophet's own "carnal and effeminate inclination" (153), where Oriental sensuality is attributed to a distinctly feminine subservience to the senses, not, as one might expect, to masculine virility. We can, however, also understand the recurrent link between polygamy and homosexuality in a second way, because one of the principal objections to slavery that Montesquieu (among others) makes is that the master "*contracts* with his slaves all kinds of bad habits" (490); it would seem therefore to follow that in the closed world of the seraglio, the despot is contaminated—that is to say, effeminized—by his excessive contact with the enslaved women who surround him.

In the course of his meditation on the seraglio, Montesquieu reviews the various factors that demand the claustration of women in different climates or political regimes. He is particularly concerned with the dangers that arise when the hot-blooded, sensual women of the tropics are permitted to circulate freely in society, and he presents his reader with a somewhat burlesque account of moral degeneracy in India: "In Patane the lechery of women is so great that men are forced to make themselves chastity-belts ['certaines garnitures'] in order to escape their advances" (516). Fear of female sexual aggression reaches a peak in the following passage, in which Montesquieu asserts that in Guinea, matters have become so bad that "the two sexes have lost their very laws" (516).

What emerges from this discussion of enclosure, as from the preceding meditation on polygamy, is anxiety about the potential erosion of sexual difference. Montesquieu voices a fear that if women circulate in society with the same freedom as men, or if the two sexes spend too much time in each other's company, they will ultimately cease to be different. This concern was by no means limited to Montesquieu or new to the Enlightenment. However, for reasons that I now want to examine, during this period anxiety about the loss of sexual difference assumed new proportions and was mustered in support of a specific set of political and social arguments.

The Shifting Grounds of Sex and Gender

In his influential work on the history of sex and gender, *Making Sex: The Body and Gender from the Greeks to Freud*, Thomas Laqueur has shown that between the late seventeenth and early nineteenth centuries, Western representations of sexual difference underwent a decisive change. Up to this point, female reproductive physiology was typically portrayed as male physiology, inverted: "In this world, the vagina is imagined as an interior penis, the labia as foreskin, the uterus as scrotum, and the ovaries as testicles" (Laqueur, *Making Sex*, 4). But by the late 1600s, this representation was being challenged by a second model that foregrounded the physiological differences of the sexes. As Laqueur shows, these biomedical models of resemblance and difference were saturated with cultural meaning.[14] Although the "one-sex model" had affirmed male physiology as the standard or norm and portrayed the female body as a deviation or inferior copy, it now began to seem fraught with dangers. Homosexuality and effeminacy were cited as evidence that if women were simply inverted men, then the differences between the sexes might themselves be subject to inversion. On the sociopolitical level, this instability threatened to undermine the hierarchy of gender, imperiling the foundations of men's authority over women. By contrast, in the "two-sex model," which represents sex as a dichotomy rather than as a hierarchy, asserting the different intellectual aptitudes of the sexes and advocating different lifestyles and forms of education, such reversals appeared less likely.

In this context of discursive change, explorations of racial alterity furnished a valuable testing ground on which different models of sexual difference could be reviewed. Notably, in the sphere of biomedical thought, the question of race played an important role in the debate over the mechanics of the human reproductive system. In 1672, Reinier de Graaf discovered the production of eggs in human ovaries.[15] Also in the 1670s, Antoine de Leuwenhook observed semen under a microscope and discovered sperm. Yet these discoveries did not resolve the mystery of embryo formation. In fact, the theory that dominated the scientific debate over human reproductive biology from the 1670s on was the idea of "preformationism," the argument that human life is preformed either in the egg or the sperm, and that the sexual encounter between male and female provides merely a stimulus to conception. In schematic terms, because it avers that humans of both sexes are preformed in the organs of either the male or the female partner, preformationist theory may be said to rest on, and reinforce, the one-sex model of the sexes.

By the middle years of the eighteenth century, dissenters, including Pierre de Maupertuis and Georges de Buffon, had begun to break away from this model, arguing that the possibility of inheriting racial characteristics from either a male or a female parent demonstrated that egg and sperm are jointly necessary to the formation of an embryo. Again in structural terms, this position can be said to be aligned with the two-sex model, for it emphasizes the complementarity of the sexes, the different material that each partner brings to the reproductive process.

A key text in this debate was Maupertuis's *Vénus physique* (*Physical Venus*; 1745). This popular scientific treatise had its roots in the author's earlier meditation, *Dissertation physique à l'occasion du nègre blanc*, on the genetic makeup of the "white Negro" ("nègre blanc"), an African albino who was exhibited in Paris in 1744. Maupertuis found seemingly irrefutable evidence of the possibility of inheriting characteristics from both parents in the study of interracial reproduction. (In fact, in the high-profile case of the "white Negro," he took this reasoning too far, erroneously attributing the albino's coloration to racial mixing or to the reemergence of buried racial traits.[16])

Scientific discourse provides only one illustration of a much broader process by which the (ostensibly) well-defined differences between Europe and the rest of the world were used to create a perspective from which to examine the (apparently) more intractable problem of the differences between the sexes. The obsessive perusal of sexual relations in the Orient effectively "Orientalized" the women of Europe in order that their difference could be magnified and assessed and the appropriate conclusions drawn. As I have begun to suggest, the outcome of this exchange was not what one might expect, for far from advocating subjugation and enclosure on the Oriental model, French writers discerned in these repressive practices a dangerous instability that threatened to undermine both sexual difference and the social fabric.

Gender and the Public Sphere

To understand more fully the use of Oriental despotism to stage concerns about gender in France, we must also consider a second historical shift, a shift that in certain respects paralleled the biomedical evolution that I have described. This metamorphosis was the rapid expansion of the public sphere that occurred in conjunction with the transition from absolutist state to bourgeois society.

In his influential account of the rise of liberal democratic society, *The Structural Transformation of the Public Sphere*, Jürgen Habermas argues that in the early modern nation-state, the "public" sphere was coextensive with the authority and institutions of the monarchy, whereas the "private" sphere was composed of individuals who did not hold public office. Over the course of the eighteenth century, these categories were transformed by the emergence, within the realm of private individuals, of a "public" that engaged in critical debate of cultural, economic, and political issues. This public was at once a partial social reality, exemplified by social institutions such as the literary salons, coffeehouses, Masonic lodges, regional academies, and the growing world of print journalism, and by a normative ideal of free and rational communication among human beings.

The coming together of private individuals to constitute a public had a secondary consequence, for as a result of this process of restructuration, the private sphere itself came to comport two distinct dimensions: the activities of public life and the domestic life of the conjugal family. In the political theory and iconography of the latter part of the century, these two domains were increasingly differentiated: the individual's participation in public affairs was rigorously separated from the conduct of his private life, laying the foundations of the model of privacy with which we are familiar today—a privacy many of us feel to be imperiled by media scrutiny and advances in the technologies of surveillance.

In principle, the constitution of a public sphere involved the recognition of the freedom and the equal right to participate in the political process of all human beings. In practice, however, such rights were often ascribed only to the class of male property owners, while women and other dependents were relegated to the status of "domestic" subjects. Thus, although women played an active role in shaping the literary public, or the "republic of letters," they were progressively excluded from the more explicitly political and economic debates conducted in coffeehouse society and the periodical press. Simultaneously, a growing number of cultural representations wove a web of images and arguments designating woman's proper place as the home or domestic sphere.

The most radical historical account of this gendering of public space has been provided by Joan Landes, who in her feminist revision of Habermas's original thesis, *Women and the Public Sphere in the Age of the French Revolution*, maintains that the growth of the bourgeois public sphere was inextricably linked to a system of cultural representation through which men came to perceive themselves as "properly political" while women were identified as "naturally domestic" (2, 4). Landes goes so far as to argue that the exclusion of women from the bourgeois public sphere was an essential rather than a merely incidental aspect of its development, and that the central categories of liberal thought—universal reason, law, and nature—must therefore be seen to be "embedded in an ideologically sanctioned order of gender differences" (11).[17] Perhaps unsurprisingly, this radical assertion has been contended from a number of quarters; notably, Keith Michael Baker, Lawrence Klein, Dena Goodman and Suzanne Desan have all argued that Landes is wont to identify the bourgeois public sphere as a whole with the ideology of sexual segregation promoted by Jean-Jacques Rousseau, and as a result paints a too homogeneous picture of the exclusion of women from the evolution of liberal democracy.[18]

I invoke these debates about gender and social space because, although I am inclined to agree with Landes's critics that neither as a matter of fact nor as a matter of cultural representation was the exclusion of women from the public sphere as uniform as she implies, I also believe that the obsessive representation in Enlightenment literature of the Oriental harem as a site in which crucial distinctions between domestic and political, male and female, are imperiled lends some support to Landes's far-reaching claims for a progressive gendering of public and private spaces and activities. When read in the light of this representational tradition, Rousseau's arguments in favor of the rigorous differentiation of the sexes, the renewal of the maternal instinct, and the circumscription of women to the domestic sphere appear not as a unique, albeit influential, prototype, but as the culmination of a long-standing meditation on the proper place of women in French society.

Rousseau himself used the theme of Oriental despotism to advance his social agenda in his polemical *Letter to d'Alembert on the Theater* (1758), a text that exploits the negative image of the harem in contemporary culture as a rhetorical device in its offensive against women's influence on the cultural life of the nation. In this diatribe, the Parisian *salonnière* is painted as a languid and indolent despot who wields her authority over a coterie of literary luminaries, themselves depicted as emasculated men, and, implicitly, as eunuchs:

> every woman gathers in her Paris apartment a harem of men more womanish
> than she. . . . But observe these same men, always constrained in these
> voluntary prisons, get up, sit down, pace continually back and forth . . .
> while the idol, stretched out motionlessly on her couch, has only her
> eyes and her tongue active. (100–101)

The antidote that Rousseau proposes to this salon-seraglio—the spatial embodiment of excessive female influence and the deleterious mixing of the sexes—is the gyneceum portrayed—and celebrated—in his novel, *La Nouvelle Héloïse*: the home (or more specifically, the nursery) that woman freely accepts as her proper domain.

It was, however, not Rousseau but Montesquieu who most fully deployed the "veil of Orient" to ponder the position of women in French society. We have seen that in his discussion of the Oriental seraglio, in the *Esprit des lois*, Montesquieu claims that polygamy itself is not the sole cause of the enclosure of women; the unbridled sexual appetite of women in warm climates and despotic government itself are also claimed as reasons for claustration. In fact, as Michèle Crampe-Casnabet claims, Montesquieu discovers all too many reasons for locking women up, raising the suspicion that under the "veil of Orient," he is pondering whether *European* women's free participation in the social life of the nation is in fact desirable.[19] Montesquieu explicitly denies the need to enclose European women, whose passions he finds to be naturally calm, but hypothetical passages such as the following, which contemplates what would occur if frivolous French women were set loose in a despotic regime, show that the discourse on the seraglio is always at the same time a discourse about gender in France:

> Let us suppose for a moment that the frivolity and indiscretion, the likes
> and dislikes of our women . . . were transported into an Oriental govern-

ment with the same activity and liberty they enjoy here: what father would feel a moment's peace? . . . rivers of blood would flow. (*Esprit des lois*, 515)

Despite these ruminations, Montesquieu does not advocate the extension of the Oriental model to France. As we have seen, he associates Oriental government not with the preservation of the social order, but with the dangerous erasure of essential differences between the sexes and between public and domestic life. The seraglio is for him an unstable environment in which the despot is effeminized by his contact with women and in which government is corrupted by its entanglement in the personal life of the ruler—a depiction whose secondary target, as I have suggested, is the court of Versailles, at once the home of the monarch's family and the center of government, a world not strictly divided between public and private sectors, a world in which women could aspire to become the "power behind the throne."

But if Montesquieu rejects the Oriental scenario, he is also manifestly disturbed by the current state of affairs in France. Although he never condemns the French social model outright, he does wag his finger at the corrupt atmosphere of the court, characterized by the immodesty of women and their unbridled influence in affairs of state:

> Women show little restraint in monarchies because the distinction of rank calls them to the court, where they develop that freedom of spirit that is the only behavior tolerated there. Each man uses their charms and their passions to advance his fortune; and, as their weakness does not lead to pride, but only to vanity, luxury always reigns there with them. (*Lettres persanes*, letters VII, IX)

As this passage illustrates, Montesquieu associates women with everything that might be considered frivolous, decadent, and elitist in French society, in particular with consumption, luxury, and fashion.[20] In this respect, the *Esprit des lois* pursues an agenda begun in 1721 in the *Lettres persanes*, where Montesquieu pokes fun at women's excessive concern with fashion and draws attention to the extraordinary, if not despotic, power that they wield in matters of taste:

> A woman decides that she must wear a certain outfit on a particular occasion, and at once it becomes impossible for fifty artisans to get

any sleep, or to have leisure to eat or drink; she gives her orders and is obeyed more promptly than our monarch, as self-interest is the greatest monarch on earth. (*Lettres persanes*, letter CVI)

The tone of these passages is undoubtedly more mocking than hostile. Montesquieu was not Rousseau, and he never explicitly advocated the regeneration of French society through the exclusion of women from public life. However, his reflection on women's excessive political and cultural influence, and his repeated complaints about women's moral laxity, are conceptually tied to more serious concerns about the decomposition of contemporary society—to themes such as declining population, abortion, filial disobedience, and the social ascension of the bourgeoisie that surface throughout his writing, as they do in the works of many of his contemporaries.

Dissatisfied with both Oriental and European models of social organization, it seems to me that Montesquieu weaves the two together to produce a third scenario, a model that is sketched out in the following passage, in which the practice of enclosing women is presented in the most general of terms, as though it in fact concerned all women, European as well as Oriental:

> Women must not only be separated from men by the enclosure of the house; they must also be separated within this enclosure, such that they constitute a *family within the family*. From this derives their whole practice of morality. . . . Women have naturally to fulfill so many duties that are proper to them that they cannot be separated enough from everything that might give them other ideas, from all that is called amusement or . . . affairs. (*Esprit des lois*, 515; my italics)

In this passage, it is argued that women should be kept inside the house—revealingly, Montesquieu says house ("maison") rather than seraglio ("sérail")—so that they can pursue their appointed tasks without distraction. But it is also argued that they should occupy a distinct sphere within the household, such that they form a "family within the family." This curious prescription reads almost as the literary correlate of a historical transformation: the gradual scission of civil society into the divergent sectors of publicity and intimacy. In other words, the call to constitute women as a "family within the family" is not merely an expression of male paranoia but also a literary transposition of ongoing changes in the organization of the social sphere.

I want to support this interpretation by comparing the passage that I have just cited to a rather similar passage that appears in the *Lettres persanes*. In this earlier passage, Montesquieu's Rica represents French women who meddle in affairs of state as a kind of political fifth column:[21]

> When I arrived in France I found the late sovereign absolutely governed by women. . . . These women all have relations with each other and form a kind of republic whose always active members help and serve each other: it is like a second *state within the state*. (*Lettres persanes*, letter CVII; my italics)

This letter typifies a widespread grafting of criticism of absolutist rule onto criticism of the political influence of elite women. Montesquieu, however, adds a new twist to the conventional complaint that the court, public institutions, and social interaction are "absolutely governed by women" by implying that women have gone so far as to constitute themselves as a distinct political entity, a "kind of republic" or "state within the state." This alarming political metaphor warns of the decomposition of the nation, vaguely alluding to the revolts of the *Fronde* during which aristocratic women played a prominent role. The comparison of Oriental and occidental models seems in fact to produce in Montesquieu at least a subliminal sense that, excluded both from affairs of state and the economic transactions of civil society, women lacked a clearly circumscribed place in the body politic. As a result, he begins to look at them as a volatile and rather dangerous class, a "state within the state" or "foreign body" that represents a potential threat to the cohesiveness of national identity.[22]

The structural similarity between the representation of women as a "state within the state" and the declaration that they should, by contrast, constitute a "family within the family" suggests that during the twenty-seven years that elapsed between the publication of the *Lettres persanes* and that of *De l'Esprit des lois*, Montesquieu, like many of his contemporaries, had tentatively begun to formulate a new model of gender relations in French society. Rejecting both the "despotic" model (by which, despite their formal sub-

jugation, women wield power as a result of the weak differentiation of public and domestic spheres) and the "monarchic" model (by which women are
perceived to exercise a preponderant influence in public affairs), he advocates
a more stringent demarcation of boundaries between public and domestic
life, male and female roles. As Joan Landes asserts, Montesquieu ultimately
turns to a "less sumptuous, more continent ideal of womanhood, one that
places women within the domestic realm," and whose prototype was the
Roman republic, a political context in which, although formally free,
women were confined to the domestic sphere by the force of custom and by
the weight of their own virtue (*Women and the Public Sphere*, 37).

Like many of his contemporaries, Montesquieu wrote extensively about
the Roman republic and admired many of its political ideals. This does not
mean, however, as Landes is wont to imply, that he was himself a proponent
of republicanism. Montesquieu's interest clearly lay in reforming the monarchy, not overhauling the political system.[23] The model of the republican family did, however, exercise an important influence on his political thought to
the extent that it guided his perception of the monarch as the father of the
nation. The belief that the monarch enjoyed a paternal relation to his subjects was by no means limited to Montesquieu: at the beginning of the eighteenth century, most French subjects probably looked up to the king as a
kind of father. However, by midcentury, as the Enlightenment gained
momentum, this metaphor of political authority was beginning to lose its
force. Montesquieu attempted to revitalize this paradigm of social relations
by subjecting it to a process of critique and by using Oriental despotism as
a *repoussoir*, a negative image of overbearing paternalism to which the
Bourbon monarchy could be likened.

In fact, it seems reasonable to argue that the central role that the concept
of despotism plays in Montesquieu's political thought derives directly from
his fundamental belief that paternal authority is the natural form of all
authority,[24] for as Voltaire pointed out in one of his numerous assaults on
Montesquieu's theory of Oriental despotism, the Greek term *despot*, unlike
the word *tyrant*, originally referred to an unjust father or master of a household, not an unjust king.[25] In building a political discourse around this term,
Montesquieu implies that royal paternalism has become corrupt and over-

bearing and that the king ought to become a different, less authoritarian kind of father.

The remedy that he proposes throughout his writings is a contractual union resembling that of the conjugal family: a political structure in which, within the parameters of a certain degree of freedom and equality, distinct social—and sexual—identities are preserved. Needless to say, the drive to reform the "national family" ultimately exceeded the goals that Montesquieu set for it. As Lynn Hunt has shown, the valorization of the benevolent patriarch in the political discourse and iconography of the midcentury was but the first step in a long process by which the "children" came to assert their own rights and to construct the model of liberty, equality, and *fraternity* that finally dislodged the father from his position of supremacy (*Family Romance*, 1–16).

THE COLONIAL FOREIGN BODY

Now that I have identified the concerns about domestic culture that underlie Montesquieu's lifelong fascination with the Orient, I want to return to his thinking on colonialism and to highlight some significant parallels between these two areas of his thought. I argued above that the discussion of the colonies in the *Esprit des lois* rests almost exclusively on the Spanish colonies in the Americas, while the attendant problem of slavery is transposed onto the Orient. I now want to show that one result of this displacement is a series of structural parallels between Montesquieu's critique of Oriental polygamy and despotism and his opposition to colonial expansion in the Atlantic.

The most evident relationship between polygamy and the colonies is that both are identified by Montesquieu, as by other contemporary thinkers, as causes of falling population.[26] Anxiety about the depopulation of Europe was a recurrent theme of Enlightenment literature, in part, as Carol Blum has shown, because it was a valuable critical device. Falling population could, after all, easily be attributed to the kinds of practices that the *philosophes* decried, notably the celibacy of the clergy, extravagant military campaigns, and the prohibition of divorce in Catholic countries. Depopulation anxiety was also woven into the debate over women's position in French society, as women's active participation in the cultural and political life of the nation was increasingly identified as a source of such social scourges as adultery, abortion, and infertile marriage. Within this discursive framework the Oriental harem functioned, not as a corrective but as a *repoussoir*, a powerful negative image of what would happen if gender boundaries were not reaffirmed.

In the *Lettres persanes*, Montesquieu devotes a block of eleven letters (letters CXII–CXXII) to the causes of global depopulation since Roman times. In one of these letters (letter CXIV), he describes the deleterious effects of Oriental polygamy, comparing the Moslem man to "an athlete destined to compete without respite, but who, quickly weakened and overcome by his first trials, languishes on the very field of his triumphs." Exhausted by polygamous marriage, the Moslem husband suffers from impotence or infertility, or is the parent of unhealthy children:

> Among us it is quite common to see a man with a sizable harem surrounded by a very small number of children. These children are, for the most part, weak and unhealthy and suffer from the languor of their father. (letter CXIV)

This diatribe pits unbridled female sexuality—represented in the context of the harem as the sexual demands of a large number of women—against the limits of male virility.[27] Subtending this account is a primitive version of the master–slave dialectic: although the Moslem husband is ostensibly the master of his enslaved wives, it is the slaves who ultimately gain the upper hand and who drain away the strength of their master. In the *Lettres persanes*, Zélis writes from the harem to her ostensibly free husband Usbek "in the very prison in which you keep me I am freer than you" (letter LXII).

In Montesquieu's depopulation letters, the establishment of far-flung colonies is also examined as a potential cause of depopulation. Focusing on the Spanish colonies in the Americas, Montesquieu argues that vast colonies drain people and resources away from the mainland. He compares empires to "a tree whose over-extended branches draw all the sap from the trunk and do nothing but give shade" (letter CXXI). In the figural economy of this analogy, the tree trunk—which represents the metropolis but also, on a subliminal level, the penis—is said to be drained by the extension of its resources to distant branches. This critique of colonial expansion illustrates the inter-mingling of colonial discourse with the thinking on sexuality that I have already noted. It is fraught with concerns about reproductive failure—or to be more precise, about the squandering of bodily fluids and demographic resources.

These were ideas with a future. Beginning with Mirabeau's 1756 *L'Ami des hommes* (a rather isolated reflection on colonialism and the slave/plantation system in the period before the 1760s), which draws on the metaphor of the tree to tie population growth and economic prosperity to human happiness, economic philosophers represented colonial agriculture as a benighted sys-tem that served only to drain the resources of the soil and argued that the introduction of free trade into the colonies would immediately expose the dispendious wastefulness of slavery and plantation agriculture. In a different, although fundamentally parallel vein, by the end of the century, the Orient itself—characterized by Montesquieu as a region of overextended empires—was consistently associated with depopulation and desertification. *L'Orient désert*, a key trope of Romanticism, signified both the deserted Orient and the Orient as desert. Ironically, through one of the reversals characteristic of colonial rhetoric, this literary metaphor of the emptiness or tabula rasa of the Orient ultimately provided a rationale for the European colonial occupation of Egypt and North Africa.

Drawing on the hallowed metaphor of the body politic, Montesquieu represents colonies as dangerous overextensions of the body of the nation.[28] In an unpublished fragment of the *Esprit des lois*, he observes that "the monarch who establishes colonies does nothing but give himself very distant states that weaken the *body* of his monarchy" (1007; my italics), while in the *Considérations sur les richesses de l'Espagne* (*Considerations on the Wealth of Spain*; c. 1724), he writes that "The vast expanse of this country [America] means that it [Spain] can derive almost nothing from it, for the strength of this great *body* is entirely spent in sustaining and defending it" (209; my ital-ics).[29] The portrayal of the colonial encounter as the meeting of two bodies is echoed in the assertion that colonialism is responsible for the global spread of disease, and in particular for the spread of syphilis, another obvious cause of depopulation. Thus, Montesquieu inveighs that "it was the thirst for gold that perpetuated this sickness; people kept going to America and on each occasion brought back new germs" (*Esprit des lois*, 485). The colonizers' figural thirst for gold causes them to ingest a "germ" that attacks and undermines the reproductive health of the nation. The very gold that the conquistadors imported to Spain is represented as a foreign body, a destabilizing force that wrought havoc on the domestic economy: "there was an *internal* and *physical* vice in the nature of these riches, which rendered them useless; and this vice increased every day," Montesquieu writes (*Esprit des lois*, 674; my italics), citing the bankruptcy of Philip II as evidence that the influx of precious metals from the New World ruined rather than improved the health of the Spanish economy. In the organicist rhetoric of these passages, colonial wealth is represented as an "internal and physical vice," a self-reproducing cancer or virus that progressively spreads throughout the healthy body politic.

The forces underlying Montesquieu's critique of colonial expansion become clearer when we consider that colonialism, like polygamy, is approached as a master–slave dialectic, an unequal, repressive, and therefore unstable bond that in the end endangers the dominant partner. The encounter between cultures, like the encounter between the sexes, is deemed dangerous where there is subjugation without true "commerce," in either the sexual or the mercantile sense of the term. Consequently, Montesquieu ultimately questions the entire structure of global trade, observing that although the gold that Europeans mine in the West Indies is applied to commerce with the East, there is absolutely no market for European products in either part of the world (*Esprit des lois*, 674). In such conditions, where there is no reciprocity, no mutual exchange, the conquered territory stands as an "other" that is neither fully distinct from the metropolitan culture, nor fully assimilated into it—an alien presence that threatens to blur the boundaries of its social and economic identity.

Given these parallels, it is unsurprising that in his writing on colonialism, Montesquieu prescribes the very remedy that he prescribes in the case of gender relations—that is to say, the replacement of repressive structures with more egalitarian practices, and the preservation of difference through a recognition of reciprocity or (re)productive complementarity. Perhaps the most striking confirmation of this consonance comes in Montesquieu's extraordinary assertion that it would have been desirable for one Native American family to move to Spain for every Spanish family that had settled in the West Indies (799), a call for miscegenation and reciprocity that betrays the thorough abstraction of Montesquieu's account of colonialism and its divorce from any concrete historical reality, but that also testifies to the latent presence of other cultural concerns.

IDENTITY, DIFFERENCE, AND LANGUAGE

The concerns about the effects of difference on identity that I have explored in this chapter are historical in nature. They testify to the fact that the Enlightenment was a period of transition which in France culminated in a radical political upheaval; they also testify to the profound impact that the discovery of other civilizations had on Europeans' perception of their own cultural identity. The structural parallels that I have identified among thinking on gender, thinking on the Orient, and thinking on the colonies are likewise, at least in part, the result of a historically specific displacement of the unpalatable truths of New World slavery onto the Oriental context. However, these parallels could also be considered in a less historical light: as symptomatic expressions of the fact that in the last analysis, the social construction of difference has typically been organized around a relatively limited number of conceptual operations. The principal point that I wish to make in this regard is that the exchanges that I have brought to light are facilitated by the fact that the one- and two-sex models are structurally equivalent to two foundational models of ethnographic thought. That is to say, the one-sex model of gender, on which the female body is approached as a variant of a male body, itself perceived as the standard or norm, can be said to correspond to the universalistic position that is often ascribed to the European Enlightenment, and in particular to Voltaire, a position that affirms the existence of a universal human nature, yet all too often identifies this shared essence with the norms of European culture. By contrast, the two-sex model of gender is roughly analogous to the emphasis on cultural difference that we encounter in Montesquieu's ethnographic thinking.

Each of these models of alterity—which, following Luce Irigaray, we could call the "other of the same" and the "other of the other"—has its defects (*Ce sexe*, esp. 98–105). Both participate, in the end, in the attempt to reduce or to contain difference, to exclude it from "the self" or "home culture," to domesticate or assimilate it. In making this observation, I do not mean to imply that these are the only available models of ethnographic inquiry—to do so would be to eliminate all the complexity and nuance of the field—but rather to suggest that the question of whether peoples, or the sexes, are fundamentally alike or profoundly different is one that surfaces in ethnographic and scientific thinking, popular and academic, even today.

In its exploration of questions of difference, *De l'Esprit des lois* consistently leans toward the firm separation of "self" and "other," men and women, metropolis and colonies, deflecting the recognition that because identity and difference are constructed in language, itself a boundless web of resemblances and differences, alterity invariably inhabits the "self." In the following chapter, I will turn to Montesquieu's Enlightenment classic, *Lettres persanes*, a novel whose subject is even more explicitly the experience of human diversity. In my reading, I will argue that although the work of fiction gives narrative expression to many of the same cultural concerns that surface in the sociological treatise, it also articulates a far more complex relation to difference. I will show that by binding the alterity of Oriental women to the perceived foreignness of language, this epistolary novel—in which language is inevitably portrayed as an indispensable constituent of human identity— tacitly acknowledges that foreignness is an integral dimension of the "self" or domestic culture.

CHAPTER TWO

Truth and Representations: Old and New Languages in the *Lettres persanes*

Although there is a certain irony in the fact that the *Lettres persanes* (*Persian Letters*; 1721), without question a classic of French literature and a staple of the eighteenth-century canon, defines what it means to be French from the perspective of a group of foreigners, the success of Montesquieu's novel, like that of many other Enlightenment representations of primitives, *ingénus*, and cultural outsiders, invites our recognition that national identities are often solidified through encounters with difference.[1] This process is, however, complex—and almost always double-edged. The *Lettres persanes* provides an exemplary illustration of the tensions that permeate ethnographic writing in the sense that it is structured around two contrasting principles: the drive to define identity in opposition to an "other" who is identified as a potential threat, and the countervailing recognition that alterity is woven into cultural identity. This tension is nowhere more apparent than in the novel's paradigmatic depiction of Oriental women, the "other's others" who embody both an extreme form of alterity against which cultural identity is measured and an otherness that resides within identity. This chapter explores this duality, focusing on the novel's central trope of unveiling as a site in which knowledge of "the other" is both accrued and problematized, and on the text's dualistic representation of language as both the instrument of knowledge and authority and a source of vulnerability—what one might call the blind spot in the epistemology of Enlightenment.

A CAUTIONARY TALE

The story told in the *Lettres persanes* is so well known that it scarcely needs retelling: two Persian travelers, Usbek and Rica, the former a married man and the latter a bachelor, travel across the Ottoman Empire and Italy to Paris.[2] The official motive for their journey appears to be scientific, but we soon learn that they are also fleeing persecution in their native land. As outsiders, the travelers enjoy a critical distance from French society, and they write their Persian friends a series of letters in which French social and political life is represented "anthropologically," as an assemblage of exotic practices that inspire interpretation and analysis. At home, under the watchful eye of his eunuchs, Usbek leaves behind him a harem of wives and concubines with whom he also corresponds. From these letters emerges a complex and overdetermined portrait of Oriental women, successively portrayed as heterosexual and homosexual, virtuous and unfaithful, submissive and defiant. Because Usbek's absence is prolonged, relations with home deteriorate, and at the end of the novel, the harem is overturned by a revolt led by Usbek's favorite and most trusted wife, Roxane (letter CLXI).

This dramatic ending has been the subject of many interpretations. Although it is most commonly read as a *cautionary* tale addressed to the absolutist monarchy of France, a prescient anticipation of the fall of Versailles, when it has come to analyzing the fact that the subjects in revolt are *women*, critics, including most recently political theorist Diana J. Schaub (*Erotic Liberalism*), have been inclined to argue that through this denouement Montesquieu *vindicates* the rights of the oppressed. There would seem to be a logical inconsistency in this interpretation, for if the novel is indeed a cautionary tale or veiled threat articulated by a disaffected monarchist, can it also be read as an unreserved affirmation of women's rights? I believe that it is more plausible to imagine that Montesquieu's parable addresses itself to a wider audience than the court; it warns not only of the dangers of political absolutism, but also of the need for a continuous reevaluation of the social position of women in France.

Montesquieu's decision to represent French society from the perspective of two outsiders perhaps reflects the fact that this society, which was undergoing a process of profound social change, in certain respects appeared new and different even to its own constituents. Notably, it seems plausible to argue that Montesquieu was responding to the unprecedented expansion in civil society that, following Jürgen Habermas, we have come to think of as the emergence of the "bourgeois public sphere." The openness of French society certainly makes a lasting impression on the Persian travelers, who are accustomed to a physically and intellectually closed environment in which social interaction is extremely limited. Given their own rigorously segregated culture, it is unsurprising that their most emphatic reaction is to the ubiquitous presence of women in French public life: as we saw in Chapter 1, their letters paint the picture of a world "absolutely governed by women" (290) and imply that women not only dictate who will be deemed witty or clever, but also who will receive political office or tokens of royal favor.

However, if Montesquieu uses the Persians' lack of familiarity with France to cast a critical glance at the social role of women, the dramatic disintegration of the harem at the end of the novel reveals, again, that he also had reservations about the Oriental model of gender relations and that he considered the unequal relationship between a master and his slaves to be dangerously unstable. In consequence, the novel may be seen to speak in favor of a middle way and to anticipate currents of gender ideology that emerged later in the century, as a result of which the differences between the sexes came to be perceived not as a matter of *indifference* or as a simple question of dominion, but as a fact of life mirrored in every aspect of the social system.[3]

I will not dwell on the details of this interpretation, both because it is presented at some length in Chapter 1 and because it has been amply explored by Joan Landes. Rather, I want to probe the sentiment that in my view underlies this anxiety about women's place in French society: the perception that women constitute a problematic class of "others" that must be carefully managed rather than violently repressed or accorded too much freedom. Although this attitude in France is by no means limited to the eighteenth century, it seems reasonable to conclude that as the country moved toward modern nationhood and began to contemplate the involvement of a broader stratum of the population in the process of government, the status of women and their integration in political life was increasingly subject to scrutiny. By using an alien culture as a lens through which to examine the position of women in France, Enlightenment social theory nurtured the perception that women constitute a "foreign element" within the body politic—a vision only intensified by the fact that the alien culture in question was the Orient, a world that had long appeared to Western spectators as enigmatic and secretive, and whose mystery was emblematized by the veiled woman.

As I argue in the Introduction, in the Western philosophical tradition, the veiled woman has served both as a figure for truth—for a foundational principle or hidden essence obscured by representation or by the structure of human perception—and as a metaphor for lies and dissimulation, notably for the perceived inscrutability of Oriental culture. This range of meanings is fully in evidence in the *Lettres persanes*, where the veil stands for both the truth of Woman and for the potential duplicity of women. The paragraphs that follow scan the scenes of literal and figural unveiling that are scattered throughout Montesquieu's novel. They propose that the narrative's repeated staging of veiling and unveiling serves as a mechanism by which the disturbing alterity of women is identified and controlled, but that at the same time the text tentatively maps out the fragility of the borders between revelation and concealment, truth and lie, knowledge and error, implicitly questioning the possibility of a definitive act of unveiling. In laying out this double reading, I draw a distinction between the *narrative* economy of the text, which propels the reader toward a closure that corresponds to the unveiling of Usbek's wives, and a less manifest *textual* economy. Following the example of Ross Chambers, I suggest that whereas the "narrative function" of the novel can be aligned with the authority of the author, the "textual function" is far more readerly in nature.[4] In the case of the *Lettres persanes*, this distinction between narrative and textuality, writing and reading, is embedded in the movement through which the closure achieved by the narrative is counteracted—although not fully negated—by the text's inscription of the futurity of its own reading. I will state from the outset that in formulating this distinction, I will no doubt overstate the differences between narrative and textual economies: the polyphonic narrative of the *Lettres persanes* is itself complex and certainly constitutes something more than an ideological address to the social concerns of the moment. My hope, however, is that by contrasting these two axes, I will avoid the tendency of many previous readers to produce a reading that determines the *Lettres persanes* to be either "positive" or "negative" in its approach to gender or in its conceptualization of cultural difference, and instead draw attention to the complex array of historical forces asserting themselves in the novel.

UNVEILING WOMEN

Unlike most of the travel narratives from which Montesquieu gathered information about the Orient, the *Lettres persanes* makes almost no attempt to describe the elaborate costumes of the women of the harem.[5] It does, however, show a pronounced interest in the veil, the piece of Oriental attire most closely associated with the difference and mystery of the Orient. From the moment that Usbek arrives in Livorno, he writes in astonishment to his friend Ibben that in Italy, women wear only a single veil (164); in a note, Montesquieu insists on this point by reminding the reader that Persian women are rigorously concealed beneath no fewer than four.[6] Immediately, then, the veil assumes the role of a cultural marker, a line of demarcation between Europe and the Orient, Christianity and Islam, secular and religious society, a powerful emblem of cultural difference that fosters the perception that to unveil the woman is to penetrate the culture.

Unveiling is first represented early in the novel when Zachi, one of the wives whom Usbek has left behind in the harem, sends her husband a sycophantic letter in which she complains of his absence and protests that his physical presence is necessary to her emotional well-being.[7] In recollecting her past fulfillment, she recreates a scene in which Usbek, surrounded by wives and concubines competing for preference, performs an Oriental version of the Judgment of Paris, offering a reward—his own person—to the lucky winner. What Zachi represents as a personal memory is in reality a topos of Oriental travel writing. European travelers ranging from Sir Paul Rycaut to Lady Mary Wortley Montagu describe a ceremony in which the sultan is surrounded by a circle of adoring concubines, all competing for his favor. According to Rycaut, the sultan drops a handkerchief before the object of his choice, and she is congratulated by envious rivals (Rycaut, *Present State of the Ottoman Empire*, 39).[8]

In her version of this custom, Zachi describes how the women at first appear before Usbek adorned "in all the clothes and ornaments that the imagination can conceive." She reminds him that he applauded their efforts and "saw with pleasure the miracles of our art" (135), then recollects that, unable to choose between them—or simply hoping for further entertainment—he commands them to "appear . . . in the simplicity of nature." The wives obediently shed all marks of artifice and are literally unveiled such that they present themselves in their "natural" or true form. Usbek now ceases to be a passive spectator, and he undertakes a probing investigation of the female body that culminates in carnal knowledge. Not only are the carefully concealed bodies of Oriental women unveiled, but the most secret recesses of their femininity are exposed to the penetration of his gaze.

The dialogue between female exhibitionism and male voyeurism that structures this scene is tellingly captured in the engraving reproduced in Figure 3. This engraving, drawn by Charles-François Édouard de Beaumont, is one that appears in a number of editions of the *Lettres persanes* published in France and England in the mid- and late nineteenth century. During the fin de siècle period, many novels of the previous century were re-edited in special series adorned with illustrations that in many instances accentuate the suggestive eroticism of the narrative (see also Figure 4, in which the corporal punishment of the wives is exploited for its erotic subtext).[9] In the set of engravings by Beaumont, Usbek is represented with his back to the viewer-reader, whereas the bodies of his wives are fully displayed, a voyeuristic position that mirrors that of the reader as he or she becomes viewer of the scene. In short, the engravings can be said to draw attention to Usbek's status as a "surrogate voyeur"—an Oriental spectator who functions as a masked figure for the voyeurism of the Western public.[10] The text itself in fact appears to acknowledge this potential for a transmission or contagion of voyeurism, for in her remembrance of the scene as a scene, Zachi herself remains detached from it, as though she too were an observer sexually stimulated by the visualization of her own past.

The immanence of the women's naked bodies apparently fails to satisfy Usbek, because, still unable to choose, he commands his wives to assume different positions as though they were models posing for a painter: "in an instant you made us adopt a thousand different postures," Zachi reminds him (135). The empirical experience of viewing the naked body is thereby transformed into an aesthetic experience in which the boundaries between observation and creation are eroded. Thus, although the baring of the wives initially promises to disclose the truth of the natural body, what the unveiling related by Zachi ultimately displays is a nude: a body that is clothed in representation.[11] This epistemological shift loosely prefigures the historical trajectory of Orientalist representation, for it previews in miniature the progression from the empiricism characteristic of seventeenth- and eighteenth-century ethnography to the aestheticization of Oriental women that dominates nineteenth-century Orientalist literature and painting. The representation of Zachi's unveiling also discloses an important political and epistemological duality, for although her body is incontestably exposed to satisfy the curiosity of the Western reader, the text complicates this act of unveiling in a way that conveys the impossibility of attaining a position of truth or objectivity beyond the veil of representation.

This duality is enacted again later in the narrative when Zachi is unveiled for a second time, this time in a figural sense. The sycophantic rhetoric of the letter cited above is progressively discredited when Zachi is chastised by Usbek, first for encouraging the advances of a white eunuch (160), and a little later in the novel for cavorting with one of her own female slaves (362). Yet although we are inclined to believe that Zachi is in fact unfaithful, the absence of a single narrative perspective means that the eunuchs' reports of Zachi's misconduct are never definitively confirmed. As a result, the act of unveiling fails yet again to establish beyond question the unmediated, unvarnished truth.

Unveiling also plays a central role in the dismantling of the harem narrated in the final letters of the text. In an uncanny anticipation of the events of 1789, Usbek's wives, perhaps in complicity with some of the eunuchs, at least for a time overthrow the authority of the master. This upheaval is precipitated by a series of unveilings by means of which the closed world of the harem is opened to the outside, in much the same way that the secretive process of French government was slowly made open to the public and subjected to its critical evaluation (notably, for example, by Finance Minister Jacques Necker's decision in 1784 to render public the royal budget). The *Lettres persanes* is in fact not the only text by Montesquieu that deploys unveiling as a metaphor for political crisis. This trope is also brought to bear

Figures 3 and 4. Illustrations for *Lettres persanes*, drawn by E. de Beaumont, engraved by E. Boilvin, circa 1869. Source: *Persian Letters*, Philadelphia: G. Barrie, 1901(?), 16, 217. Courtesy of General Research Division, New York Public Library, Astor, Lenox and Tilden Foundations.

in *Arsace et Isménie*, a highly politicized Oriental fiction that Montesquieu wrote in the early 1740s. The comparison of these two works proves instructive because although they are broadly parallel, they are in certain key respects different, and these differences provide a valuable perspective on the epistemological and political stakes of the *Lettres persanes* and a small window on the historical evolution of Montesquieu's political thinking.[12]

Arsace et Isménie opens with an autobiographical narrative. Arsace, a young foreigner who has just defended the state of Bactriane against an invasion, recounts the story of his life to Aspar, the chief eunuch of Bactriane. Unlike the eunuchs of the *Lettres persanes*, who are suspect both in their ability to govern and in their fidelity to their master, Aspar is a model of statesmanship and loyalty—the first in a series of contrasts that defines the relationship between *Arsace et Isménie* and the *Lettres persanes* as one of optimistic inversion. The story that Aspar hears is the somewhat convoluted tale of Arsace's relationship with his wife, Ardasire, whom he abandoned for motives of political ambition and who subsequently died. Having listened to his guilt-ridden tale, Aspar hints to his young protégé that it may yet have an unexpected ending. Several days later, a mob gathers outside the palace of Bactriane in response to a rumor that the queen has been replaced by an impostor. Aspar steps to the fore and admits that the queen has indeed died, but that he has placed on the throne her twin sister Isménie, whom he had earlier sent to a foreign country in the interests of national security. With the crisis averted, he makes preparations for a ceremony in which Arsace is to be invested as a general. It is during this ceremony that the plot reaches its denouement: the new queen unveils herself, revealing to the assembled crowd "the face of beauty itself" (*Arsace et Isménie*, 489). In fact, this climactic unveiling not only proves once and for all that Isménie is the rightful queen—she is identical to her sister—but also reveals to Arsace that she is none other than his wife Ardasire (whose death turns out to have been a feint orchestrated by Aspar). In all its points, this narrative conforms to what I describe in my Introduction as the "correspondence" theory of truth—the model that takes truth to be the correlation of a representation or perception with a principle that exists beyond representation. The woman who is unveiled is not only the rightful ruler and Arsace's wife, but also a "true," unimpeachably faithful woman.[13]

J'allais.....j'allais la préférer à elle même.

Figure 5.   Illustration for *Arsace et Isménie*, drawn by Le Barbier,
engraved by Courbe. Source: *Arsace et Isménie* in *Le Temple de Gnide*,
Paris: Didot Jeune, 1795, 156. Courtesy of Pierpont Morgan Library,
New York.

This final unveiling echoes an episode that occurs earlier in the story in which, to test her husband's love, Ardasire disguises herself as a foreign princess. As the drawing of this scene by Le Barbier, which first appeared in an edition of the tale published posthumously in 1796, suggests (Figure 5), this attempted seduction thoroughly confuses Arsace because the veiled stranger to whom he is so powerfully attracted is in reality none other than the wife he loves (480).[14] Erotic substitutions of this type—a woman disguises herself in order to test or recover the affection of a lover—are a recurrent theme of eighteenth-century literature. Perhaps the best known example is Beaumarchais's *Mariage de Figaro* (*The Marriage of Figaro*), in which the Countess Almaviva disguises herself as her own maid to win back the count's love. What is interesting about these scenes is that the pleasure attached to the substitution derives not only from the moment of disguise— the metaphorical exchange of one woman for another—but also from the final unveiling of identity, the revelation that the beautiful stranger is none other than Ardasire, or that the soubrette is really the countess. In other words, the substitution is appealing, not only, as we might suppose, because it confirms men's power to exchange women, but also because it affirms the reassuring figure of Woman as truth and the attendant conviction that Woman "corresponds" to herself.

The denouement of *Arsace et Isménie* is particularly reassuring from the masculine perspective because Arsace is made a general and then king, such that love and political power, forces opposed throughout the narrative, are reconciled. Indeed, the very name "Ardasire" suggests the union of royal power and erotic love. Following his ascension, Ardasire-Isménie abdicates her authority and retires to private life, thereby assuaging any residual anxiety about women's participation in the political affairs of the nation. In fact, with a single gesture, the ending of the story erases residual fears both about women's participation in public life and about the erosion of sexual difference: the queen buckles around her husband's waist a sword—symbol of both political power and sexual prowess—and proceeds to delegate her authority to him.

As we have begun to see, the *Lettres persanes* approaches the act of unveiling with considerably less confidence. Whereas Isménie drops her veil to assure the survival of the monarchy and to affirm her fidelity to Arsace,

Usbek's wives drop theirs in flagrant transgression not only of his authority but also of the moral traditions of Islam.

Things in the harem begin to deteriorate when Usbek learns from one of his eunuchs that a young man has been sighted on the grounds, that a secret correspondence has been surprised, and that "several days ago on her way to the mosque, Zélis allowed her veil to fall and appeared before the people with her face almost uncovered" (362). Zélis's transgression is disturbing, but it pales in comparison with the figural unveiling of another of Usbek's wives, the one woman in whose virtue Usbek had always believed. Despite the fact that her name resonates with the literary history of perfidious Oriental women,[15] for much of the novel, Roxane appears to her husband to be modest and dutiful, the very embodiment of the masculine ideal of the truth of woman. As late as letter CLI, the eunuch Solim assures Usbek that "Roxane alone has remained dutiful and maintained her modesty" (365). He is, however, soon obliged to tell his master that he was mistaken, and that her virtue was in reality "the veil of her perfidy" (371).

The radically different outcomes of Montesquieu's two harem tales are in part attributable to the fact that whereas the *Lettres persanes* explores the vicissitudes of despotism and polygamous marriage, *Arsace et Isménie* narrates the abandonment of these practices in favor of more stable and egalitarian structures: enlightened monarchy and the complementarity of the sexes within the couple. Indeed, after the completion of the plot proper, *Arsace et Isménie* continues as a treatise on enlightened monarchy. As I suggested in the previous chapter, we can also, very tentatively, ascribe this change in outcome to a change in cultural atmosphere between the early 1720s, when concern over the biological and political differences between the sexes existed only in latent form, and the 1740s, a decade in which Montesquieu, like many of his contemporaries, began to gravitate toward a new ideological resolution of the problem of gender.

But the ending of the *Lettres persanes* does not simply show that polygamy and despotism breed flattery and dissimulation, or that a less hierarchical, more harmonious relationship in which the roles of the sexes are more evenly apportioned is socially advantageous. It also makes an epistemological point that subverts this very type of conclusion. Although the news of Roxane's infidelity is unquestionably hard for Usbek to bear, from the perspective of the wider readership of the novel, the unveiling of her deception would still appear reassuring were it certain that her lies had been exposed and the truth reestablished. The text, however, obstructs this certainty by presenting the relation between veracity and deception, revelation and concealment, in a more complex light. Roxane's imposture is described, as we have noted, as "the *veil* of her perfidy" (371; my italics), such that within the textual econ-omy of the novel, the veil stands both for virtue or truth, and for infidelity or lies. This linguistic convergence signals not only the epistemological com-plexity of a denouement in which Roxane tells the truth about her own deception while giving the lie to Usbek's self-representation as the embodi-ment of truth, but also the fact that the veil of fidelity and the veil of decep-tion are both veils of rhetoric. The ending of the *Lettres persanes* thus departs radically from the "correspondence" model of truth narrativized in *Arsace et Isménie*, approximating rather the conception that Heidegger called *aletheia*—an unceasing process of veiling and unveiling that occurs within rather than beyond language.[16] This *textual* subversion of the *narrative* of unveiling, as I now propose to show, is the cornerstone of a much more extensive movement by which the text defers its own ideological closure through the self-reflexive representation of language.

DESPOTIC AND NEW LANGUAGES

Usbek's letters from Europe play on two registers. Those destined for male friends and acquaintances are referential and discursive; they raise a wide range of political and philosophical questions, including issues pertaining to gender.[17] By contrast, the letters that he sends to the harem draw primarily on the performative register of language and are marked by the use of imper-atives and exclamation marks. This tone is established early in the novel when, alerted to an affair between Zachi and a white eunuch, he writes men-acingly to the chief of the white eunuchs, telling him that "You should trem-ble on opening this letter" (161). As this injunction suggests, Usbek perceives the letter itself to be invested with a symbolic significance that is in no way dependent on reading: the eunuch need merely open it for the desired per-locutionary effect to be achieved. Later in the novel, when the order of the harem has begun to crumble, Usbek again writes to his eunuchs, demanding that his written word assume the force of "thunder that strikes in the midst of lightning and storms" (367). He characterizes his orders as "bloody" (364), identifying them with the effects that he anticipates and overlooking the intermediary necessity that his addressee read and interpret his demands. Usbek's unquestioning belief in his own power is manifestly accompanied by a strong conviction in the authority of language. He experiences no doubt whatsoever that language will convey his intentions and produce the extralinguistic effects that he anticipates.

This representation of the power of the letter plays on a number of contemporary fears about the abuse of language in Bourbon France. It is in part a satirical condemnation of the *lettres de cachet* through which the French monarchy summarily exercised its power. (In ancien régime France, the very appearance of the royal seal was sufficient to warrant the arrest and imprisonment of a political troublemaker or the wayward son of a prominent family.) It can also be read as an allusion to the controversial papal bull Unigenitus, which sought to eradicate Jansenism in Europe by proscribing all biblical interpretations not officially sanctioned by Rome (letter CI), and which, in addition, contested women's right to read the Scriptures. Like the bull, which is explicitly attacked in several letters, Usbek's writing forecloses on the reader's right to read and interpret for him- or herself.[18]

The novel's critique of linguistic authoritarianism also bears an ethnographic dimension, because Usbek's conception of writing can be said to correspond to innumerable Western representations of the Oriental despot who exercises his unbridled authority through the medium of the pure sign.[19] The *Lettres persanes* simply summarizes on this issue the information purveyed by contemporary travel writers from Chardin and Baudier to Thévenot and Du Vignau,[20] all of whom depict Islam as a literalist dogma that demands obedience to the letter of the sacred text. Michael Harbsmeier, in "Early Travels to Europe," has persuasively argued that the prevalence of this characterization reflects the fact that by the late seventeenth century the threat of religious conflict no longer provided a powerful incentive for highlighting differences between Islamic and Christian societies, and that as a result, travel writers began to register other signs of cultural diversity, notably widespread illiteracy in Turkey and Persia and the persistence of outmoded rote-learning techniques in these countries' schools. This characterization of Islamic culture supports the view, still held by some contemporary Orientalists, that Islam is little more than a literalistic dogma that precludes self-reflexivity and impedes the growth of democracy in the Arab world, a belief whose correlate is that Western writing must undertake the critical representation that cannot occur within Islam.[21] In its juxtaposition of "Islamic dogmatism" with a less authoritarian, more self-reflexive discourse, Montesquieu's novel offers a tacit staging of this ethnographic view of the cultural politics of language.

Unfortunately for Usbek, the letters sent to the harem fail to achieve their goal. Instead of reaching their addressees, they are circulated from hand to hand and exposed to being stolen or lost, an uncontrollable dissemination that figures the fact that the "pure sign" is in reality embedded in a network of signifiers and consequently open to interpretation and misinterpretation. As he struggles to regain control over the harem, he learns that the letters that he has dispatched to quell dissent are not even being read. One eunuch reports, with a touch of what has become known, after Freud, as "kettle logic,"[22] that a letter from Usbek has been stolen *and* lost: "I sent a slave to find it; he was *robbed* on his return and the letter is *lost*" (366). Likewise, the successor to the "Great Eunuch" writes deferentially that he has not dared to read a letter addressed to his predecessor, and instead has kept it "*enveloped* with respect" while awaiting further orders. Usbek responds vehemently: "you miserable creature! In your hands you have letters that contain prompt and violent orders; the slightest delay causes me to despair and you wait on a vain *pretext*!" (364; my italics). Never texts, but only *envelopes* or *pre-texts*, Usbek's orders are, in the end, dead letters that teach him that to be meaningful, writing must be complemented by an act of reading.

Roxane does not pick up the pen until the end of the novel. Her long silence, which sets her apart from Usbek and from the other wives and concubines (who all write obsequious letters in which they flatter Usbek or complain about mistreatment), renders her an enigma that is not unraveled until the final lines of the text. This enigma is intensified by the fact that in the first of the two letters that she writes, Roxane defends her fellow wives against the accusations made by the eunuchs and protests the unwarranted punishments that are being meted out in the harem, whereas in the second—

the last of the novel—she admits her own betrayal and informs Usbek that she is committing suicide because his eunuchs have murdered the only man she ever truly loved.

Roxane's death raises a number of interpretative questions. Because, as many feminist scholars have noted, eighteenth-century novels typically achieve closure by narrating either the death or marriage of the heroine, it is certainly possible to view Roxane's suicide as a conventionally masculine ending by which the troublesome heroine is killed off before she can cause further trouble, rather than as a courageous act of female rebellion. Arguing in this vein that the death of Roxane serves to bring a swift end to the subversive expression of women's erotic and political desire, Julia Douthwaite (*Exotic Women*, 129) contrasts the denouement of Montesquieu's novel with that of a text that is in many ways a feminist rewriting of the Persian classic, Françoise de Graffigny's *Lettres d'une Péruvienne* (*Letters of a Peruvian Woman*; 1747). Far from killing her heroine off or marrying him to the hero, Graffigny defies novelistic convention by presenting the reader with a heroine who neither dies nor marries, but rather chooses to live independently as a writer.

With an eye to how the major French novels of this period dispose of their female characters, it is possible (in the most general terms) to chart a progression from Madame de Lafayette's *Princesse de Clèves* (1678), whose protagonist withdraws from the world in order to die, through the *Lettres persanes*, whose heroine dies as she writes her renunciation of the values imposed by her world, to the *Lettres d'une Péruvienne*, whose heroine lives on as a writer.[23] This evolution is clearly significant: narratives shape the ways in which we think about our lives and the opportunities that are available to us, and the death of Roxane conveys a message in much the same way that Graffigny's depiction of a heroine who lives independently and publishes her memoirs does. Yet although I want to acknowledge the broad cultural impact of the narrative of Roxane's death, I also want to suggest that on a textual level, the closure imposed by the story's dramatic ending is subtly deferred.

In the final letter of the novel, Roxane admits to Usbek that her virtue has been an imposture and that she has always loved another man. This is, however, no ordinary confession. Subverting the rhetoric of confession, which conventionally bespeaks a belief in truth and in the saving power of a privileged authority figure, Roxane questions Usbek's authority to judge her—implicitly questioning all of the social structures through which men legislate women's lives. In confessing, she therefore not only tells the truth about her own lies, but also exposes the lie by which Usbek represents himself as the arbiter of truth.

Although Usbek never pauses to reflect on Roxane's response to his writing, she provocatively anticipates his reading of her "confession," surmising that her defiant, philosophical tone must "seem new" to a man accustomed only to flattery and submission. It seems to me that her reference to a "new" language, one of several allusions to "new" or "unknown" languages scattered throughout the text,[24] must be understood metaphorically as a commentary on language. To speak a new language is to ponder the relation between words and ideas, and as a result, to recognize the contingency of meanings that have become ingrained or naturalized. It is, as Suzanne Rodin Pucci observes, to affirm the separation of signifier and signified on which the novel's technique of defamiliarization—the presentation of French practices and institutions from the perspective of a foreigner—rests ("Letters from the Harem," 129).

In a certain sense, however, Roxane's critical discourse constitutes not so much a new language as a feminist appropriation of the Enlightenment rhetoric of the Persian travelers (Pucci, "Letters from the Harem," 129–30). When she didactically tells Usbek that "I have reformed your laws on those of nature," she speaks, like him, as a *philosophe*—a social reformer on a mission to unveil the cultural contingency of laws and institutions through an appeal to "natural law." Her claim in fact closely echoes Rica's account of a conversation he has had with a "very gallant philosopher"—perhaps intended to represent the amorous philosopher-scientist Bernard de Fontenelle, or François Poulain de la Barre,[25] the author of a treatise on sexual equality—about whether "natural law subordinates women to men." Roxane's final letter essentially reiterates the philosopher's response that "nature never dictated such a law. Our empire over them is a veritable tyranny" (186).

The sense that a woman is appropriating an existing critical discourse is reinforced by the fact that her claim to speak a "new language" echoes

Usbek's own claim to have spoken, at the court of Ispahan, an "unknown language," a language of truth and sincerity that has unmasked the lies uttered at court (140) and "brought truth to the very foot of the throne" (letter VIII). Roxane's subsequent claim to speak a language that unmasks *Usbek's* pretension to authority compels the reader to question whether vice has, or can be, definitively unmasked by virtue, and whether rhetoric, appearances, can be uncovered. This indeterminacy casts a retrospective shadow over the novel, necessitating a reevaluation of Usbek's epistemological self-positioning as an impartial observer who exposes the blind spots of French society.

This demand for rereading is by no means merely formal. Indeed, it produces substantive changes in the way that we interpret certain letters. Perhaps the strongest illustration of how the meaning of the narrative shifts in light of Roxane's final missive is provided by letter XXVI, in which, having recently arrived in Paris, Usbek writes to Roxane, contrasting her austere virtue with the sexual availability of French women. He recollects in some detail her vehement resistance to his sexual advances in the weeks after their marriage, seemingly titillated by the memory of her "powerless tears" and by the fact that she went so far as to try to stab him rather than permitting him to deflower her (169). He attributes her resistance to modesty and is obviously enticed rather than discouraged by her refusals.[26] After reading Roxane's final letter, we understand that these refusals were in reality born of her contempt for Usbek and her desire for another lover, not of a concept of female chastity promoted by and for men.

From the perspective of the contemporary reader, Usbek's persistence in deflowering Roxane, the impervious violence of his desire, can only be read as a rape. Although, as one would expect, the novel does not show any special sensitivity to Roxane's experience as a victim of sexual violence, it does open itself to this modern interpretation by inscribing the need for rereading and thereby acknowledging that writing has a history—that representations evolve in accordance with the historical and cultural perspective of their readership. Perhaps more clearly than any other epistolary novel, the *Lettres persanes* instructs us that texts signify through the interpretations of readers, and in consequence, despite the achievement of narrative resolution, can never truly be considered closed. This deferral of closure is in fact registered in the chronology of the novel: the final letters of the text, in which the overthrow of the harem is narrated, predate the last critical letters.[27] In other words, while Usbek continues to reflect upon the state of affairs in France, the foundations of his own political and epistemological authority have already been profoundly shaken.

In the final letter of the novel, Roxane articulates her rejection of Usbek's authority in a writing that she equates with death. She dramatically tells Usbek that poison flows through her veins as she writes, such that the flow of ink is caught in a metaphorical exchange with blood—her own blood, and the blood lately shed in the harem—and with poison. Writing thus emerges in this letter as what Jacques Derrida calls a *pharmakon*, a poisonous venom that spells out the death of the writing subject, yet at the same time the only available remedy—a cure that bears at least the potential for life and political change.[28] The temporality of this letter is also worthy of our notice, for whereas Roxane at first tells Usbek that "the poison will flow in my veins," she subsequently informs him that "the poison is consuming me" and ends with the statement "I am dying." Given the metaphorical exchange between ink and poison that runs throughout this letter, I want to suggest that this last statement must be read as a speech act, an act in which language *performs* rather than simply *describes*, an extralinguistic effect, the death of Roxane. Through a progressive shift in tenses, the performative dimension of her letter overtakes the referential mode, and writing itself comes to represent first rebellion and finally death and escape. In this regard, her language is, as she asserts, "new," for rather than simply describing her death and in so doing reaffirming the conventional relationship between signifier and signified, it enacts it, signaling the intralinguistic creation of meaning and the destabilization of the naturalized system of reference. In strong contrast to Usbek's performative writing, which fuses signifier and signified to the exclusion of interpretation, Roxane's writing highlights the contingency of meaning and the absolute necessity of reading.

Suzanne Rodin Pucci has aptly described the women of Usbek's harem as "veiled figures of writing" ("Letters from the Harem"). Building on this characterization, I now want to suggest that a determinate analogy may be drawn between the position that Roxane occupies in the narrative and the text's representation of its own language. For much of the novel, Roxane is portrayed as the submissive woman who subscribes to the "official discourse" propagated by the master; certainly Usbek never suffers the apprehension about her that he feels about his other wives. Yet it is ultimately she who leads the revolt in the harem, undermining Usbek's power from the very place in which he felt most secure. In this regard, she constitutes the quintessential "foreign body," an alien presence that undermines from within the controlled environment of the harem. In a parallel way, language, which for most of the novel functions as the instrument of both despotism and enlightened critique, is at the end of the text represented as a "new" and "unknown" force, the epistemological blind spot within the terrain of knowledge in all its manifestations.[29]

POSTSCRIPTS

In concluding, I want to consider the issue of textual and ideological closure from a different perspective: that of the critical reception of the text. In 1754, shortly before his death, Montesquieu wrote a preface for a new edition of his novel that he entitled *Quelques réflexions sur les Lettres persanes* (*Some Reflections on the Persian Letters*). It is in this preface that he makes the famous assertion that the narrative is organized in accordance with a "secret and in some sense unknown chain" that links "philosophy, politics and morality to a novel" (62; my italics). This secret chain is generally held to denote the allegorical relationship between Oriental despotism and French absolutism, although the precise extent to which the *Lettres persanes* is a roman à clef has been the subject of extensive critical debate—so much so, in fact, that in 1988, Theodore Braun published an article entitled "'La chaîne secrète': A Decade of Interpretations" summarizing and evaluating the conclusions of the previous decade of interpretations of the secret chain. This critical preoccupation undoubtedly flows from the seductive possibility that Montesquieu is tendering, from the external perspective of a postscript, a key to the meaning of his novel—or to be more exact, to his own intention as author. The effect of this enticing promise is a criticism of *enchaînement*, a reading praxis whose ultimate objective is to fix once and for all the "authoritative" meaning of the text.

Critical discussions of *Some Reflections* have almost invariably concentrated on its allusion to a secret chain,[30] overlooking a passage toward the end of the text in which Montesquieu appears to contradict himself by writing that "certainly the nature and design of the *Persian Letters* are so evident [*à découvert*] that they will deceive only those who wish to deceive [*tromper*] themselves" (131). With these words, he seems to imply that the novel is in no way esoteric and that readers will only deceive themselves if they embark on a quest for secret meanings. In the context of the novel, the association of the expression "à découvert," which suggests uncovering, with the verb "tromper," which means not only to deceive but also to be unfaithful, implicitly binds the existence of a hidden meaning to the issue of the fidelity or truth of women. However, the text insinuates that it is not women who deceive, but the reader who deceives himself by looking for the one "true" meaning of the text, or, one might venture to say, the truth of Woman. Like the novel itself, the preface questions whether truth can in fact be established from a metaperspective beyond the text, or from beyond the error and uncertainty inherent to language. Indeed, the two apparently contradictory moments of the preface—the allusion to a secret chain and the counterclaim that there is no submerged meaning—parallel the double structure of the novel. By this I mean that as a classic of Enlightenment literature, the *Lettres persanes* exemplifies the Enlightenment's will to expose the prejudices and distortions of ancien régime France and to replace them with an alternative vision of politics and society. Yet at the same time it registers, with a more modern, if not timeless, sensibility, the impossibility of definitively establishing an objective standpoint or an unimpeachable truth.

CHAPTER THREE

Intimacy Exposed: Gender, Race, and Language in the Oriental Tale

The preceding chapters show how representations of the Oriental, feminine "other" participated in the transformation of the cultural field, notably in the invention of the more open political process which, following Jürgen Habermas, we have come to call the "bourgeois public sphere." I now want to build on this analysis by examining how Oriental imagery—not only in literature but also in the decorative arts—contributed to a related shift in cultural boundaries, the progressive differentiation of public life from intimate existence, of the economic investments of commodity culture from the emotive investments of the conjugal family. The terrain of this analysis will be the *conte oriental* ("Oriental tale"), one of the many forms of "tale" that became popular in Enlightenment France, a genre almost universally neglected in critical discussions of literary Orientalism, but which was in fact the most popular form of eighteenth-century writing on the Orient. I will take as my focus two Oriental tales published at midcentury, Crébillon-fils's *Le Sopha* (*The Sofa*; 1742) and Denis Diderot's *Les Bijoux indiscrets* (*The Indiscreet Jewels*; 1748), probably the best known and most epistemologically complex examples of this brazenly frivolous genre.

The two works in question are in many respects parallel: in both narratives, a male protagonist is magically accorded a voyeuristic position from which he can observe the intimate lives of women, a position from which he is able to unmask appearances and reveal the secrets of the bedchamber; in both instances, truth—and, conversely, lies, representation, and appearance—are embodied in female figures; and finally, in both narratives, the promise of an unmediated truth is ultimately withdrawn and the protagonist is obliged to reconcile himself to the absence of transparency that is inherent to social and sexual relations. Maintaining my practice of double reading, I argue that it is important to lend weight to each of these two narrative axes: the historical impact of narratives that unveil the sex lives of Oriental women before a voyeuristic Western public, and the texts' deconstruction of their own epistemological grounds.

This chapter does two further things. First, it insists on the importance of Oriental context, which has been largely disregarded by previous readers of the Oriental tale: most critical studies of this genre have focused on the representation of gender, dismissing the Oriental setting as little more than a veiled representation of French politics and society. I argue, by contrast, that the global forces of travel, exploration, colonial expansion, and international commerce play a central role in fashioning the epistemological framework and critical message of these texts. The second concern of this chapter is to connect the analysis of literary texts to the broader arena of material culture. Beginning with the sofa celebrated in the title of Crébillon's novella, it explores the significance of the Oriental and feminine names given to the comfortable reclining chairs that epitomize the decorative taste of the age.

THE COMMODIFICATION OF INTIMACY

Le Sopha is the best known and most sophisticated of a series of Oriental tales[1] written by the libertine novelist Crébillon-fils in the 1730s and 1740s.[2] Like all examples of the genre, it betrays the influence of the *Thousand and One Nights*, translated into French by Antoine Galland some three decades earlier (between 1704 and 1717), both in its episodic structure and in its vision of the Orient as a world of fabulous characters and fantastic events. Crébillon in fact acknowledges this influence by providing a genealogy that identifies his protagonist, Sultan Schah-Baham, as the grandson of Scheherezade.[3]

Schah-Baham is the consummate Oriental despot: indolent and effeminate, he has an insatiable appetite for fictions, and he exercises a parodic form of absolute rule by commanding his courtiers to tell him stories. His preoccupation with *contes*—a word that means both stories and lies—serves as a metaphor for his worldview, for as Crébillon emphasizes, this Oriental ruler has no interest in affairs of state and rejects all knowledge that is not inherently fictional. In fact, Crébillon's depiction of the court of Schah-Baham provides an exemplary illustration of the process by which in the French literature of this period the fantastic ambiance of the Oriental tale is extended to all aspects of Oriental culture, politics, and religion.

The particular story narrated in *Le Sopha* is told by Amanzéï, a courtier who, unlike the Sultan, is a Hindu rather than a Moslem. He informs his audience that in order to punish him for liking sofas too well, for indulging in the type of pleasures that in eighteenth-century French literature are associated with Oriental furnishings, Brahma turned him into a sofa. The compensation for this unusual punishment was that Amanzéï found himself in a privileged position from which he was able to spy on the private lives of women. This metamorphosis would seem to represent the ultimate manifestation of the voyeuristic fantasy that pervades Orientalism, but in reality, what Amanzéï offers his audience is not so much a titillating glimpse of Oriental sexuality as a sustained exposure of the moral corruption of the female sex. Concealed in a sofa, he discovers the false appearance that women present to the world and takes it upon himself to lay bare their true moral condition.

Like many Oriental fictions, this narrative is built around the metaphor of truth as a veiled woman, the implication of which, as we have seen, is that when the veil is removed, "Truth" is revealed. The centrality of this trope to Crébillon's novella provides a first indication of the importance of Oriental context: the "Orientalization" of women shapes the manner in which they are perceived in the sense that it envelops them in a complex relation to both veracity and deception. At first glance, this "veil of Orient" appears aligned with what I have identified as the "correspondence" model of truth, for it suggests that woman can be unveiled and Truth definitively established. However, as the story unfolds, it begins to show more affinity with another conception of truth: the Heideggerian model of *aletheia*, which apprehends truth not as a definitive moment of revelation, but as a ceaseless process of veiling and unveiling unfolding within, rather than beyond, representation. This epistemological shift is of course not articulated in the abstract terms of philosophical reflection, but rather takes shape through the narrative's reconfiguration of the social categories of intimacy and publicity.

The first adventure that Amanzéï relates exposes the hypocrisy of a pious woman named Fatmé, who, although affecting an austere virtue in public, indulges her sexual appetites to the fullest in the privacy of her *cabinet*. Fatmé's *cabinet* is portrayed as a place in which private passions are sheltered from the public gaze, and the lovers she receives there—a brahmin (priest) and a house slave—are carefully selected to protect her social reputation. The choice of a domestic worker as a sexual partner particularly reinforces the sense of privacy attached to the *cabinet* because it conveys Fatmé's desire to conduct her sex life beyond the judgmental gaze of society. This pattern of behavior is repeated in the second episode of the novella, in which a wealthy overseer named Abdelathif takes a low-class dancer as his mistress, while the latter in turn enjoys a "private" liaison with a black slave. The narrator explains that Abdelathif finds the company of Amine less demanding than that of the society women with whom he has affairs (48), and we can perhaps assume that Amine in turn relaxes in the company of her slave. These representations seem to capture a widespread sentiment of the period. Let us consider, for example, an observation made by the narrator of another libertine novel—Charles Duclos's *Confessions du Comte de**** (1742)—who says that he too sometimes likes to frequent lower-class women who compensate him for "the constraint imposed by ladies" (140). Such accounts of sexual relationships with inferiors, in which desire is satisfied outside of the accepted networks of social and sexual exchange, convey the sense that intimacy has become mired in representation; that it is relentlessly monitored by the public gaze; and that to achieve a feeling approximating intimacy, one must stoop to relationships with one's social inferiors.

The exposure of Fatmé's duplicity in the first episode of Crébillon's novella is tempered by the narrator's claim that women are obliged to be artificial because of the hypocritical emphasis that society places on their virtue (563).[4] In the episodes that follow, the process of social unveiling is repeatedly problematized as women's motivations for promiscuity and infidelity are shown to be less a matter of unbridled sensuality than the result of pressures both material and social. As in other libertine novels, sexual exchange is rendered not as the fulfillment of erotic desire, but as the metaphorical terrain on which social status is won or lost.

This structure becomes most evident in a lengthy episode toward the end of the novel, during which Amanzéï probes the duplicitous character of a woman named Zulica. This scrutiny actually occurs on two levels: Zulica is blindsided by Mazulhim and Nassès, two libertines working in tandem, and their triumph is observed and reported by the sofa, a double exposure that creates a position from which the different rules that apply to men and women in the erotic fiction of the midcentury are elucidated. Whereas men, within the confines of social decorum, are expected to advertise their conquests, the female libertine is required, as Judith Butler (*Gender Trouble*) would have it, to "perform" her gender by presenting the appearance of virtue and feigning that she has succumbed out of invincible passion rather than mere lust or— worse—out of blind obedience to the social system of *libertinage*.[5] This pretension of virtue is laid out as a more or less transparent veil over a woman's sexual conquests, such that concealment operates as a socially sanctioned form of advertisement. As a result, although Mazulhim and Nassès persistently strive to unmask Zulica's infidelities and the lies she weaves about them, what is really unveiled here is not so much the falseness of women—a concealed yet discoverable referent—as the workings of the social code itself.

In another episode, as I have already noted, Amanzéï spies on Amine, a common dancer who has recently become the mistress of Abdelathif, the wealthy and powerful overseer of the emperor's estates. Amine's motives in this relationship are obviously venal, but Abdelathif's are less clear, for as the narrator emphasizes from the outset, he experiences more "*libertinage*" than real "desire" (49).[6] Early in their relationship, Abdelathif expresses dissatisfaction with his mistress's humble living quarters and tells her, "You cannot live here . . . you must be properly lodged. . . . I would be ridiculed if a girl in whom I have an interest did not live in a style that commands respect." As he is leaving her for the evening, he remarks that "you are not *furnished* well enough for me to dine with you tonight" (49; my italics), a parting slight that confirms the reader's suspicion that Amanzéï's desire for Amine's person has swiftly been transported to her living quarters.[7] Given this apparent transfer of libido, it is unsurprising that Abdelathif loses little time in installing his mistress in a *petite maison*, a lavishly furnished house in which he can entertain his fashionable friends.[8] As the passage cited above implies, he wants his relationship with the dancer to be known so that he can enjoy the reputation of a successful libertine, or *homme à bonnes fortunes*.

The ostensible purpose of a *petite maison* was to provide a discreet setting in which desires could be indulged beyond the public eye: "These private houses, commonly known as *petites maisons*, were introduced in Paris by lovers who were obliged to show caution and to see each other in secret, and by those who sought a refuge for parties of debauchery that they would have feared to conduct in public houses," writes the narrator of Duclos's *Confessions du Comte de**** (88). Yet in *Le Sopha*, the possession of a *petite maison* is represented not as a guilty secret, but as the absolute prerequisite of a certain kind of social status. The perception that *petites maisons* were becoming objects of public display was by no means limited to Crébillon. Indeed, Duclos's hero proceeds to observe that the purpose of a *petite maison* had gradually shifted, and that if in the beginning "One took them . . . to conceal one's affairs from the public, soon many started taking them to feign invented affairs." The same observation is made in Président Hénault's comedy *La Petite maison*, a work staged privately in the 1740s. In this play, Frozine (a maid) asks La Montagne (a valet) why his master keeps a *petite maison* if not discreetly to pursue romantic conquests: "What good is a *petite maison* to him? It seems to me that they were invented for those who wanted to come in secret and wait for persons whom they could not visit at home." La Montagne brings her up to date with the news that "That was true in the days of Old King Guillemot. Today a *petite maison* is just another indiscretion: one knows whom they belong to and who goes there, just as one knows the comings and goings of a house in town."[9] This shift in perceptions echoes the dynamic at work throughout *Le Sopha*: concealment is disclosed to be a form of revelation, whereas revelation is apprehended as something other than the polar opposite of concealment.

In reality, almost every episode of *Le Sopha* conveys the sense that sexual intimacy has become little more than a means of securing a social reputation, and that as a result, the secrecy in which it is enveloped constitutes an indirect form of disclosure. Some two centuries before Michel Foucault formulated in his *History of Sexuality* the provocative argument that one of the central characteristics of modern societies is to speak of sex ad infinitum while exploiting it as *the* secret, Crébillon's novel "exposes" the secrecy surrounding sex as an indirect form of social discourse (1:35).

The sophistication of *Le Sopha* in this regard is highlighted when one compares it with another midcentury novella whose narrator is also turned

into a couch, *Le Canapé couleur de feu* (*The Fire-Colored Canapé*; 1741), usually attributed to Fougeret de Montbron.[10] The protagonist of this second
novella is punished for his failure to gratify Crapaudine, an old and ugly
fairy, and is only released from his enchantment when he encounters a similar failure on the part of another man. The imposition of this condition suggests that sexual impotence is a condition rarely encountered, and indeed
until the end of the narrative, when an elderly lawyer fails to satisfy his
young bride, the couch meets with nothing but ribald sexual hedonism: in
its unfolding, the narrative decries the lechery of the clergy and the prevalence of cuckoldry, both time-honored targets of social satire. In complete
contrast, Crébillon's protagonist is told that he will only be freed from his
enchantment when he witnesses two people losing their virginity to each
other. This stipulation turns out to be a double condition involving sincerity as well as sex. The reciprocal loss of virginity stands for an authentic experience of intimacy in which neither party is misleading the other, an originary moment of union or unmediated exchange between the other and the
self. Because most of the novella's protagonists are accomplished liars—and
indeed derive erotic pleasure from lying and manipulating others—the satisfaction of this condition is repeatedly deferred.[11] The second aspect of the
condition is that intercourse occur at all, and perhaps surprisingly, this also
turns out to be an obstacle. As Amanzéï reflects halfway through his narrative, "in all the time that I was a sofa, I saw more opportunities squandered
than seized" (79). To emphasize this point, he devotes three episodes to the
adventures of the libertine Mazulhim (purportedly modeled on that aging
libertine, the duc de Richelieu), who, despite his reputation as a masterful
seducer, actually suffers from impotence.[12] The reader is thus forced to conclude that Mazulhim's unrelenting pursuit of women has less to do with private acts of consummation than with the quintessentially public process of
conspicuous consumption.[13]

The libertine appropriation of sexual exchange as the medium of social
relationships can in part be attributed to the new, and indeed unprecedented, permeability of social boundaries in eighteenth-century France. As
Peter Brooks argues in *The Novel of Worldliness*, the fiction of this period
obsessively stages social differences, placing the greatest emphasis on sexual
relationships and marriage because these are the acts through which the

established hierarchy is either perpetuated or rearranged. I believe that this appropriation also bespeaks a new consciousness of another type of social boundary: the distinction between public and private experience, or between the conduct of personal relationships and the economic transactions of civil society. Along these lines, I want to argue that in Crébillon's novella, the central figure of the sofa embodies a conflict between intimacy and publicity that is the recurrent theme of the libertine narrative. By this I mean that although the sofa is presented as a voyeuristic device that offers privileged access to the secrets of the bedchamber or the *cabinet*, it is concurrently a fashionable commodity, an outward and ostentatious marker of social status.

WOMEN, THE ORIENT, AND EIGHTEENTH-CENTURY FURNITURE

However far-fetched the transformation narrated in *Le Sopha* may appear, Crébillon's novella is not the only text of the period to relate the metamorphosis of a human being into a domestic object. In addition to Fougeret's *Canapé couleur de feu*, there is the Abbé de Voisenon's *Le Sultan Misapouf et la Princesse Grisemine* (1746), whose hero becomes a bathtub, and a series of English and American novellas—many inspired by the English translation of *Le Sopha*—whose heroes are similarly transformed into bedsteads and chairs.[14] Yet despite the abundance of these narratives, critical studies of Crébillon have never directly addressed the cultural implications of Amanzéï's transformation into a piece of furniture. This reticence is perhaps attributable to the widespread although insufficiently nuanced perception that unlike their nineteenth-century successors, eighteenth-century novels simply do not represent material contexts. Going against the grain of this critical commonplace, I want to argue that the recurrent representation of talking domestic objects in eighteenth-century fiction reflects a strong awareness of the social significance of certain domestic commodities.[15]

The literary metamorphosis of human beings into household objects testifies to the anthropomorphic quality of furniture also expressed in the use of terms such as feet, arms, and in French, *joues* (cheeks), to describe its different components. The abundance of these improbable narratives illustrates the degree to which in eighteenth-century France decorative objects were implicated in a dialectic with social identity by which, as Katie Scott has argued, people reciprocally interpreted furniture in terms of self, gender, social station, and fortune, and themselves in terms of their possessions (*Rococo Interior*, 81). Crébillon's narrative translates into the sphere of literature the contemporary vogue for a new type of chair—the armchairs, sofas, and chaise longues that in the seventeenth and eighteenth centuries introduced a new level of comfort into the homes of the upper classes—and more importantly, conveys the correlation between these pieces of furniture, which were often given Oriental or feminine names, and several different, although overlapping, perceptions of women's place in French society.

The first avatar of the contemporary couch was the *canapé* (canapé or settee), which appeared in France in the 1650s, probably inspired by travelers' descriptions of the Turkish *divan*.[16] Although *lits de repos*, or daybeds, had existed before this time, the *canapé* represented a new hybrid of the chair and the bed, and as such, it bespeaks important changes in the organization of social life. Whereas the seating arrangements of Louis XIV's Versailles mirrored the formality and hierarchy of the court—to occupy a *fauteuil* (armchair)[17] was the prerogative of royalty, and only the highest ranking courtiers could lay claim to even a *tabouret* (stool)[18]—toward the end of the reign, a gradual relaxation of decorum, combined with the growth of spheres of sociability beyond the court, created a market both in Paris and the provinces for chairs whose comfortable forms espoused the contours of the body and facilitated informal conversation.

From the 1680s on, the name "sofa" was given to a *canapé* with *accotoirs* (arms) or *joues* (wings) (Figure 6).[19] François de Caillières's *Des mots à la mode et des nouvelles façons de parler* (*On Fashionable Words and New Ways of Speaking*; 1692) identifies the word as a fashionable term and defines it as "a kind of bed in the manner of the Turks."[20] Other variants of the *canapé* included the *causeuse*, a four-place couch that came into fashion in around 1725 and whose name testifies to the association between comfortable furniture and the pleasures of conversation, and the *ottomane*, shown in Figure 7, which is basically a sofa with incurved sides, otherwise known as a *canapé corbeille*, which made its appearance toward the end of the seventeenth century.[21] In the Louis XVI period, *ottomanes* were generally called *paphoses* or *sultanes* (illustrated in Figure 8), or, if they were destined for an alcove—in other words, intended to function as a bed—*turquoises*. One variant of the *ottomane* was the *veilleuse* or *veilleuse à la turque* shown in Figure 9, a reclining chair with sides of different heights that formed a gracious curve around the person stretched out on the chair. Finally, the more traditional daybed or chaise longue was known by the late 1600s as a *duchesse*, suggestively defined in the *Dictionnaire de Trévoux* (1704) as "a seat for incommoded women."[22]

Over the course of the eighteenth century, chairs created for a single occupant also underwent a series of changes; their lines progressively became more fluid and ornate, and they were adapted to make the sitter feel more at ease. The appearance of the *fauteuil* was transformed as its classically straight lines gave way to rococo curves, as backs and arms were lowered, and as arms were set back from legs. But perhaps the most significant development was the introduction, around 1725, of the *bergère*, which, as can been seen in Figure 10, was a low, cushioned armchair with an upholstered back and wings. Inevitably, there were also variants of the *bergère*, including the charmingly named *obligeante*, whose wide arms created a welcoming appearance (Figure 10), and the *bergère à la turque*, a hybrid combining the *bergère* with the *duchesse*, which permitted the sitter to lie back (the Turkish quality claimed in the name consisting presumably of the invitation to the sitter to recline and repose).[23]

These changes to the form of the chair were perceived by many contemporaries as gendered changes: the recessing of the arms was typically attributed to the need to accommodate the *robes à panier* (hoopskirts) that came into fashion in around 1717,[24] and for André Roubo, furniture maker and author of *L'Art du menuisier en meubles* (*The Art of the Cabinet Maker*; 1769), the whole move toward larger, more comfortable chairs was a function of female fashions: "women's garments demand this shape, for they would otherwise become creased, and ladies would not be able to sit in comfort," he states with authority (1772 edition, 642–43).[25]

In reviewing this chapter in the history of the decorative arts, two questions that clearly impose themselves are, first, why the new kinds of chair were regularly given Oriental and feminine names, and second, why they were often associated by contemporaries such as Roubo with the female sex (assuming that we do not take his pronouncements about the practical implications of female fashions at face value). In the following paragraphs, I

Figure 6. *Sopha,* drawn by Jean-Charles Delafosse, engraved by Daumont. Source: *Recueil de différents artistes,* Paris, circa 1770, 105. Photograph courtesy of Bibliothèque Nationale de France, Paris.

Figure 7. *Ottomane ceintrée,* drawn by Delafosse, engraved by Daumont. Source: *Recueil de différents artistes,* Paris, circa 1770, 99. Photograph courtesy of Bibliothèque Nationale de France, Paris.

Figure 8. *Paphose en gondole*, drawn by Delafosse, engraved by Daumont. Source: *Recueil de différents artistes*, Paris, circa 1770, 107. Photograph courtesy of Bibliothèque Nationale de France, Paris.

Figure 9. *Veilleuse à la turque*, drawn by Delafosse, engraved by Daumont. Source: *Oeuvre de Delafosse relative à l'ameublement*, Paris, 189?, vol. 3, cahier F. Reprint of work published circa 1770. Courtesy of General Research Division, New York Public Library, Astor, Lenox and Tilden Foundations.

Figure 10.   Bergère and *obligeante,* drawn by Delafosse, engraved by Daumont.
Source: *Recueil de différents artistes,* Paris, circa 1770, 132. Photograph courtesy
of Bibliothèque Nationale de France, Paris.

suggest, perhaps contrary to expectation, that the use of Oriental names is
essentially a secondary phenomenon, subordinate to the process of feminization, and that the feminization of furniture can be traced to several contrasting perceptions of the position women occupied in French society.

In the early eighteenth century, the salon and the dining room replaced
the bedroom as the principal receiving rooms of the aristocratic or bourgeois
residence or *hôtel.* This displacement was one of a series of changes in the
organization of the home: rooms were gradually becoming more specialized,
and as this occurred, certain spaces, notably the salon and dining room, were
devoted to social gatherings, whereas others were reserved for the private use
of members of the family. The tendency toward more strictly demarcated
rooms loosely mirrored the progressive demarcation of public life and
domestic intimacy in society as a whole: as Jürgen Habermas writes, in eighteenth-century Europe, the boundary between public and private, social and
domestic was being redrawn in such a way that it ran "right through the
home" (*Structural Transformation,* 45).

The vogue for comfortable chairs that facilitated informal conversation can be correlated with this relocation of social gatherings to rooms in which guests no longer gathered in the alcove area surrounding the bed. That is to say, the new furniture carried the alcove's aura of intimacy and informality into a more formal space. The fact that these new chairs were given feminine names testifies to the prominent role of women in shaping the Enlightenment salon with its ideals of sociability and intellectual exchange. The close association of this ideal with the "civilizing influence" of the female sex is captured in Mme. de Genlis's description of the salon, the theater of French society, as the forum in which manners shine, enhanced by the "charming grace of women." Perhaps unsurprisingly, in her *Manuel de la jeune femme* (*Manual for the Young Lady*; 1829), Genlis, a politically conservative writer of the latter part of the century, advises the would-be hostess to fill this social space with commodious "feminine" furniture. She recommends "two causeuses, a large canapé, six armchairs, two bergères, four chairs . . . and a few cushions for the feet" (50–52).

As Dena Goodman has shown, the Enlightenment salon was governed by principles of reciprocity and equality that stood in marked contrast to the hierarchical values of the court (*Republic of Letters*). The leading *salon-nières*[26]—women such as Mme. du Deffand, Mlle. de Lespinasse, and Mme. Necker—served as intermediaries between aristocrats and *philosophes* and consequently presided over the mixing of worldly manners with intellectual ideas (Goodman, *Republic of Letters*, 83). The chairs of the period mirror this trend toward more fluid and conjunctive social relations: whereas high-backed armchairs fostered formality and maintained social distinctions, Turkish-inspired sofas and *canapés*—the first chairs to accommodate more than a single sitter[27]—encouraged nonhierarchical sociability by fostering a sense of enmeshed identities.[28] Ironically, in the particular sphere of furnishings, the Orient, viewed in most other cultural contexts as a terrain of unmediated hierarchy, served as a metaphor for social fluidity and democratic exchange.

Fictional representations were remarkably attuned to furniture's capacity to serve as an index of social change. In Jean-François Regnard's comedy *Le Distrait*, performed at the end of the seventeenth century, a maid called Lisette deplores the decadent fashion for disporting oneself in an armchair placed in the alcove or *ruelle*, and she recalls with nostalgia the *escabelles* (stools) and rigid wooden chairs of her ancestors. By contrast, in a work written a half century later, Charles de la Morlière's Oriental novella *Angola* (1746), *tabourets* are banished from the court of the fairy Lumineuse precisely because they instill respect and reinforce social distinctions. Unlike the wooden stools and rigid armchairs of the court of Louis XIV, the comfortable Oriental furniture which adorns her palace promotes a sense of equality and an ambiance of sensuality.

The Oriental decor of Lumineuse's palace in many respects prefigures the style of Bellevue, the Paris home of Louis XV's official mistress, Mme. de Pompadour. This house, decorated for the marquise in the early 1750s, featured a Turkish salon adorned with exotic overdoors (*dessus-de-portes*) by Carle Van Loo. In at least one of these wall paintings, Mme. de Pompadour herself is represented in the guise of a sultana who lounges on comfortable sofas and takes coffee from the hand of a black servant (Figure 11 shows a reproduction by Beauvarlet of Van Loo's painting). Although in this overdoor the harem setting serves as a rather transparent metaphor for Pompadour's status as royal mistress, the marquise is by no means shown as a submissive or indolent figure, subject to the whims of the harem master. Rather, like La Morlière's Lumineuse, Pompadour's sultana is represented as both a sexualized figure and a woman very much in control of her environment. In the rococo world of Lumineuse and Pompadour, Oriental decor connotes a relaxation of decorum and a new freedom in social relations, while also expressing the fact that the boundary between social interaction and sexual intimacy was a permeable one.

Not all contemporaries found sex and sociability to be so easily reconcilable. During the second half of the century, the critiques of the social privilege and the sexual laxity of the royal circle that appear in latent form in Montesquieu's *Lettres persanes* (*Persian Letters*; 1721) intensified, generating demands that the serious business of Enlightenment be distinguished from more frivolous modes of social exchange. As we have begun to see, such criticisms of the corruption of the ruling classes and the moral vacuity of rococo art frequently entailed an attack on women's social influence. In one of the most celebrated sallies of this cultural campaign, the *Lettre à d'Alembert sur le théâtre* (*Letter to d'Alembert on the Theatre*; 1758), Jean-Jacques Rousseau rails that "every woman in Paris gathers in her apartments a harem of men

Figure 11. Beauvarlet, *La Sultane* (date unknown, mid- to late eighteenth century), after Carle Van Loo. Color lithograph. Courtesy of the Stewart Museum, Montreal, Canada.

more womanish than she." He invites the reader to imagine these guests pacing up and down in frustration, "while the idol lays stretched out motionless on her chaise longue, with only her tongue and her eyes active" (100–101). Rousseau's invective draws on literary stereotypes of the Orient and the voluptuous furnishings of the harem to attack women's prominence in cultural affairs. Exploiting the topos of the harem as a site in which men are emasculated by their excessive contact with women, he inverts gender roles, portraying the salon hostess herself as the Oriental despot, stretched out languidly on a sofa, exercising an unjustified and arbitrary power over a coterie of literary eunuchs. The use of Oriental tropes thus enables him simultaneously to question the democratic principles of the salons and to devalue social exchanges mediated by women by casting them in a subtly erotic light.

Libertine fiction, by far the most abundant literary source of references to Oriental furniture, also consistently depicts comfortable lounging chairs in an erotic light. Choderlos de Laclos's *Dangerous Liaisons* (1787), certainly the best known libertine novel, notes on several occasions the suggestive presence of a reclining chair,[29] and in Marivaux's *Le Paysan parvenu* (*The Fortunate Peasant*; 1735), the seduction of the ingenu Jacob by Mme. de Ferval is facilitated by a conveniently placed sofa (708). The profusion of such references confirms the fact that the close resemblance between sofas and beds in this period served as a reminder of the permeable boundary between social and sexual exchange that is the perennial theme of libertine writing.

Libertine fiction also consistently connects Oriental furnishings and experiences that are private, even intimate, and that are carefully differentiated from the formal engagements of social life. When, at the beginning of his narrative in *Le Sopha*, Amanzéï observes that "a sofa has never belonged in the antechamber" (23), he is giving the nod to his audience that his tale will unfold in the *cabinet* and the bedroom, intimate spaces associated with sex and, as we have seen, with women. Certainly the most radical contemporary statement of commodity furniture's association with both eroticism and intimate experience is to be found in Stanislas de Boufflers's poem "La Bergère."[30] In this piece (cited in full in the Notes), the soft and pliant armchair not only resembles a woman, but thanks to the intimate bond between furniture and the feminine conveyed by the very word *bergère*, it is transformed into a woman, desired, possessed, and "used" by the poet. In this metaphor/metonymy, which extends the anthropomorphism of furniture to its logical limit, the chair/woman is identified not only with sexuality, but also with every form of informality, intimacy, and repose. Indeed, it is portrayed as an almost womblike space that envelops the sitter in warmth and comfort as he abandons himself to a private reverie.

The diverse literary representations that I have cited show that as a cultural practice, the feminization of commodity furniture arose not from a single and unified perception of gender, but from a range of competing constructions of the feminine. Women and Oriental furnishings are associated with social gatherings conducted in an atmosphere of informality and equality; they are invoked in narratives that depict sexual commerce as a natural extension of sociability; and finally, in texts such as Rousseau's *Lettre à d'Alembert*, Oriental furniture is integrated into a critique that attacks the cultural influence of *salonnières* by implying that the salon is fundamentally a private, privileged, degenerately sensualized institution, rather than a truly public forum for critical debate.

I have cited arguments to the effect that Rousseau's attack on women's influence in the cultural sphere was not an isolated phenomenon, but rather an illustration of a broader social tendency of the second half of the eighteenth century. Building on Jürgen Habermas's seminal account of the constitution within the sphere of private individuals of an authentic "public sphere" of critical debate, Joan Landes and others have argued that at least on the level of cultural representations, the scission of the private sphere into public and private functions engendered not a convergence of these two categories, but rather a polarized and gendered opposition between social interaction and intimate life. Thus, although women and in particular the *salonnières* played an important role in the genesis of the public sphere of critical debate, the prevailing ideology increasingly called for their confinement to the domestic realm of the family. One of the crucial points that Habermas himself makes about this realignment of cultural categories is that the ideal of a harmonious family bound by ties of love and mutual respect was, from the outset, an ideological construct predicated on the repression of economic relations among family members, and between the household and the wider market (*Structural Transformation*, 55–56). The tensions arising out of this repression of socioeconomic relations, I would argue, are clearly legible in the conflict between intimacy and publicity that permeates eighteenth-century fiction, and that is particularly manifest in representations of commodity furniture.

How, then, may the Orientalization of commodity furniture be inter- preted? It seems reasonable to propose that the ascription of Oriental names to comfortable reclining chairs reflects not simply Europeans' primitive knowledge of Oriental furnishings and domestic habits, but also a wide- spread association of Oriental culture with indolent behavior and pervasive eroticism. In the nineteenth century, Oriental furniture, notably the Turkish *divan*, a word that signifies both council and sofa, would in fact become a leading metaphor for the passivity and stagnation of Oriental culture (for example, Sir William Duckett, an English traveler writing about a century after Crébillon, denotes the "decadence" of the Ottoman Empire by claim- ing that "the other nations had progressed while Turkey remained squatting on its *divan*" [*La Turquie pittoresque*, viii]). But I think that the Orientaliza- tion of commodity furniture reflects something more than a generalized impression of Oriental indolence. As I argue in Chapters 1 and 2, by the mid-eighteenth century tropes of Oriental life had become woven into dis- cussions of the social roles of the sexes. This interaction initially took hold because polygamy and the harem offered a radical model of female subjuga- tion and women's confinement to a domestic interior. Increasingly, how- ever—and in large measure due to the cultural resonance of Montesquieu's *Lettres persanes*—the seraglio became less the ultimate fantasy of male sexual dominance than a disturbing illustration of what happens when men sur- round themselves with women (or allow themselves to be governed by them), or when public and domestic life are not strictly demarcated. In this context, the Orientalization of commodity furniture can be viewed as one facet of a broad-based attempt to differentiate publicity from intimacy and to circumscribe a concept of domestic intimacy that was linked to erotic life—and for many contemporaries, to the sphere of the feminine.

POSSESSIONS AND DESIRES

The chairs that I describe in the previous section are (in one sense of the word) "commodities"—they are not only commodious, but they also exemplify the process by which raw materials are transformed by artisanal labor into luxury goods with high market value. A number of points must be made about this transformation as it concerns the production of commodity furniture. The first of these concerns the relationship between the burgeoning of capitalism and commodity culture in Europe, and the history of colonial expansion. As Habermas observes, "The exchange of imported raw materials for finished new and semi-finished domestic goods must be viewed as a function of the process in which the old mode of production was transformed into the capitalist mode" (*Structural Transformation*, 18–19). Imports from and exports to the colonies created, in Europe, conditions conducive to the development and marketing of new products. For example, raw materials such as cane, which was widely used in furniture making (for example, *duchesses* were often made from cane), entered France as a result of the Dutch East India Company's commerce in Indonesia. The proliferation of chairs loosely resembling the Turkish divan and endowed with Oriental names exemplifies the process by which the expansion of global trade and travelers' exposure to different cultures stimulated the invention of new French products. However, it should also be noted that although the raw materials for these items were usually imported from existing French colonies or from colonies maintained by other European powers, the finished products were represented as Oriental. In this regard, the history of furniture can be viewed as an exemplary illustration of the displacement of colonial history onto exotic representations of the Orient that I describe in Chapter 1.

My second point concerns the phenomenon generally known as "commodity fetishism," the perceived excess of exchange value over use value, or—in the revised terms of structural linguistics—of signifier over signified.[31] When eighteenth-century artisans describe the luxuries they consider characteristic of their age, they often caution the reader/consumer that the enticing names given to these commodities do not correspond in any clear way to a signified. For example, in his *L'Art du menuisier en meubles*, the furniture maker André Roubo cites "ottomanes, veilleuses à la Turque, pafoses, turqoises and gondoles" as "bizarre names whose only etymology is the cupidity of artisans and merchants" (652).[32] His remarks not only convey his perception that the exchange value of the new furniture exceeds its use value, but also suggest that names (or signifiers) no longer correspond to a determinate referent: the exotic names given to chairs reflect neither substantial changes in morphology nor the relationship of French furniture to Oriental origins. This disjunction, which Roubo, among others, bemoans, is in fact one of the prevailing features of commodity culture, for the cycle of acqui-sition, exchange, and transformation that characterizes capitalist economies does nothing if not translate the final absence of anything but a provisional and continually changing referent or benchmark of value.

The commodity status of the new furniture is brilliantly captured in Jean-François de Bastide's novella *La Petite maison* (1758; first published in the journal *Le Nouveau Spectateur* in Paris), an extraordinary narrative that com-bines an aesthete's account of the latest fashions in architecture, furnishings, and the decorative arts with a libertine narrative of seduction. In this novella, the Marquis de Trémicour gives a woman named Mélite a tour of his tastefully appointed home, during which he directs her attention toward architectural features and decorations executed by famous contemporary architects, artisans, and artists. Trémicour's explicit purpose in giving this tour is to seduce Mélite, who is equally firm in her resolve to resist his advances. Unfortunately for her, the taste and refinement of his *hôtel* mirror and perhaps magnify the sensuality of his person. The fusion of owner and possessions ultimately has the desired effect, for Mélite finally succumbs to the seduction of tapestries, paintings, furniture, and objets d'art. The final surrender occurs as she sinks into a *bergère*, an anthropomorphized chair that reflects back—and indeed enhances—her own state of desire and self-aban-donment (*La Petite maison*, 66).

On a secondary level, the seduction that Bastide narrates may be read as an allegory for the seduction of the reader/consumer by the furniture that he describes. Analyzing the link between commodities and desire, *La Petite maison* shows how the endless novelties generated by commodity culture act as conduits for a desire that can never be fully satisfied. Bastide intimates that consumption is endless because it consists not of the satisfaction of needs by means of material objects, but rather of the consumer's absorption in an ideal system of sign-objects. As Baudrillard writes, "In their ideality sign-objects are all equivalent and may multiply infinitely; indeed they must multiply in order at every moment to make up for a reality that is absent"(*System of Objects*, 205).[33] This structure is of course also that of

Crébillon's novella, in which Amanzéï's desire—like Schah-Baham's and the reader's—is conducted along an endless chain of women, figures for the impossibility of satisfaction or of a plenitude of knowledge.

DISPOSSESSION

At the end of *Le Sopha*, Amanzéï is restored to a human identity. As a consequence, his audience must infer that the last two lovers whom he encounters—Zéïnis and her partner Phéléas—fulfill the conditions of the enchantment by losing their virginity to each other. Disappointingly, however, the moment of transparency or reciprocal "knowledge" that unites the two lovers corresponds to a frustrating failure of knowledge insofar as Amanzéï himself is concerned.

Finding Zéïnis to be eminently desirable, Amanzéï squirms around the sofa, trying to overcome his impediment by rubbing against the object of his desire (333–35).[34] He comes surprisingly close to passing from the status of mere voyeur to possessing the elusive "Oriental woman" because his cavorting inspires erotic dreams in the sleeping Zéïnis, and the arousal that she experiences in her dream paves the way for her sexual union with Phéléas. Frustratingly, however, in the very moment that the lovers consummate their passion and achieve knowledge of each other, Amanzéï is whisked away by Brahma. In what might be viewed as a telling metaphor for the epistemological quicksand that is Orientalist representation, the subject is dispossessed of his own identity just as he is about to grasp that of the other.

This anticlimactic ending articulates a distinction between the type of knowledge that consists of a complete loss of self in other—the reciprocal absorption of Zéïnis and Phéléas, for example—and the cognizance that is dependent on representation, and thus predicated on mediation and distance. Although Amanzéï's metamorphosis seems to permit him and his listeners to get beyond mere representation and to grasp the "truth in itself," the closing scene of the novella finally lays to rest the belief that one can overcome the barred access to plenitude that is constitutive of language— and indeed, of desire. This conclusion is in fact anticipated throughout the novel, for as we have noted, Amanzéï's attempts to know and expose the secrets of Oriental women are repeatedly impeded by his encounters with a complex web of concealment and revelation, encounters which teach him that the "real" cannot definitively be distinguished from its representation. The roots of this tension, as we have seen, are located in the central figure of the sofa, at once a marker of intimacy and informality and a key constituent of commodity culture.

This said, I want to suggest that two levels of meaning should be identified in this denouement. Despite its epistemological complexity, there remains a level on which the conclusion of this novel merely confirms the view (uttered by Schah-Baham at the very beginning of Amanzéï's narrative), that (Oriental) women simply cannot be known; that, as Flaubert would later intone, "Neither you nor I, no ancient and no modern, can know Oriental woman" (letter to Sainte-Beuve in *Correspondance*, 3:277). This myth of radical alterity is the necessary correlate to the desire to know and unveil Oriental women that pervades the novel, albeit in the guise of a frivolous social satire. As we have observed, this desire does not go wholly unsatisfied—although the reader may grasp the epistemological subtext of the narrative and as a result be inspired to question the authentic, uncensored portrait of the female sex that the narrative seems to offer—it is by no means clear that this awareness negates the satirical account of the faithlessness and dissimulation of Oriental women that emanates from Amanzéï's testimony. In fact, I would submit that precisely *because* this tale suggests that representations, and not concealed truths, are the legitimate objects of social analysis, it becomes incumbent on us to take these representations seriously. This opening in the relationship between text and interpretation is one I want to return to later in the context of my reading of a second Oriental tale, Denis Diderot's *Bijoux indiscrets*.

THE GLOBAL ECONOMY OF THE 'BIJOUX INDISCRETS'

Diderot's first novel tells a tale that in many respects parallels and echoes the one told in *Le Sopha*. It is the story of Mangogul, a sultan who is bored because he has it all—absolute power, a seraglio of compliant women, and Mirzoza, the official favorite, with whom he enjoys a relationship of reciprocal love and trust. Like Crébillon's Schah-Baham, he turns to stories about women's infidelity for relief from his ennui; unlike Schah-Baham, however, Mangogul wants to hear stories that are true—to apprehend once and for all the unvarnished truth about the women of his court. In keeping with the whole Orientalist tradition, to achieve knowledge of the other means to surmount a powerful obstacle: to attain it, Mangogul requires the assistance of a voyeuristic device akin to Crébillon's sofa. His wish is fulfilled when the genie Cucufa gives him a magic ring that has the power to make women's genitals speak and that can also render its bearer invisible—a power that, although it is not always exploited by Mangogul, accentuates the voyeuristic dimension of his enterprise. But although the ring yields a wealth of information about the secret lives of the women of his court, Mangogul is in the end induced to throw it away. Abandoning his dream of unmediated knowledge, he is forced to recognize the dangers inherent to his project and to reconcile himself to the lack of transparency that is constitutive of human relations.

Although Diderot's novel can be read as a pastiche of several of the Oriental tales of the period, including the Comte de Caylus's *Nocrion, conte allobroge* (1747)[35] and Crébillon's *Le Sopha*, Diderot does not hesitate to parody Crébillon's style, which he describes as "entortillé": convoluted, impenetrable, essentially vacuous. This gesture of distancing conveys the fact that in writing *Les Bijoux indiscrets*, Diderot intended to go beyond his predecessors by bringing explicitly philosophical and political questions to a hitherto frivolous genre.[36] The principal result of this revisioning is that whereas in *Le Sopha* the failure to penetrate social appearances and grasp the underlying truth engenders only a sense of disappointment and futility, in Diderot's novel, an epistemological and political conclusion about the pursuit of truth is drawn in the narrative itself.[37]

Diderot's early novel has been the object of considerable critical attention in recent years. The greatest part of this critical discussion has centered on the narrative's reduction of female subjects to talking bodies—a device rightly considered to foreshadow the psychoanalytic discourse on feminine hysteria—or conversely, on Mangogul's ultimate recognition that the speech of the body is still speech: that however objective knowledge may be, it can never definitively be separated from modes of representation.[38] What critics have largely neglected, however, is the fact that the female bodies in question are Oriental bodies. This is, however, a significant detail, because as we have observed already, the deployment of the "veil of Orient" automatically confers on women in the Oriental tale the status of figures of both veracity and dissimulation. In what follows, I want to redirect the discussion of *Les Bijoux indiscrets* to show that on almost every level, Diderot's critical perspective is informed by a sustained reflection on cultural as well as sexual difference.

As Edward Said has tirelessly argued, we are wont to presume that English works are about England, French works about France, and so on, while minimizing references to global cultural forces (*Culture and Imperialism*, 14). Thus, although a text such as the *Bijoux indiscrets* is set in the Orient, it is read only for what it says about French society. My reading of the novel reverses this trend by foregrounding instead the global economy of Diderot's writing, considering how France's colonial history reverberates within its domestic economy, and emphasizing the fact that *Les Bijoux indiscrets* was written in an age of exploration and international commerce—more precisely, at the end of a decade in which France, under the leadership of Joseph-François Dupleix, consolidated and extended its colonial presence in India, the purported site of Mangogul's court. This "globalization" of a text conventionally studied within the frame of national literary history is, within the limited framework of literary criticism, a political gesture with resonance for our own time, a small reminder of the inevitable contingency of boundaries erected against the international circulation of bodies, ideas, and goods.

I begin by reexamining one of the most frequently discussed sections of the text. Defending his use of the ring to the favorite Mirzoza, Mangogul solemnly states that the ring knows no "chimeras," that it is "not the site of prejudice" (54); it is therefore interesting that in an episode that is usually read as a *mise-en-abime* of the primary narrative, Mangogul has a dream in which he finds himself traveling in the realm of "hypotheses," a "chimerical" world populated by systematic philosophers whose ragged clothes and decrepit bodies serve as metaphors for the deficiencies of their thought (131–32). The edifice that these thinkers inhabit, itself decrepit and precariously suspended in midair, is violently destroyed upon the arrival of Experience, represented in the guise of a child who carries in his hand the torch of Enlightenment along with an array of scientific instruments, including a navigational device—a telescope. The child grows as it advances toward the edifice of systematic philosophy, finally assuming global proportions: "his head touched the sky, his feet were lost in the abyss, and his arms stretched from pole to pole" (133).

Enlightenment literature typically portrays empiricism as a decentering of human rationality, a contestation of Cartesian rationalism and its anthropocentric doctrine of innate ideas. In stark contrast to rationalism, empiricism is praised for situating man in the natural world and—at least in the sensualist and materialist epistemologies that flourished from the 1740s on— for locating the mechanism of thought in the body as well as in the mind. Mangogul's dream, however, offers a different and in some ways darker exploration of the success of empiricism as a philosophical and scientific method by drawing attention to its capacity to extend human knowledge geographically, and therefore to its central importance to the history of exploration and conquest.

In Diderot's allegory of Experience's triumph over metaphysics, the progress realized by European technology is conveyed in an explicit figure of global expansion. Although the doctrine of the *mission civilisatrice* was only formalized in the mid–nineteenth century, French colonial expansion was from its inception clearly premised on the belief that non-European civilizations were less advanced, that their truths were mere "hypotheses." Mangogul's dream lends expression to this cultural conviction by staging the encounter between truth and prejudice or mystification as a violent struggle that pits European empiricism and scientific progress against the ignorance and prejudice that shrouds the rest of the world. The gesture by which Experience destroys the crumbling edifices of a waning civilization—the realm of hypotheses—and sheds light on its failure to advance resonates for readers through its resemblance to the historical process by which French colonialism set about eradicating indigenous cultural practices and replacing them with enlightened French ones. The reading of this passage has implications for the rest of the novel, for if, following the lead of previous critics, we view Mangogul's dream as a paradigmatic rendition of the primary narrative, the sultan's reduction of female subjects to the objects of their own discourse assumes a further dimension: it begins to resemble, and indeed to fulfill, the Western ethnographic fantasy on which beliefs about Oriental sexuality receive empirical confirmation from the direct testimony of "native informants."

But in reading the chapter of Mangogul's dream, it is also important to pay attention to detail and to note that the sultan's attention is focused not on the dazzling figure of Experience, but on the shreds of material worn by the schematic philosophers, said to be fragments of the robe of Socrates, remnants of the ethical and humanistic heritage of classical philosophy.[39] This detail suggests that the triumph of Experience does not occur to the exclusion of all other modes of thought. Rather, the sultan's concern with reconstituting the robe of Socrates may be seen to convey Diderot's own recognition that experience alone is not a sufficient foundation for philosophy.[40] In a similar way, as we shall see, the primary narrative of *Bijoux indiscrets* ultimately invites the conclusion that despite its power to unveil lies and overturn established beliefs, Mangogul's ring cannot provide ethical guidance about relationships with others; nor can it set aside the robe of language as the medium of interpersonal, or intercultural, communication. In what follows, I propose that global forces play a significant role in shaping the contrasting principles that underlie this episode, and by extension the narrative as a whole: on the one hand the empiricist drive to unveil appearances and determine truth, and on the other the critical dismantling of the ideal of unmediated knowledge.

CULTURAL OTHERS AND FRAGMENTED SELVES

The problem confronting Mangogul—as James Creech, Thomas Kavanagh, and others have noted—is that he can only get behind the veil of representation by having recourse to more representation. That is to say, to "get beyond language," the sultan is forced to lend authority to the speech of the jewels. As Creech observes in *Diderot: Thresholds of Representation*, the ring ultimately represents a double bind, for although it creates the desire for transparency, it also generates representation, effectively negating the possibility of direct and unmediated knowledge.

In a text of the same period, the *Lettre sur les sourds et muets* (*Letter on the Deaf and Dumb*; 1751), Diderot ponders the fact that to get behind thoughts expressed—or as he repeatedly puts it in this work, "dressed" or "robed" (*habillés*)—in language, to catch thought in itself, one would have to be "two-headed" (*dicéphale*).[41] This dicephalous figure makes explicit what the split between mouth and sex in *Bijoux indiscrets* all along suggests—in other words, that the condition for all-encompassing knowledge of identity is a fracturing of identity that renders such knowledge impossible.

As we take cognizance of this point, we begin to realize that the central split between mind and sex is by no means the only image of fractured identity to appear in *Bijoux indiscrets*. In fact, the novel abounds in distorted figures and dismembered bodies. I want to mention just a few of these, beginning with those that we have already encountered: the philosophers of the realm of hypotheses, who, if not fancy-free, are at least "foot-less" and in some cases even "leg-less." In a second dream, the sultan imagines Mirzoza with the head of a dog (182), and Bloculocus (a courtier) has to stop and explain this alarming hallucination by suggesting that each being enjoys an infinite number of relationships to other beings; that these relationships constitute identities when they are grouped together in terms of similarity or difference; and that in dreams, as in the minds of madmen, identities are reconfigured because the infinite web of difference is freed from the conventions of meaning. In a third example, Sélim, a courtier who has lived through the reign of Mangogul's father Kanoglou (Louis XIV), makes a parodic attempt to explain historical changes in women's fashions by claiming that petticoats had to be shortened and dresses split in the front because the ladies of the court suddenly took to standing on their hands, and without these alterations, they simply could not see (238–39). Finally, Sélim tells Mirzoza the story of a young Egyptian punished for a religious transgression by the loss of his genitals. This unfortunate youth is only made whole again when he meets a woman who has been punished in a similar manner and who loves him despite his mutilation—that is to say, who loves him for his fragmented self (251–55).[42]

These allusions to mutilated, fragmented, "foreign" bodies are accommodated by the exotic context of the novel as a whole. As we have seen, the Oriental tale is an almost limitlessly flexible medium in which all manner of fantastic transformations and eccentric figures can be presented without eliciting the cry of *invraisemblance*. Yet within this already exotic economy, fragmented figures appear with most frequency in passages that deal with travel, and in particular with the ways in which language and culture shape the perception of reality. This is because in these episodes the body is portrayed, not as empiricist and sensualist epistemology generally have it, as the ultimate source of human perception, but as a fragile and variable construct whose very form is shaped by linguistic structures and cultural forces.

Given this tendency, it is interesting to note that in the early 1770s, Diderot added two new chapters to the *Bijoux indiscrets*. This was a decade in which questions of global relations and cultural difference suddenly took on a new importance and began to occupy the national consciousness in a way that they had not in the 1740s, when the bulk of the novel was written. As I suggest in the Introduction, this was largely because after the signing of the Treaty of Paris (1763), by which France surrendered many of its American colonies to England and Spain, French thinkers began for the first time to reflect critically on France's colonial venture. Diderot was one of many thinkers who in this period became actively preoccupied with colonial questions. He collaborated with the Abbé Raynal on the multivolume *Histoire des deux Indes* (1770), the first attempt to write a comprehensive history of colonialism, and further explored the global implications of European voyages of discovery in his *Supplément au Voyage de Bougainville* (*Supplement to Bougainville's Voyage*; 1772, first published 1796).

In one of the two new chapters added in the 1770s, Mangogul receives ethnographic reports from travelers returning to his court after a long absence (267).[43] These reports focus primarily on the exotic bodies, and more particularly the exotic genitalia, of the inhabitants of an unnamed island. The account made of these reports should be read as a parodic rendition of the aims and methods of the exploratory voyages of the age, and even the sultan—who, like the monarchs of France, is the nominal patron of these expeditions to distant parts of the globe—is inclined to find the travelers' testimony more entertaining than credible. Yet despite Diderot's satirical tone, the travelers' reports, with their emphasis on exotic genitalia, call to mind Europe's *historical* fascination with the sexual parts of exotic others, notably the veritable obsession with the Hottentot body that galvanized ethnography from the mid–eighteenth to the late nineteenth centuries, reaching its apogee in the early nineteenth century with the public exhibition of Sarah Bartmann, the so-called Hottentot Venus.[44] This fascination receives one of its early formulations in the article "Hottentots" in Diderot's own *Encyclopédie*, a text that explores the distinctive reproductive anatomy of this ethnic group at length and with considerable distaste. Diderot's objective in describing the islanders' sexuality was doubtless to promote a concept of cultural relativism. But when we read this episode against the historical context of contemporary ethnography, it begins to seem charged with an undercurrent of disdain for the differences exhibited by other races. As we take a closer look at the travelers' account, the presence of this strain of ambivalence becomes increasingly evident.

Through the intermediary of a "native informant" named Cyclophile, the travelers learn that the genitals of the islanders manifest different geometrical shapes (*figures*) and must therefore be carefully matched in order to guarantee conjugal felicity (268). As a prophylactic against infidelity, the islanders not only enforce a taxonomy of shapes but also monitor body temperature, thought to be a good indication of an individual's libido. This regimentation of sex is overseen by a state religion bent on the good of society. Here, as in *Supplément au Voyage de Bougainville*, Diderot contrasts Christian moralism with the less condemnatory, more socially useful attitudes toward sex demonstrated by other religions. However, as in the *Supplément*, this state intervention in reproduction is made to appear less than wholly benevolent: the islanders' bodies—much like those of the women of Mangogul's court— are reduced to their genitalia so that they can be instrumentalized in the name of science and in the interests of public welfare.

The exotic alterity of the islanders is further underscored when the travelers relate that they are born with the signs of their vocation inscribed on their bodies. Thus, the hands of a future geometrician are shaped like a compass, and the index finger of a surgeon takes the form of a scalpel (275). The voyagers' island utopia appears therefore as the ideal habitat of the materialist *machine-man* (*homme machine*), a species in which the boundary between body and instrument is eroded, generating figures that reflect the growing impact of technology on the perception of the human body.[45] The islanders' unusual "birthmarks" do not, however, increase the travelers' respect for them or lead them to view them as the embodiment of human technological progress. Rather, these vocational markings are read as dehumanizing signs that lend the islanders "the air of automata" (276). Here again, we need to invoke a larger historical picture and to situate this representation in the context of the history of transcultural exploration, a context in which the travelers' perception of the islanders as hyperproductive automata transmits a distant but disturbing echo of the history of colonial exploitation and forced labor.

The travelers' narrative is a darker, more overtly ethnographic version of an episode included in the original version of the text, in which Mirzoza presents to Mangogul and the court of Banza her own "metaphysical" fantasy about instrumentalized bodies (118–25). Like Mangogul's explorers, Mirzoza dreams of a body reduced to its essential parts, but in her thinking, these parts are determined not by an individual's technical or physical aptitudes, but rather by his or her leading passion; the coquette is thus reduced to her eyes, the singer to his throat, the card player to his hands, and so forth (124–25). The favorite's purpose in expounding this rather fanciful "doctrine" before the court seems to be that she wants to offer her listeners an alternative to Mangogul's fixation on a singular identity located in the feminine sex. Thus, she argues that the soul does not occupy a single, constant location, but rather migrates around the body in accordance with the age and passions of the individual.

Despite their shared materialism,[46] the two lovers follow opposed anthropological principles: whereas Mangogul believes in the fundamental similarity of all women, Mirzoza is attentive to the differences among people. As Elisabeth de Fontenay observes, she effects an Oriental, feminine displacement of her master's metaphysics by theorizing a mobile, decentered identity constituted in the pluralism of difference (*Diderot, Reason and Resonance*, 161). This displacement or decentering of identity is manifestly geographic as well as corporeal: in her reform of Mangogul's system, Mirzoza calls the conviction that the soul is located in the head a "geographical error" similar to confusing east with west (120). Sélim, the elder statesman of Mangogul's court, immediately picks up on the political implications of this metaphor and cautions her that her philosophy is subversive in that it displaces the geographic center of authority from the head—which for him corresponds to the Sublime Porte—to different parts of the body-empire. In fact, his astute observation draws attention not only to the political implications of Mirzoza's system, but also to the geopolitics of identity: to the fact that identities are in reality constituted across as well as within cultural borders, and to the fact that cultural groups and gender categories, far from being homogeneous, comprise internal differences that are suppressed in ethnocentrist or misogynistic models such as Mangogul's.

TRANSLATIONS

Mangogul's efforts to reduce difference to a singular coherent identity have the unforeseen effect of creating a strong sense of the *instability* of identity and its capacity for fragmentation. As we have seen, the inaugural split between mind and sex serves as the paradigm for a proliferation of corporeal divisions that disclose the fracturing of identity in representation and that tacitly acknowledge that each human voice, each language, provides only a partial representation of the world. What I now want to show is that this countermodel is self-reflexively inscribed in the novel as it alludes to its *own* displacement and fragmentation in representation—a displacement that is conveyed through the intercultural trope of translation.

References to translation in eighteenth-century fiction are sites of complexity. In many instances, novels that represent themselves as translations, for example Montesquieu's *Lettres persanes* or Françoise de Graffigny's *Lettres d'une Péruvienne* (*Letters of a Peruvian Woman*; 1747), align themselves with the history of cultural expropriation by claiming to have "eliminated" the superfluous rhetoric of less prestigious languages. At the same time, however, allusions to translation automatically connote a drifting away from the presumed authority of an original meaning. *Les Bijoux indiscrets* is exemplary in this regard. Having employed the pronoun "I" throughout the narrative, in the ninth chapter of the novel, the narrator suddenly, yet unobtrusively, announces that the text is the translation of a work by an African author and criticizes the translators—apparently not the narrator himself—for their failure to render a portion of a scientific argument (59).[47] Because of this sudden and unexpected allusion to another author, the reader is confronted with the very question that faces Mangogul—in other words, who is speaking?— and in consequence invited to question the integrity of the text, seemingly undercut by the mention of untranslated and therefore missing parts.

This passing reference to the intercultural process of translation immediately raises questions about the "identity" of author and text that mirror the decentering and fragmentation of body and self repeatedly recounted in the narrative. In light of these questions, the authority of the writer over the text is subverted in much the same way that Mangogul's attempts to control representation ultimately founder. Drawing the global implications of this parallel, I think it is important to observe that the translation of "African" into "Congolese"—that is, French—culture is inscribed not as a successful act of cultural appropriation, but rather as a process of loss and fragmentation that betrays the author's fundamental lack of mastery over the language in which he writes.

The sense that language exceeds authorial control reverberates in all of the novel's (many) allusions to translation.[48] In some of these references, Diderot seems to raise the question of translation primarily to parody the erudition of scholarly Orientalists. Thus, when asked to render the discourse that emanates from the jewel of the sultan's mare, the assembled "interpreters and professors of foreign languages of the Congo" variously identify what they have heard as a touching scene from a Greek tragedy, an important fragment of Egyptian theology, Hannibal's funeral oration in "Carthaginese," and a Chinese prayer to Confucius! (129). In another instance, Bloculocus (who has just offered a plausible translation of Mangogul's dream) announces that he has been busy translating a Greek treatise on dreams. He explains to Mangogul that he does not view his unfamiliarity with Greek as a handicap because his readers don't know it either! (186). These episodes are, however, more than just amusing jibes at the vain presumption of contemporary Oriental scholarship; they are also signposts that direct the reader's attention to the impenetrable foreignness of language, conveying a profound sense that man is trapped in a language that he doesn't really "know" and can never fully master.

THE POLITICS OF TRANSPARENCY

The trials of the ring come to an end in the final chapter of the novel, when Mirzoza succumbs to a near-fatal attack of the vapors. The favorite had always been disturbed by the sultan's enterprise and had made him promise never to turn the ring on her. This had inevitably been his first temptation, and, as Thomas Kavanagh notes, the jewels he does test can be seen as substitutes for the questioning of Mirzoza herself. The favorite is, however, adamant in her refusal to be questioned; indeed, she firmly states that should Mangogul turn his ring on her, the confidence between them would be broken and her affection for him forever compromised (45–46). The narrator makes it clear that her motive for resisting is not, as Mangogul might surmise, that she has something to hide (for instance, that she has been unfaithful or does not truly love him). Rather, she simply does not want her jewel to prove what she says is true. In other words, what she is resisting is Mangogul's misogynistic desire to circumvent her subjectivity to satisfy his own fantasy of objective truth.

As James Creech observes in *Diderot: Thresholds of Representation*, from Mangogul's perspective, the existence of the ring transforms Mirzoza from a lover into "a woman," a sociological category which in the economy of the narrative is scientifically broken down into an infinite number of subcategories: the "tender woman," the "virtuous woman," the "gallant woman," and so forth. The novel in this sense anticipates the taxonomic enterprise of the *Encyclopédie*, in which the article "Woman" is similarly divided into a series of subcategories—the "abandoned woman," the "adulterous woman," the "divorced woman," and so on. I want to bring an additional dimension to Creech's observation by arguing that the taxonomic project of the ring, which makes everything, in his words, "representational . . . mediate and . . . *alien*" (Creech, *Diderot*, 29; my italics) turns Mirzoza into an Oriental woman: a woman who is other, lost, and desired, an idealized figure of truth and knowledge, yet at the same time a debased cultural category that participates in the scientific classification of race and sexuality.[49] Indeed, Mirzoza exemplifies the tension at the core of the figure of Oriental woman, for she is at once ethnographic example and foreign body, a figure for the foreignness of language and of the irremediable alienation of the self in representation.

Mangogul finally turns the ring on Mirzoza when he believes that she is dying, justifying his act with the claim that if it is already too late, then her jewel, like her mouth, will stay silent (257). This observation bespeaks recognition on his part, first, that self-identity (the mouth and the jewel say the same thing) occurs only in death and that he could only truly know Mirzoza if she were dead; and second, that if this were the case, then she would be irremediably lost, beyond the reach of human knowledge. This conclusion echoes the ending of *Le Sopha* in the sense that, like Amanzéï, Mangogul discovers that he cannot *possess* another human being, if possession means acquiring unmediated knowledge of his or her heart. However, in *Bijoux indiscrets*, this conclusion is drawn by the sultan himself, and it inspires a specific course of action: Mangogul abandons the ring and is happily reconciled with Mirzoza.

As several scholars, beginning with Diderot's nineteenth-century editor Assézat, have noted, Mangogul's use of the ring operates on one level as a thinly veiled allegory of Louis XV's use of police reports to garner information about the goings-on at his court. The king purportedly devoted his *petits levers* to hearing the accounts of scandalous behavior gathered in the course of the previous evening by his chiefs of police. This practice of espionage may have served primarily as an amusement, but it certainly also fulfilled the king's will to exercise control over his subjects by learning their secrets, a technique that has been a feature of all authoritarian regimes. Diderot's narrative in this regard anticipates a political discourse that took shape toward the end of the aging monarch's reign[50] and intensified during the prerevolutionary period, when writers, including the Marquis de Sade and Pierre Manuel, looked back on the surveillance tactics of Louis XV, portraying them both as manifestations of political despotism and as signs of the monarch's pornographic tastes, the symptom of a corrupt, oversexed, and effeminate royal body.[51]

Viewed in this light, Mangogul begins to look like an "Oriental despot": a figure for the absolutist tendencies and social and political corruption of the Bourbon monarchy. Once an enlightened prince who opened the doors of the harem and enjoyed cordial and informal relations with his subjects, he is corrupted by a fantasy of absolute power and succumbs to the temptation to place his own entertainment, and his desire for psychological control, above the good of his subjects: "Am I a sultan for nothing, then?" he barks back when Mirzoza cites the good of his people as an argument against the use of the ring (50). As the novel progresses, the initially flattering portrait of an enlightened Louis XV gradually disintegrates, evolving into a warning about the abuse of power. Unsurprisingly, therefore, when Mangogul finally agrees to give up the ring, Mirzoza assures him that he is doing it for the good of both court and empire, and Cucufa similarly promises that both his heart and his glory will henceforth be secure (258).

It is helpful to compare this use of the ring as a metaphor for the misuse of political power with a text in which Diderot's contemporary and nemesis, Rousseau, speculates on what he would do if he possessed a similar object. In the Sixth Reverie of his *Rêveries du promeneur solitaire* (*Reveries of the Solitary Walker*; 1780), Rousseau writes that "If I had possessed Gyges' ring it would have freed me from my dependence on other men and made them dependent on me. In my day-dreams I have often asked myself what use I would have made of this ring, for it is in this situation that the temptation to abuse is closest to the power to do so" (117). Whereas Diderot rejects the ring, Rousseau, at least at first, says that he would have kept it, arguing that goodness is the product of strength and freedom, never that of "slavery" or dependence on other men. Pursuing this logic, he claims that he would have acted impartially, showing clemency rather than severity, and performing miraculous acts beneficial to his fellow man. If Rousseau finally determines that he would do better not to retain the ring, it is because he admits to human frailties that might lead him astray in his use of it, not because he questions the ideal of transparency in human relations. The difference between Rousseau's position and the conclusion drawn in *Les Bijoux indiscrets* provides a succinct illustration of the contrast between Rousseau's epistemology of self-sufficiency and Diderot's relational and intersubjective model of human identity, an epistemological and political model that was elaborated in the mode of negative knowledge in *Les Bijoux indiscrets* and later developed in works such as *Le Neveu de Rameau* (*Rameau's Nephew*; c. 1762, first published 1805), which proposes that a monarch or a philosopher must not set himself above, or outside of, the rest of humanity to observe or rule it.

A CAVEAT

I have suggested that the metaphorical exchange of Oriental world for domestic culture in the exotic fiction of the midcentury produces a height-

ened awareness of the self's alienation in the foreign medium of representation. However, I want to end this chapter by once again introducing a caveat
about this recognition of the foreignness of language and the accompanying
dispossession of the self. As we have observed, several contemporary critics
argue that the underlying message of *Les Bijoux indiscrets* is that the attempt
to get beyond the veil of representation falters on the irreducibility of representation. Although I support this interpretation and have attempted to
relate this conclusion to the novel's exotic context, I also want to argue
against the tendency to reduce this and other Orientalist works to critiques
of the conceptual formations that support essentialist thinking about gender
or cultural difference.

Although the fixation on knowledge and identity is ultimately deconstructed in both *Les Bijoux indiscrets* and *Le Sopha*, it is far from clear that
this problematization neutralizes the exposure of female identity that these
narratives perform. Deconstructive accounts of the *Bijoux indiscrets*, notably
those of James Creech, Jane Gallop, and Thomas Kavanagh, have in fact
curiously avoided the important question of whether and in what sense the
final *mise-en-cause* of the ring retroactively discredits the unflattering testimony of the jewels. Certainly it is important that it is Mirzoza, a woman,
who ultimately occasions the defeat of the ring. But it is equally necessary to
note that by the end of the narrative, Mirzoza, who could be described as the
"exceptional woman," the faithful yet desirable, brainy but compliant
femme-philosophe or woman-man, has herself been made to think the worst
of her sex and to distinguish herself from all "other women." "The more you
use the ring the more odious my sex becomes to me," she tells Mangogul
after one particularly shocking revelation (96). This unsisterly reaction
forces us to reflect that objectifications and satirical portrayals of women and
Orientals have historically proved incomparably more powerful than the
critical examination of ethnographic "knowledge," and that the issue of the
historical reception of narratives such as *Les Bijoux indiscrets* and *Le Sopha* is
therefore an urgent one. I therefore want to argue that if—as Crébillon and
Diderot's novels amply demonstrate—the metaphysics that sustains ethnocentrism also sustains deconstruction,[52] the proposition that the deconstruction of identity is the ironic complement to its consolidation is

reversible. In other words, I want to argue a pressing need for critics to acknowledge that deconstruction and ethnocentrism (or indeed all other forms of binaristic social thought) go hand in hand, and that as students of literature, we must acknowledge and assess both sides of this textual, and political, equation.

CHAPTER FOUR

Split Figures: Women and Language in the Oriental Travelogue

In the early 1840s, a somewhat obscure European traveler, the Egyptologist Théodore de Fonfrède, bought a Javanese woman in a Cairo slave market.[1] Some years later, the man who had accompanied Fonfrède on his travels, the poet Gérard de Nerval, immortalized this "yellow woman" by making her a central figure in his travel narrative, *Voyage en Orient* (*Voyage to the Orient*; 1851).[2] In the narrative of the *Voyage en Orient*, it is Nerval himself and not his traveling companion who buys the slave, and as he completes the transaction, he carelessly asks the slave dealer, the enigmatic Abd-el-Kérim, for the woman's name, observing that he is, after all, "buying the name too." Yet the name that he is given ("Z'n'b"), and which he claims to own, immediately becomes an obstacle, for he cannot pronounce it, and it takes him some time to ascertain how vowel sounds complement the triliteral root of the Arabic name Zeynab.

Within in the broader economy of the *Voyage en Orient*, the inscription of this act of naming has multiple resonances. It serves, notably, to cement the transformation of the Javanese slave from historical personage into literary legend. But it also discloses the fragile authority of European travel writing because the unpronounceable name of the Oriental feminine other figures the much wider sense in which the writer does not master the language of his own authority. Nerval's relationship with his slave in fact quickly becomes a complex power struggle that unfolds on the terrain of language. Failing to recognize or appreciate what her master perceives to be liberal behavior on his part, she brands him, in Arabic, "giaour" (infidel) and "pharaon" (pharaoh, tyrant), words that have considerable resonance in

French because they are those conventionally used in relation to the Orient. Disturbed by his inability to control her language, he tries to teach her French, but she in turn shrewdly recognizes that a cultural politics of literacy is at stake in these lessons and rejects what she rightly perceives as the ideological transmission of European ideas along with European words.

This chapter reconstructs the environment—historical and literary—in which this drama of language and power could unfold. It explores the representation of race, gender, and language in the Oriental travelogue, the dominant genre of writing on the Orient in the first half of the nineteenth century, focusing on Nerval's *Voyage en Orient*, an extraordinary fusion of political ideology, comedic writing, and poetic irony, published at the end of several decades in which travel writing established itself as a key romantic genre. In the *Voyage en Orient*, Nerval built on the ideological and aesthetic foundations laid by such illustrious precursors as Volney, Chateaubriand, and Lamartine, but he also transformed travel writing by redefining the political and spiritual quest that it had come to entail as the pursuit—at once philosophic and amorous—of "Oriental woman," and by foregrounding the rhetorical foundations on which Western representations of the Oriental other were built.

ORIENTAL REALISM AND THE COLONIAL REAL

In the final decade of the eighteenth century, the arc of French colonial interest swung eastward from North America and the Caribbean to Egypt and North Africa. Although the incursion into Egypt led by the young Napoléon Bonaparte in 1798 was short-lived, it nonetheless established a foundation for French political and cultural influence in the region. In the years that followed the *Expédition* France sided with the Egyptian viceroy Mehemet-Ali in his struggle against Ottoman rule and committed itself to training and equipping the Egyptian army. In 1830, French forces made a second, more enduring incursion into the Orient, occupying Algiers and Oran and laying the foundations for the later annexation of the whole of Algeria.

In this context of territorial expansion, the Oriental travelogue, immensely popular during the seventeenth century but eclipsed in the eighteenth by the fictionalized Orient of the tale, came back into vogue.[3] Constantin Chassebeuf de Volney's *Voyage en Égypte et en Syrie* (*Voyage to Egypt and Syria*; 1787), François René de Chateaubriand's *Itinéraire de Paris à Jérusalem* (*Itinerary from Paris to Jerusalem*; 1811), and Alphonse de Lamartine's *Souvenirs, impressions, pensées et paysages pendant un Voyage en Orient, 1823–1833* (*Memories, Impressions, Thoughts and Landscapes during a Voyage to the Orient*; 1835) were the works that set the tone for the French reflection on the Orient in the first half of the nineteenth century. This consecration of the travel narrative connoted a discursive swing away from fantasy toward observation and description: Volney, Chateaubriand, and Lamartine's writing on the Orient is characterized by an abundance of painterly metaphors and descriptive details that reconstruct for the reader the region's landscapes and principal monuments. Following the lead of the *Description de l'Égypte* (*Description of Egypt*; France, 1809–1828), the massive project of scientific observation undertaken by the coterie of Orientalists and archaeologists that accompanied Bonaparte to Egypt, these early nineteenth-century travel narratives sought to capture all the aspects of the physical appearance of Oriental civilization that were deemed to be of interest, paving the way for the photographic attempts to "capture" the Orient that began almost immediately after the invention of the daguerreotype in the early 1840s.[4] A key feature of the picturesque style shared by travel writing, Orientalist painting, and photography was a virtual erasure of the organizing gaze of the Western spectator, resulting in the tacit affirmation of the objectivity of Orientalist representation.

The shift from fictional fantasy to realist description also signaled a break with the tradition of the *Orient galant*, the fascination with women, polygamy, and the harem that had dominated eighteenth-century exoticism. Intent on establishing the intellectual and spiritual gravity of travel writing, early nineteenth-century writers studiously avoided anything resembling the previous century's voyeuristic accounts of Oriental sexuality. Whereas Edward Said claims that after 1800, virtually all Western travelers to the Orient were embarking on an erotic quest, pursuing sexual experiences unavailable in the West, I would contend rather that in the French context, it was only in the latter part of the century that eroticized narratives really became prevalent.

A brief survey of the canonical travel narratives of the romantic period uncovers only peripheral interest in exotic sexual practices and mysterious Oriental women. Volney observes, from a fastidious distance, the presence of veiled women whom he describes as "walking phantoms," shrouded forms that show nothing human but a pair of eyes (*Voyage en Égypte et en Syrie*, 116). He also reiterates the basic conclusions of the Enlightenment medita- tion on Oriental sexuality by arguing that polygamy leads to depopulation, and that the enclosure of women in the harem impedes the growth of the kind of public life enjoyed in France (306). Chateaubriand is, if possible, even less loquacious on the subject of Oriental women. The encounters with representatives of the Ottoman Empire related in his *Itinéraire* are all encounters with men, and for the most part, they are charged with an air of hostility and reciprocal aggression. His narrative in fact quickly establishes a paradigm by which the upright, mobile, implicitly energetic French traveler presents himself to a Pacha or Aga who is squatting on a mat or reclining on a sofa—sedentary attitudes expressive of indolence, dissolution, and in cer- tain cases of the vicious cruelty of the "Oriental despot." But although this contrast between vertical and horizontal, active and passive, implicitly fem- inizes the Oriental other, the relation between Europe and Turkey is consis- tently constructed as a conflictual rather than an amatory one—an irrecon- cilable conflict of values and beliefs rather than the irresistible attraction of opposites. Finally, Lamartine, the celebrated poet of love and loss, has little to say on the attractions of women in the Orient. With the exception of the account he provides of his stay in Lebanon with the English eccentric and religious visionary Lady Esther Stanhope, women are observed in the *Souvenirs* only from a distance, as picturesque figures bearing baskets of grapes (374), or, more frequently, as shrouded forms whose drab uniformity mirrors the monotony of the Oriental landscape (335).

Nerval's *Voyage en Orient*, published in 1851 on the basis of a voyage undertaken in 1843,[5] builds on the legacy of Volney, Chateaubriand, and Lamartine, but at the same time departs in significant ways from the para- digm established by these illustrious forebears. From the beginning of his narrative, Nerval announces that he will present his reader with "sentimen- tal impressions" rather than a "picturesque description," and as promised, the account he gives of his travels is driven not by the description of landscape but by narrative, dialogue, and self-dramatization (1:84). These differences in structure and poetic form communicate a decided change in political perspective: whereas the descriptive emphasis of earlier travelogues conveys the narrators' detachment from—and indeed, aversion to—Islam and Ottoman rule, the lively engagement of Nerval's narrator communicates the author's comparative openness to Oriental culture and religion. Along these lines, it is important to note that Nerval's writing also departs from his predecessors' in the sense that it freely merges the empirical bent of travel writing with the narrative conventions of the novel, thereby subverting the realist Orientation of the genre and any political—strategic or military— application of the information it contains. This subversion may be said to have yielded both direct and indirect political consequences. Whereas Volney's *Voyage en Égypte et en Syrie* was adopted virtually as a guide by the *grande armée* during Bonaparte's Egyptian campaign, it would have been unthinkable to try to exploit Nerval's narrative in this manner. In a broader sense, Nerval's self-conscious representation of the artistry of travel writing had the effect of foregrounding the Western gaze that is all but erased in the picturesque style of his predecessors, thereby raising the crucial question of the real existence of "the Orient" as it had been represented in Western art and letters.

Of most importance for the present study is the fact that Nerval's narrative is propelled by the pursuit of a seemingly endless parade of women. From the opening section, suggestively titled "Les amours de Vienne" ("Love in Vienna") to the chapter devoted to "Les femmes du Caire" ("The Women of Cairo"), women are placed at the center of the narrative, which unfolds as a series of romantic episodes and culminates in a marriage plot. The narrator's profound interest in women—which, as I have noted, contrasts radically with the more masculine preoccupations of his precursors—is also slyly claimed as an excuse for another significant deviation from the conventions of Oriental travel writing. Nerval explains that he was unable to follow his illustrious predecessors to the Holy Land because of the expense incurred in acquiring Zeynab, the Javanese woman purchased in the slave markets of Cairo. A Moslem woman is thus made responsible for the *Voyage en Orient*'s break with the tradition of the spiritual pilgrimage, a break more plausibly attributable to the antipathy that Nerval felt for the political conservatism of contemporary Catholicism (as he observes, the majority of Christian pilgrims in this period were French legitimists [2:22]) and to his self-proclaimed openness to Oriental religions.

Whereas Chateaubriand and Lamartine represent themselves explicitly as Christian travelers and approach Oriental travel as a form of spiritual pilgrimage, Nerval's text repeatedly juxtaposes Judeo-Christian monotheism with Oriental religion, and consistently favors the latter. Christianity is recurrently shown to be monolithic, repressive, and patriarchal, whereas Oriental religion is portrayed as pluralistic, tolerant, and essentially feminine. Thus the narrator observes of the entire Mediterranean region that

> the feminine principle, and as Goethe says, the celestial feminine, will always reign on these shores. The sinister and cruel Diana of the Bosphorus, the prudent Minerva of Athens, the armed Venus of Sparta— these were their most sincere religions. The Greece of today replaces with a single virgin all of these holy virgins, and sets little store in the masculine trinity and all the saints of Christian legend. (1:134)

He makes it abundantly clear that he is equally unmoved by the masculine trinity and that one of the key motivations for his voyage is the desire to rediscover and embrace the feminine pluralism of Oriental religion.

THE "FEMINIST" TRADITION IN ORIENTALISM

Nerval's many deviations from the paradigm established by his predecessors were, however, less the product of a distinct set of personal experiences than the result of the writer's ideological affinity for a different tradition of writing on the Orient. As Michel Jeanneret has demonstrated, Nerval's knowledge of the Orient was not so much "lived" as "read"—the author spent more time perusing the European libraries and scholarly institutes of Cairo than the narrator of the *Voyage en Orient* spends out on the streets drinking in Oriental culture (introduction to *Voyage en Orient*, 1:22–23). One of the strongest literary influences on Nerval's perception of Oriental culture was the *Turkish Embassy Letters* of Lady Mary Wortley Montagu, an English aristocrat who accompanied her husband to Constantinople when he was named ambassador to the Sublime Porte in 1717. Montagu's letters, published posthumously in 1765, established what may be viewed as an alternative tradition within Orientalism, a feminocentric tradition that challenges received beliefs about the Orient, including the (still widely held) view that Islam is uniformly oppressive to women.[6] Like Montagu, Nerval takes issue with cultural stereotypes that alternately eroticize and condemn polygamy, and he insists instead on the extensive marital and property rights enjoyed by women in Islam. He also follows Montagu in suggesting that rather than constituting an insurmountable obstacle to gallantry, as Western writers had previously suggested, the veil facilitates flirtation and even adultery. Thus, although he announces at the beginning of his stay in Cairo that "Cairo is the city of the Levant in which women are the most hermetically veiled" (1:149), he quickly reaches the conclusion that "the veil is perhaps not as severe a barrier as one might suppose" (1:150). Ultimately, he outdoes Montagu in suggesting that, far from constituting an impediment, the veil is a powerful stimulant of curiosity and desire. In one episode, for example, he recounts his frenzied pursuit of two mysterious black "dominos" through the streets of Cairo, a chase that ends with the disappointing but ironic discovery that the women concealed beneath these capes are themselves French (1:179–80). Anticipating the Nietzschean analysis of the seduction exercised by the mirage of truth as a veiled woman, Nerval repeatedly insinuates that it is the veil itself, and not the woman concealed beneath it, that attracts.

Yet although it is clear that Nerval is keen to challenge the Western reader's sense of cultural superiority by providing new perspectives on practices such as polygamy, slavery, and the veil, I would hesitate to follow a number of recent Nerval scholars, including most prominently Kari Lokke, in interpreting this revisioning as the product of a distinctly feminist outlook (*Gérard de Nerval*, 65–103). Whereas Mary Wortley Montagu subjects Western perceptions of gender relations in the Orient to scrutiny to highlight the lack of self-determination enjoyed by women in Europe, Nerval never makes this essential connection; on the contrary, his narrator on several occasions observes that in Europe, women have grown "too strong," and expresses a desire to unite with "some ingenuous girl of this sacred land" (2:41–42). A number of texts signed by Nerval do, as Lokke asserts, draw connections between patriarchal authority and the social victimization of women—a critique that is most evident in his novella *Angélique* (1850), which recounts the suffering of the spirited Angélique de Longueval at the hands of her father and husband, but which is also to be found in the *Voyage en Orient*'s insistent critique of Christian patriarchalism and in its narrator's self-deprecating account of his own patriarchal relations with his Javanese slave.

Lokke is also right to say that Nerval is drawn to the iconoclastic power of mythical feminine figures and that he represents this feminine power as an appealing alternative to the paternalism of male authority, a contrast rendered with greatest force in the three long Oriental tales embedded in the primary narrative, and particularly in the last of these tales, a retelling of the biblical story of the courtship of Solomon and the queen of Sheba. In Nerval's rewriting of this story, Balkis rejects Solomon because she finds him overly materialistic and suspects that he would treat her as a chattel rather than a consort. Her reservations about the match express not only Nerval's distaste for Judeo-Christian monotheism, but also his penetrating analysis of the contradictory status of women in the emergent bourgeois-capitalist order of mid-nineteenth-century France. However, it is important to set this celebration of mythic female power in its textual context, and to observe that the primary function of these powerful feminine figures is to act as muses to the figures of *male* creativity that are the true protagonists of almost all of Nerval's texts: the queen of Sheba, for instance, unleashes the Promethean power of the blacksmith Adoniram, legendary founder of the Freemasons, of which Nerval liked to consider himself an initiate. It is also important to observe that the endorsement of feminine power almost always occurs in the context of a polarized relation to woman as real and woman as ideal, a dichotomy that runs throughout nineteenth-century literature but that is particularly acute in the writing of Nerval.

I therefore propose that the apparent feminocentrism of Nerval's *Voyage en Orient* is less the expression of a protofeminist outlook than the product of several other factors. These include Nerval's Nietzschean drive to subvert the quest for truth encoded in travel writing by showing that the pursuit of knowledge is always an erotic pursuit, and on a more philosophical plane, the quest for an originary unity that Nerval, following the German romantics, identified as a feminine principle. But what I principally want to argue in these pages is that Nerval's feminization of the Orient reflects an attitude toward colonial expansion that became very prevalent in opposition circles in the 1830s and 1840s.

Whereas in the years after the Expédition d'Égypte colonial expansion was typically portrayed in French literature as the product of conquest—the outcome of a violent encounter between two groups of men—by the 1830s, it was just as often naturalized as a spiritual or erotic union. On this new model, both colonizer and colonized were (implicitly or explicitly) gendered: the Orient and Africa were portrayed as feminine, whereas Europe was assigned the more active role of the energetic male suitor. Thus, for example, in his popular history *La Femme* (*Woman*; 1859), Jules Michelet describes Africa as a woman and claims that "the negress adores the white man" and particularly the Frenchman, superior both as a soldier and as a lover to his colonial rivals, the Englishman and the German (181–82). Nerval's *Voyage en Orient* was one of the earliest and boldest literary statements of this new sexualization of colonial discourse, and as such, it established a set of defining metaphors of miscegenation, erotic union, and cultural unveiling that strongly influenced subsequent thinking on colonial relations.

UTOPIAN SOCIALISM AND COLONIAL IDEOLOGY

In *Orientalism*, Edward Said claims that for Nerval the Orient was less a concrete geopolitical reality than a screen onto which he could project his own imaginative vision (179–84). Although there is much truth to this observation—as Said suggests, Nerval saw travel writing not as a descriptive medium but as a forum for philosophical reflection and textual experimentation—it adheres too narrowly to a rather traditional view of Nerval as a "pure poet"[7] and consequently misses the intense political engagement manifested throughout the narrative. A close reading of the *Voyage en Orient* suggests that Nerval's detachment from geopolitical reality was not as complete as Said suggests. Indeed, it shows that the sentimental and philosophical narrative is interwoven with an energetic endorsement of France's involvement in foreign affairs: although Nerval is less disdainful of Oriental culture than his precursors, the *Voyage en Orient* is nonetheless peppered with remarks on the subservience of Arabs and the racial inferiority of Africans that tacitly justify the project of colonial intervention.

Recent critical approaches to Nerval have converged in identifying his texts as sites of multiple splittings: the psychological scission of the subject in mental illness; the splitting in political perspective and literary form that arises from what Ross Chambers, in "Literature Deterritorialized," calls "political deterritorialization"—living and writing in a hostile political environment—and, most importantly for the present study, the ideological duplicity of the Western traveler who entertains the fantasy of self-abandonment in an idealized "elsewhere" but also reiterates established ethnocentric stereotypes about alien cultures and religions. Ali Behdad, in *Belated Travelers*, in particular has argued that Nerval's *Voyage en Orient* is torn between "Orientalist desire"—the drive to comprehend, control, and possess the Orient—and "desire for the Orient" (18)—the contrasting imperative for immersion or absorption in the Oriental other. I follow Behdad in emphasizing the ideological splitting of Nerval's writing on the Orient. However, I also want to modify the account he provides of this political hybridity by arguing that the fault lines discernible in the text are not simply the product of an unconscious tension in Nerval's thinking or the expression of the perennial contradictions of Orientalism, but rather the manifestation of the new currents in left-wing thinking on the "Eastern Question" that gained force in the 1830s and 1840s. I have suggested that a central facet of this thinking was the idea that colonial expansion constituted a form of erotic union. What I will now propose is that the tensions manifested in the *Voyage en Orient* between the drive to appropriate and control the Orient and the countervailing desire to idealize the Oriental other stem directly from the modeling of colonial relations on sexual relations. In other words, I will suggest that in the 1830s and 1840s thinking on the Orient became infused with the contradictory mix of idealization and proprietary attitudes characteristic of gender relations in nineteenth-century France.

Early in the *Voyage en Orient*, Nerval takes a critical stance toward European colonial rule by presenting it in an overtly negative light. Having observed that the Cycladic island of Cerigo (the Cythera of myth) is now ruled by England, he laments that "the earth is dead, it has died at the hands of man . . . the gods have flown" (1:139), insinuating a direct connection between the English occupation and the destruction of ancient religious traditions. On another Adriatic island, San-Nicolo, he notes the incongruity of a sign proclaiming that England is there for the love of Europe, pointing to the presence of a gibbet as a sign of the true character of English rule. What Nerval is attacking, however, is precisely *English* rule. The fact that his criticisms are as much nationalistic as they are anticolonialist becomes apparent a little later, when he contrasts the islanders' oppression under the English with the positive memory, said still to be alive in the minds of the elderly, of Bonaparte and the French Republic. Nerval thereby becomes one of the earliest commentators on colonialism to formulate the often-repeated claim that "England does not make Englishmen out of the peoples it has conquered . . . it turns them into slaves or sometimes into servants" (1:129), an observation with the implied correlate that France embraces its colonial subjects and generously absorbs into itself their cultural and religious traditions. (It must be emphasized that such claims, however integral a part of French colonial ideology, are the product of nationalist mythology, rather than an accurate interpretation of France's history in the Levant. In reality, in the seventeenth and eighteenth centuries, when France's mercantile and military presence in the Mediterranean was more organized and extensive than that of any of its European rivals, it was also more closely regulated; notably, ordinances published by the government and by the Conseil de Commerce de Marseille prohibited interracial marriage and discouraged French merchants and diplomats from wearing Oriental costume, a practice favored by English expatriates.[8])

Nerval's perspective on French involvement in the Orient emerges with greatest force in his account of his stay in Syria-Lebanon, a region that had been a focus of French strategic and commercial interest since the time of the Crusades. As he catches his first glimpse of the Palestinian coast, the narrator rapturously describes the city of Beirut as "Europe and Asia melting in soft caresses" (1:350), a figure that constructs the union of East and West as a reciprocal embrace rather than as the fruit of military conquest, setting the tone for a narrative in which geopolitical reflection is intertwined with the unfolding of a marriage plot. The discussion of Lebanese politics in the *Voyage en Orient* centers on topical contemporary issues, notably the disintegration of Ottoman authority and the escalating regional conflict between

Moslem Druze and Christian Maronite minorities. As elsewhere in the text, the narrator painstakingly establishes the colonial politics that frame this dispute, explaining that since 1830, France, Austria, and Sardinia have acted as protectors of the Maronites, whereas England has supported the Druze. He goes so far as to accuse the European powers of stirring up this ethnic conflict to further their own territorial ambitions (2:35), although he subsequently disculpates France by observing that it has lost much of the influence it once enjoyed in Syria-Lebanon. As I will show, this subtle exoneration paves the way for a series of arguments in favor of a strong French presence in the region.

When he first arrives in Lebanon, the narrator moves in Maronite circles. He is invited to stay at the home of a Maronite prince, and he even becomes embroiled in a skirmish with a Druze village. But his sympathies begin to shift when he falls in love with Saléma, the beautiful and intellectually gifted daughter of a Druze Cheikh incarcerated by the Turks for his political activities. He meets her at the school where he has placed his Javanese slave in the hope that its principal, Mme. Carlès, will be able to effect a "gentle conversion" (1:362; on this point, too, the narrative is grounded in a concrete historical reality; in 1831, France was in fact accorded special rights to establish Catholic missionary schools in Syria-Lebanon), and he is immediately attracted to this woman who corresponds to the type of unattainable feminine figure—the actress, the poetess, the queen—that he has always idolized (2:50). There is, however, a formidable obstacle to his union with Saléma: the Druze sect is, he claims, endogamous and does not recognize the conversion of outsiders. The narrator, however, compensates by drawing resourcefully on his knowledge of Friedrich Creuzer's *Symbolik und Mythologie* (1810–1812), a repository of Orientalist learning popular among the French romantics, to convince Saléma's father of the existence of close historical and spiritual connections between the Druze, the Knights Templar, and the Freemasons, of which he presents himself as an initiate.[9]

If this episode allows Nerval to show off the Orientalist learning gleaned from his extensive reading of Friedrich Creuzer and Silvestre de Sacy's *Exposé de la religion des Druzes* (*Exposé of the Druze Religion*; 1838), it also provides him with a forum for the expression of political views. The narrator claims that his marriage "is becoming high politics" and muses that it may "hold the key to renewing the ties that once bound the Druze to France" (2:143). Behind these rather grandiose claims is the suggestion that Syria-Lebanon is the region of the Orient in which Europe could establish itself with the least difficulty, because of its large contingent of Christians and "enlightened Moslems" (1:131), a covert reference to the recent occupation of Syria by the French-trained troops of Mehemet-Ali. Nerval also complains that France has hitherto focused only on the Maronites, neglecting the Druze and a whole series of "intermediary beliefs" that would be capable of "attaching themselves to the principles of Northern Civilization, and little by little, of bringing in the Arabs" (2:130). In other words, he points to the fact that the Druze are of interest from a political as well as an intellectual perspective because they represent a potential link in a chain binding "the Arabs" to the principles of the French Enlightenment. Through these scattered observations, Nerval represents Syria-Lebanon as a terrain ripe for colonization; indeed, he seems to exhort the French authorities to recommit themselves to the expansionist and (at least on the surface of things) pro-Moslem policies espoused by Bonaparte.

The French government did not act on Nerval's suggestions. On the contrary, in 1856, France became a signatory to a European treaty that mandated nonintervention in disputes involving the vassals of the Ottoman Empire.[10] To understand France's decision to sign this treaty and its reluctance to wage an aggressive campaign of territorial expansion, it is necessary to look back to the French defeat of 1815. In the wake of this overwhelming rout at the hands of England, Austria, and Russia, France was hesitant to reignite the animosity of its European neighbors. Louis XVIII and Charles X were, unsurprisingly, particularly loathe to alienate the foreign powers that had restored the Bourbon dynasty to the throne of France. This tentativeness in foreign policy did not, however, recommend itself to all segments of the political spectrum. Bonapartist and left-wing opponents of the Restoration and July monarchies expressed their opposition to the ruling regime by asserting France's national autonomy and espousing militant or expansionist principles. The conquest of Algiers in 1830, ostensibly undertaken in response to an insult offered in 1827 to the French consul general by the dey of Algiers, was in reality largely a last-ditch attempt to save the monarchy of Charles X through a display of nationalistic fervor calculated to appease the opponents of the regime.[11] Following the July Revolution of that same year, the government of Louis-Philippe elected to prolong the occupation, doubtless for similar motives. However, demonstrating the same conservatism as the previous regime, it waited until 1840 before venturing to extend French rule to Algeria as a whole.

In the 1830s and 1840s, France did mark out a small niche of independence in foreign policy by establishing itself as the sole European ally of Mehemet-Ali Pacha, the Egyptian viceroy who in 1839 led a victorious army against the Turks and occupied part of Syria. This action, which brought the Eastern Question sharply into focus, presented France with a difficult alternative between supporting the viceroy and expanding French influence—at the risk of inciting a war in Europe—and joining the other European powers in their efforts to pacify the Egyptian ruler. The nationalistic appeal of supporting the viceroy was intensified by the fact that this diplomatic crisis coincided with French maneuvers to return the remains of Napoléon Bonaparte from the British-controlled island of Saint-Helena to France.

At this delicate historical moment, Louis-Philippe's cabinet was headed by the historian Adolphe Thiers, a moderate liberal and committed nationalist who advocated support for Egypt, and who, in preparation for a European war, began a process of French rearmament. But the king himself was alarmed by these preparations and resisted the idea of involving France in a new international conflict. In the face of his resistance, the cabinet was forced to resign, and Thiers was replaced by the more conservative, less belligerent François Guizot, who joined England, Russia, and Austria in bringing Mehemet-Ali to a compromise. In the aftermath of this crisis, Guizot continued to exercise a moderating influence on French foreign policy. Notably, in a famous speech delivered before the National Assembly in 1842—just months before Nerval's departure for the Orient—he reactivated Montesquieu's arguments against the extension of the body politic to far-flung colonies, advocating instead the establishment of *points d'appui*, strategically located bases that would facilitate France's participation in international commerce.

Recent theoretical studies of nineteenth-century colonialism have portrayed colonial discourse as one element of a broader dominant discourse comprising the values and belief systems of bourgeois liberal capitalism. This is, most notably, the position of Richard Terdiman (*Discourse/Counter-Discourse*), who has developed a provocative and influential model that asserts that mid-nineteenth-century intellectuals sought to oppose or resist the prevailing discourse, including colonial ideology, yet found themselves helplessly replicating the dominant cultural attitudes they set out to attack as a result of the constant expansion of media culture, which progressively spun the dominant discourse into a seamless web, capable of absorbing all expressions of resistance. Although Terdiman's model of ideology and resistance in nineteenth-century France focuses on the writing of Gustave Flaubert, it has been applied by Ali Behdad to the case of Nerval, and in particular to Nerval's complex relationship to French colonial ideology.

The difficulty with this model from my perspective is that insofar as colonialism is concerned, it does not adequately render the complexity of the domestic political field. Until the 1870s, when colonialism became an official policy that enjoyed government support, it was, like nationalism, primarily the province of the left-wing opposition. It is therefore difficult to speak of a dominant discourse that includes colonial ideology without acknowledging the existence of important discursive breaks among the views of the governments and its supporters and those of the political opposition. The application of the discourse/counterdiscourse model is also problematic in the sense that it presupposes that oppositional writers, including Flaubert and Nerval, were by and large opposed to French expansion into the Orient, even if their writing on this topic falls back into hegemonic positions. As I have observed in the case of Nerval, and as I will later argue of his friend Théophile Gautier, this claim fails to take account of the extent to which writers who took an oppositional perspective on domestic matters actively *advocated* colonial expansion into the Orient.

The model advanced by Terdiman and Behdad approaches nineteenth-century colonialism from an essentially twentieth-century perspective. At least since Lenin's characterization of colonialism as the overseas extension of industrial capitalism, critics have been wont to view it as a right-wing ideology, predicated on the acceptance of inequality and belief in the inherent superiority of one ethnic group over another. But in the mid–nineteenth century, colonial expansion was advocated by groups that supported social and political reform and championed the rights of the politically disenfranchised, such as the working class and women. In these circles—which included the Bonapartists, Utopian Socialists (notably the Saint-Simonians and Fourierists), and Freemasons, French expansion into the Orient was approached not as a conquest predicated on the innate superiority of Europe, but as the symbiotic union of two cultures.

The Saint-Simonians were particularly active proponents of colonial expansion. Aggressively promoting the view that feudal economy was a thing of the past, they advocated territorial expansion as a preliminary to sharing the material resources of the earth—a redistribution justified by an assertion of the underlying unity of humanity. Although Saint-Simon himself had been opposed to the establishment of colonies, in the 1830s and 1840s, several of his leading followers emerged as strong advocates of French expansion. The most prominent among these was the eccentric Père Prosper Enfantin, who in 1838 embarked for Egypt with a group of followers who called themselves the "Compagnons de la Femme" ("Companions of Woman") and whose objective—not entirely unlike Nerval's—was to discover the female messiah and pave the way for the mystical union of East and West. As in Nerval, this quest involved a blend of protofeminist thinking and eroticism; Enfantin and his followers embraced a doctrine of free love and perceived Egypt as a place in which this credo could be actualized. In 1840, after failing to establish a colony in Egypt, Enfantin traveled to Algeria and returned to France with an elaborate plan for colonization.

Nerval himself was not a Utopian Socialist. Like many members of the literary avant-garde, by the early 1830s, he had become suspicious of political attempts to prescribe the social role of the artist, and at least one of his narratives of this period, *L'Ane d'or* (*The Golden Ass*; *Oeuvres complètes* vol.2, 1841), explicitly satirizes the doctrinaire exponents of Utopian Socialism and feminism.[12] There are nonetheless clear affinities between his vision of colonialism and that of a figure such as Prosper Enfantin. The contradictions of this conception, in the writing of Nerval as in the case of the Socialists, were in large measure those of a conception of gender relations that mixed conventional patriarchal thinking with mystical eroticism, thereby producing something akin to an ideological denial of the power dynamics and economic forces that permeate sexual relations just as they permeate relations among nations and cultures.

WOMEN, REAL AND IDEAL

The quest for women that is narrated in the *Voyage en Orient* is alternately a philosophical quest for truth, understood as a feminine principle of unity obscured beneath a veil of difference—"primitive Isis of the eternal veil and changing mask" (1:124)—and a more mundane pursuit of romantic involvement with "real" women. These different levels are repeatedly interwoven because here, as in other texts, Nerval's writing inhabits the boundary between the real and the imaginary, the referential and the symbolic. The narrator is, for example, repeatedly drawn to women whom he perceives as the material instantiation of ideal types. He describes Munich as a city of painters in which "all the types created by the great artists of the world have a material existence . . . the Judith of Caravaggio . . . the Madeleine of Rubens" (1:77); he portrays Catarina Colossa, a woman encountered in Vienna, as "the ideal woman of the Italian school" (1:86); and he extols Madame Bonhomme, director of the French reading room in Cairo, as the type of blonde beauty celebrated by Gozzi (1:297). The fact that he is unable in the end to achieve a sexual union with any of these artistic types translates a recognition that the ideal is by definition unattainable—or, more philosophically, that there can be no definitive revelation of an eternal truth or fundamental aesthetic principle. But this frustrating antinarrative also registers something more mundane, that is to say, the disappointment engendered by real women when they are measured against the perfection of an ideal—a comparison that unfailingly diminishes women as real, material subjects and reinforces social perceptions of female inferiority.

This effect is intensified by the fact that in Nerval's writing, as in many other nineteenth-century texts, the contrast between real and ideal women is permeated with ideas about class and racial difference. Perhaps the clearest illustration of this articulation of differences is Nerval's late text *Sylvie* (1853), whose narrator finds himself divided among three contrasting female figures: the haunting Adrienne, a fair-haired aristocrat whom he had admired as a child; the blonde actress Aurélie, whom he desires because she rekindles the memory of Adrienne; and the more tangible Sylvie, a dark-haired peasant girl whose warm affection he is unable to reciprocate fully. But the *Voyage en Orient*, too, repeatedly returns to an opposition between real and ideal that is predicated on the contrast between ethereal blonde women and more earthy brunettes. Seeking a bride in Cairo, the narrator is introduced to two girls, one dark the other fair; he is immediately drawn to the blonde and only abandons the idea of marrying her when he learns that she has been divorced and is thus not quite as ideal as he had initially supposed (1:186). His decision to purchased Zeynab, a Javanese slave, comes after several days spent roaming through the Cairo slave markets inspecting African women. In his eyes, this "yellow woman" eclipses the black faces that he has hitherto examined and that he describes as "masks," a common trope of nineteenth-century racial discourse. However, once he has purchased Zeynab, he ruefully compares her ebony hair and severe features to the ideal blondeness of the French Madame Bonhomme (1:298).

Nerval's account of his visits to the slave markets—a topos of both the midcentury travelogue and of Orientalist painting, and a site in which, as Linda Nochlin asserts in "The Imaginary Orient," Western erotic fantasy is typically masked by the overlay of a moralizing reflection on the vicissitudes of slavery and sexual relations in the Orient—provides an important key to understanding the structure underpinning these repeated contrasts between real and ideal, fair and dark (44). At first the narrator insists on the absolute alterity of African women, dwelling on their "barbaric dress" and "strange," "almost bestial" features, but he ultimately concludes that they are not "absolutely ugly" and condescendingly remarks that if he were acquiring an entire harem rather than just a single woman, he would not hesitate to buy one, because they form a charming *contrast* with white women. This idea is so compelling that he is moved to reflect that African women really seem "destined to serve" (1:217). Anticipating the ethnographic images produced later in the century by painters such as Jean-Léon Gérôme (see Chapter 5, Figure 12), the *Voyage en Orient* legitimizes the *hierarchical* relationship between mistress and slave by constructing it as an *aesthetic* contrast between black and white.

Nerval's obvious appreciation of this contrast suggests that his preoccupation with split feminine figures—the Adrienne–Aurélie–Sylvie triad of *Sylvie*; Zeynab and Saléma or Zeynab and Madame Bonhomme in the *Voyage en Orient*—does not simply translate an impulse to overcome difference and restore an originary unity, as scholars of Nerval have often maintained, but rather expresses a powerful predilection *for* difference. By the same token, it is important to recognize that if Nerval's writing embraces difference, it is not simply, as Kari Lokke suggests, in an idyllic celebration of feminine pluralism. Rather, difference functions in Nerval's writing as an essential component in the construction of ethnic and class identities. The construction of the transcendent ideal of the white, aristocratic blonde woman, for instance, is rooted in the experience of racial diversity and class difference.

The poetics of what I propose here is that the impetus to symbolic form—to the gathering together of difference to produce unity that critics have considered characteristic of Nerval's style—arises from, and is dependent on, the differential structure of language, and, further, that this necessary relationship between symbol and signs, unity and plurality is inscribed in Nerval's writing through the representation of split feminine figures.

I now turn to an episode in which the poetics as well as the politics of difference come to the fore, as the narrator recounts his efforts to teach his slave to write, a self-reflexive episode in which, as I will show, the text represents its own rhetorical structure and concurrently its own construction of racial and sexual difference.

WOMEN, LANGUAGE, AND THE CIVILIZING MISSION

Critical studies of the poetics of the *Voyage en Orient,* notably the existing book-length studies by Ross Chambers (*Gérard de Nerval et la poétique du voyage*) and Gérald Schaeffer (*Le Voyage en Orient de Nerval. Étude des structures*), have devoted considerable attention to the structural function of the three Oriental tales embedded in the primary narrative, arguing that these tales represent a *mise-en-abime* of the creative process and that the male protagonists of these stories, notably the blacksmith Adoniram and Caliph Hakem, the founder of the Druze sect, both iconoclastic figures who break with the paternalism of monotheism, constitute specular figures of the author. This critical emphasis, although it has much to recommend it, has had several problematic effects, one of which has been to privilege the structural circularity and thematic closure of the *Voyage en Orient* over the open-ended movement of the narrative, which, as we have seen, is propelled by the representation of women. It has also, I think, obscured the existence of a number of passages in which the text represents its own creative impulse by means of *feminine* figures. These figures differ significantly from the specular figures of male creativity identified by Schaeffer and Chambers. Notably, the fact that they are feminine and Oriental means they are invested with an aura of alterity that suggests the autonomy or alterity of language—its capacity to shape, rather than to be shaped, by the writing subject.

From the beginning of the *Voyage en Orient*, women figure the foreignness of language and the resultant precarity of intersubjective and intercultural communication. When the narrator first arrives in Vienna, he decides, on the advice of Lord Byron, to take some "pretty person" as an interpreter (1:85). He picks a lady's maid named Catarina Colossa who seems well qualified because she was born in Italy and brought to Austria by a French mistress. In reality, this cosmopolitan figure turns out to be all but ideal, for she embodies not the transparency of translation but the insurmountable opacity of linguistic difference: the narrator admits that she "does not know any language well, but rather speaks a little of three languages" (1:87), and he adds that her handwriting is "as hard to make out as her speech" (1:87). Later in this same section, when the narrator is about to leave Vienna, he admits that the romance he has been conducting has "ended badly" but makes light of the whole affair by stating that the women represented in his account of Vienna are "women who speak almost no European language" (1:115), a perplexing claim whose principal function seems to be the reassertion of a link between the otherness of women and the foreignness of language. This linkage is strongly reestablished later in the text in the narrator's account of his relationship with the Javanese slave, Zeynab.

The narrator acquires a slave in response to pressures exerted by his Cairene neighbors. Protesting that a bachelor living alone represents a threat to the honor and security of their wives, these neighbors insist that he either bring a woman into his home or else leave the neighborhood. After several frustrating attempts to meet a woman that he both wants and can afford to marry, he decides to abandon the scheme and to buy a slave instead. Throughout this narrative, Nerval represents himself as a hapless victim, bullied and swindled by everyone from his *drogman* (guide) and his landlord to the blind matchmaker who acts as an intermediary with the families of marriageable girls, an admission of vulnerability that no doubt conveys the genuine instability of colonial relations, but which also exemplifies the rhetoric that Mary Louise Pratt, in *Imperial Eyes*, has called "anti-conquest," the strategic admission of weakness and naiveté on the part of a Western traveler.

The Javanese woman is alluring because she evokes an ideal elsewhere within the already exotic space of Egypt: "In Africa one dreams of India just as in Europe one dreams of Africa: the ideal always beckons from beyond our present horizon," as the narrator observes (1:262). But her allure is also, he implies, that of a foreign language, a set of alien signs with the capacity to transfigure the banality of everyday thoughts and objects: "there is something very seductive in a woman from a distant country who speaks an unknown language and who in consequence shows none of the vulgar banality of women of one's own country" (1:244). The attraction of the exotic, however, quickly wears off, and in the narrator's eyes, this idealized feminine other begins to seem all too real. Notably, despite the language barrier between them, Zeynab manages to barrage her master with vestimental requests that in his eyes render her as vulgar and trivial as the women of his own country.

Particularly distressing are Zeynab's repeated pleas to be dressed in European clothes. In the boutique owned by Madame Bonhomme, for example, she tries on a white beribboned bonnet that in his view merely highlights her yellow coloring, making her look ill and confirming him in his view that the mixing of European and Oriental cultures, white and colored races is unhealthy and not to be sanctioned. Yet if he seems anxious to preserve cultural distinctions, he is also, by contrast, clearly disturbed by the *otherness* of Zeynab's body and sets about vainly trying to mitigate it by concealing the hennaed hands, pierced nostril, and solar tattoos that betray her cultural difference. The ambivalence that he feels in relation to her body in fact captures a key dilemma of European colonialism, which, as Homi K. Bhabha observes in "Signs Taken for Wonders," has typically been torn between the drive to assert a clear distinction between colonizer and colonized and the competing desire to eradicate cultural alterity and universalize European standards and norms (172–73).

In a famous meditation on the experience of cultural difference, *Nous et les autres* (*On Human Diversity*), Tzvetan Todorov argues that the most promising candidates for exoticism are the cultures or ethnicities most alien to our own (298). Yet in reality, as the predominantly negative representation[13] (or simple nonrepresentation) of black Africans in the Western literary tradition demonstrates, radical difference has more frequently given rise to incomprehension and revulsion than benign exoticism. The narrator's reaction when confronted with the foreignness of Zeynab's body marks out this boundary between the exotic ideal and an alterity that, because it cannot be assimilated, is invested with fear and disgust. It also points to the fact that if alterity appears inassimilable, it is in part because the European observer senses, at least subliminally, that the "other" has a history that is beyond his apprehension. That is to say, what Nerval's narrator reacts to is not simply the foreignness of Zeynab's body, but also the fact that the tattoos and burn marks embossed on her skin are signs of a personal and cultural history whose existence he had not considered. His cognizance of this history—the recognition that Zeynab is not simply a blank text that awaits his creative imprint—immediately becomes a barrier to the imposition of his fantasy of exotic difference.

Signs, or more precisely the issue of who controls and disseminates them, are at the center of Nerval's account of his dealings with Zeynab. From the very beginning of their relationship, signs are represented both as the medium through which authority is exercised and as the potential limit of that authority. As I noted at the start of this chapter, when the narrator purchases Zeynab, he chivalrously inquires after her name, commenting that he is, after all, "buying the name as well" (1:236). But the name he is given immediately becomes a stumbling block because he cannot pronounce it, and it takes him some time to determine how vowel sounds complete the triliteral root "Z'n'b." This narrative detail signals broader concerns about language; the narrator's inability to pronounce the name he believes he owns can be read as a metaphor for the more general sense in which he does not enjoy mastery over the language of his own authority and, indirectly, for the fact that he does not at the end of the day enjoy unrestricted power over his slave.

Frustrated by the language barrier between them, the narrator decides to teach Zeynab how to speak and write French, thereby becoming a virtual *porte-parole* for the *mission civilisatrice*, the ideology that legitimized French colonial expansion in the latter part of the nineteenth century by investing it with the moral purpose of a pedagogical program. The politics of literacy at stake in these lessons are clarified when we reflect that although in the slave-holding colonies of the Caribbean, as on North American plantations, writing was often withheld from slaves—both because it was viewed as a potential source of autonomy and because Africans' inability to write was interpreted as evidence of their limited intelligence—the spread of French and of literacy was a key component of French rule in Africa and the Maghreb. As Volney predicted in his *Voyage en Égypte et en Syrie*, the printing press rapidly became a valuable instrument in the campaign to eradicate "religious obscurantism" and to inculcate "enlightened European beliefs" (299–301). But the effort to transmit literacy was fraught with the barbed ambiguities that characterized the colonial project as a whole, because although it conferred dignity on the colonized subject by "raising" him or her to the level of the colonizer, it did so by denying the value of indigenous traditions and replacing them with European ones. The duplicity of this process is vividly captured in Nerval's account of the lessons he gives to Zeynab: his pedagogy consists of having her repeat after him the words "I am a little savage" (1:273). This exercise in mimicry conveys not only a contemptuous sense of superiority, but it also conveys the fact that in the colonial education system, European signs were taught not so that the individual could develop his or her own ideas, but because they were the medium of European ones—in this instance, the belief that a Javanese woman is little more than a savage.

When Zeynab discovers the meaning of this phrase, she rebukes her master in Arabic, using an exclamation, *mafisch* (i.e., "not at all, by no means!"), whose meaning he learns only later. Rejecting his notion of pedagogy, she determines that to express her *own* thoughts, she must bypass the sign system he wants to teach her because it has proved to be all but neutral. She therefore sets about tracing a pen filled with ink across a piece of paper, falsely believing that writing has the power to communicate thought directly. The narrator laughs at her naiveté, comparing her to a cat that has dipped its paw in ink, a figure of animality that reminds us of Henry Louis Gates, Jr.'s observation that illiteracy has often been established as a standard dividing human from animal, white from black ("Writing 'Race,'" 8–11). But Zeynab's attempt to commit her thoughts directly to paper, although conveying her lack of sophistication, also draws attention to the fact that language is not a transparent medium but a codified and therefore potentially alienating system of signs. This "scene of writing" encapsulates an important duality by capturing the power of the sign to shape attitudes and perceptions, but also the inevitable alienation of the subject in his or her own language.

As Homi K. Bhabha has argued at length, the colonial system is oriented toward the production of mimicry. That is to say, it cultivates the replication of European values, ideas, and discourses, *with a difference* ("Signs Taken for Wonders," 169). This kind of repetition is possible only when ideas and beliefs are divorced from the cultural context in which their meaning coalesced, or, to put this another way, when they shed their symbolic status and the organic connection to a specific time or place, and become iterable signs. The writing lesson narrated in the *Voyage en Orient* offers an exemplary illustration of Bhabha's observation that the shift from an economy of symbols to an economy of signs is double-edged because the "repetition with a difference" that subtends colonial authority has the secondary and unintended effect of subverting the authority of the original. This double bind of colonial mimicry is thematized throughout the episodes involving Zeynab: through his attempts to transmit his own priorities, values, and language to his slave, the narrator is gradually turned into a self-parody, a ridiculous "Arnolphe" figure, a character from a Molière comedy who jealously parades his authority to defend the illegitimacy of his possession.

Like many episodes of the *Voyage en Orient*, the narrator's account of his relations with Zeynab is almost entirely fictional. In reality, it was Nerval's traveling companion, the Egyptologist Théodore de Fonfrède, and not Nerval himself who bought a slave. The writer's correspondence suggests that he was in fact unhappy with this decision, albeit primarily for economic reasons (Nerval, letter to Théophile Gautier, May 2, 1843, *Oeuvres complètes*, 1:924). Given that Nerval did not himself buy Zeynab and that he essentially disapproved of his companion's acquisition, it is certainly significant that in the *Voyage en Orient* he assumes full responsibility for the purchase. When we consider the rather unflattering account he gives of his dealings with Zeynab, it seems implausible to attribute this decision to the mere desire to add color to the narrative. Rather, this complex staging suggests that Nerval was conscious of the inherently problematic nature of relations between a comparatively wealthy European man and a subjugated Oriental woman, and perhaps of the wider contradictions of French colonial ideology.

But the fact that Nerval was able to recognize and represent the contradictions of colonialism does not automatically signify that he was able to transcend the assumptions that fuel them. It would in fact be impossible to reclaim all the energetic colonialist rhetoric and all the ethnic slurs scattered throughout the text as the inverted signs of critical self-consciousness. The diffuse presence of allusions to the simian appearance of Africans, or to the Arab who is like "the dog that bites when you step back, but who licks the hand lifted against it" (1:348) suggest rather a deeper, less resolved anxiety about racial and cultural identity. In this regard, the *Voyage en Orient* must be approached as an immanent critique, a critique articulated *within* the framework of colonial discourse, rather than as a metadiscursive analysis.

The ambivalence of the text in this regard centers on issues of hybridity and cultural fusion, the ideas which, as we have seen, lie at the very core of Nerval's colonial vision. For although Nerval's account of his dealings with Zeynab appears to diagnose the fear attached to cultural mixing, other parts of the text manifest precisely this anxiety.

Let us consider by way of example the explanation the narrator offers of his ultimate failure to marry the Druze princess Saléma and to consecrate a union that he had hailed as the harbinger of political and religious unity between Europe and the Orient, Islam and Christianity. As previous readers have suggested, this failure to marry corresponds to a lack of resolution in the text as a whole and reflects the narrator's need to preserve the ideality of at least one Oriental woman. However, the manner in which this anticlimax is articulated suggests that cultural as well as textual forces are at work in this episode. Writing from Constantinople after a period spent in quarantine, the narrator explains that he came down with fever—a term that in Nerval often signifies madness and the loss of identity[14]—which compelled him to leave Lebanon. He further states that he decided not to bring his fiancée with him because "fevers carry off three quarters of the Oriental women transplanted to Europe" (2:149). This proliferation of metaphors of contamination and disease suggests that on a deep psychological and cultural level, Nerval, like many of his literary forbears, perceived political and sexual miscegenation not as the fertile union of opposites, but as a dangerous opening of the self to the foreign body of the other.

In sum, Nerval's writing on the Orient is fraught with the very ambivalence that it tentatively begins to diagnose in colonial discourse. This is notably true insofar as the colonial deployment of language is concerned, for language in the *Voyage en Orient* functions rather as it does in the parodic "scene of writing." That is to say, it functions both as an instrument of cultural hegemony—a medium for the dissemination of colonialist propaganda and for the authorization from an eyewitness perspective of prevalent racial stereotypes—and as a site in which control is relinquished and identities called into question. In this respect, it is like all language—for language is always at one and the same time the medium of knowledge and power (as Foucauldian theory has asserted) and an obstacle to knowledge, a field of barred access, loss, and dispossession (as Lacanian and deconstructive theory have maintained). This duality is, however, brought into focus as a result of the protocolonial context in which the narrative unfolds. That is to say, although colonialism constituted an environment in which cultural identity and cultural power were consolidated and transmitted through language, it also created a context in which entrenched meanings and hierarchies were challenged as a result of the transcultural conversion of symbolic authority into an economy of signs. This economy is inherently an unstable, open system that fosters the proliferation of ambiguity, the reconfiguration of ideas and values, and, slowly but irresistibly, the redistribution of power.

CHAPTER FIVE

The Modernist Turn in Orientalism:
Gautier's Egyptian Tales

UNDRESSING THE MUMMY

In 1867, ten years after the writer Théophile Gautier published his novel *Le Roman de la momie* (*The Romance of the Mummy*; 1857), he was invited to participate in a special session of the Exposition universelle (Universal Exhibition) in Paris in which a female mummy—the mummy of Nes-Khons—was undressed, or as Gautier puts it in his account of the event, "démaillottée" (a term that means, literally, to remove an infant's diaper; "Autour de l'exposition universelle. L'Orient," *Le Moniteur universel*, April 25, 1867, in *Voyage en Égypte*, 142–50). It seems fair to suppose that this private undressing, attended by a number of scholars and scientists as well as by the Goncourt brothers and Maxime Du Camp—men of letters known for their writing on the Orient—would not have taken place but for the publication of Gautier's novel. The presence of Gautier and his literary friends confirms that the purportedly "scientific" aims of this session (illustrative of the culture of display that successive *expositions universelles* built around non-European artifacts), were shaped by the Orientalist fantasy of the fiction. What is compelling about this episode, however, is not simply the metalepsis by which a fiction inspires a historical event—a minor victory for Gautier's own modernist aesthetic—but also the double relation to Oriental woman that is articulated here. On the one hand, Gautier's account rehearses the erotic tension of the undressing and relates the fear engendered in the spectators when a sudden storm gave rise to fears about a "mummy's curse." It also relates the surprises that the mummy held in store for the viewers: the unexpected discovery of flowers placed tenderly beneath the armpits and of a piece of cloth bearing the name of an unknown and unsuspected dynasty— surprises disquietingly similar to those that Gautier had described in his novel. On the other hand, it demystifies and in a sense denigrates the whole proceedings by emphasizing that the mummy was caked in bitumen, by alluding to the "sad nudity" of the body when it was finally exposed to the air, and by observing that every bric-a-brac store in Paris can sell you a "bijou funéraire" (funereal jewel) akin to the one worn by Nes-Khons. In short, his account of the undressing oscillates between veneration and revulsion, fetishism and phobia, inscribing the double relation by which, in this age of colonial expansion, the Orient/woman was at once overfamiliar and still capable of surprising, possessed and yet still anticipated.

To comprehend the profound ambivalence articulated in this scene of undressing, the complex and highly charged relationship to the Orient and to woman to which it testifies, it is necessary to trace the historical and aes- thetic roots of the European fascination with Egyptian mummies, particu- larly female mummies. In this final chapter, I propose to perform this kind of cultural genealogy by examining the nexus of connections that in mid- nineteenth-century France bound the emergence of literary modernism to the experience of colonial expansion and to the representation of Oriental women as rigidly perfect figures, frozen in time. In exploring these connec- tions, I focus on the career of Théophile Gautier, one of the leading Orientalists of the period and one of its most aggressive proponents of liter- ary formalism.

THE COLONIAL AESTHETIC

As Edward Said and others have argued, any serious reflection on represen- tations of the Orient in nineteenth-century art and literature must invoke the relationship between this corpus of images and the history of European colonial expansion. It must acknowledge that by their very multitude, these representations signal the presence of "interests" that were political and eco- nomic as well as cultural in nature. However, as I have already established, this argument must be qualified by the observation that, at least until the final quarter of the century, what we predominantly encounter in Orientalist representation is not a celebration or even a record of colonial conquest, but a marked aestheticization of both Oriental culture and colonial experience. In this respect, we can draw a parallel between the eighteenth and nineteenth centuries. Just as it was only in the aftermath of France's humiliating defeat at the hands of England and Prussia in 1763 that Enlightenment writers began to reflect actively on the Atlantic colonies, so it was only after the traumatic Prussian victory of 1871 that France for the first time developed a coherent national policy of expansion, and that colonial expansion and its impact on the Orient were seriously addressed in the cultural sphere. Military defeat in Europe thus seems to have galvanized policy on the colonial front. In making this argument, I do not mean to say that before this period writers did not represent, or express judgments about, Europe's military and cultural influence in the Orient. Rather, I want to argue that when considered together, these references present an extremely fragmentary account of colonial experience and give little or no play to the primary preoccupations of French foreign policy.

Characteristic of mid-nineteenth-century Orientalism is a structure of relative *dissociation* by which creative artists acknowledged Europe's encroachment into the Orient yet failed to address the military or political consequences of this venture. For example, few of the illustrious literary travelers of the age undertook to visit or to depict Algeria, although after the conquest of 1830, Algeria was the primary focus of foreign policy in the region; indeed, as I mention in the Introduction, for Gustave Flaubert and Maxime Du Camp, the term "Orient" no longer even encompassed the overfamiliar Maghreb. A similar pattern can be traced in the visual arts, in which, as Linda Nochlin asserts, the gaze of Western tourists or colonial occupiers is almost never registered, and the material changes resulting from this presence are correspondingly occluded by the nostalgic construction of a picturesque and unchanging Orient ("Imaginary Orient," 36–37). One of the clearest imprints of this process is found in the canvases of neoclassical painters such as Jean-Dominique Ingres and Jean-Léon Gérôme, who produced a series of serene and stylized images of an unchanged and unchanging Orient.[1]

But where several contemporary art historians (such as Marilyn R. Brown in "The Harem Dehistoricized") see an anomalous dehistoricization of the Orient, I see rather an extreme statement of a much broader disjunction between Orientalist representation and colonial history. If we consider the Orientalist production of Romantic painters whose aesthetic style and political ideals were diametrically opposed to the neoclassicism of Ingres and Gérôme, we encounter a comparable although less manifest tendency toward aestheticization and displacement. For example, the Oriental canvases of Eugène Delacroix, who visited Morocco in 1832 shortly after the French occupation of Algiers and Oran, depict not the pomp of French military conquest but "local color": the sensuous but suffocating interior of the harem, the cruel beauty of lion hunts and fantasias—stealthy projections of Western colonial violence onto the Orient itself.[2] In a parallel fashion, the celebrated *Radeau de la Méduse* (*Raft of the Medusa*; 1816) by the socially progressive painter Théodore Géricault, depicts the dramatic plight of the survivors of the wreck of the *Medusa* without giving any indication that the unfortunate victims of this catastrophe were bound for Senegal on a mission to reestablish a colony lost to England during the Napoleonic wars.

Throughout the nineteenth century, French colonial expansion progressed at a fairly steady rate, despite the absence of a coherent official policy of territorial expansion. In this political context, the aesthetic "sublimation" performed by art and literature fulfilled several important functions.[3] Among artists and intellectuals, it sustained an ambivalent relation to French colonialism and deferred the need for a definitive assessment of Europe's involvement in the Orient. In a broader political frame, it helped to render French foreign policy palatable to the literate public by occluding the more negative aspects of the colonial process and emphasizing instead the timeless attractions of the Orient.

This situation began to change in the early 1870s, when the European "Scramble for Africa" heated up and French colonial ideology was cemented. In this new political climate, the delicate balancing act between colonialism and aestheticism ceased to be viable, and the tension between exotic quest and colonial reality became the central theme of a number of works of fiction, including most notably Pierre Loti's *Aziyade* (1879) and Alphonse Daudet's popular satire *Tartarin de Tarascon* (1872). In this entertaining novella, Daudet takes aim at both the glorification of the French conquest of

Algeria and the selective representation of the Orient in literary works by narrating the misadventures of Tartarin, a meridional hunter who, inspired by literary example, sets off for the Orient in pursuit of high adventure only to find himself in a modernized country bereft of ferocious *turs* (Turks) and untamed lions, but overrun by duplicitous Frenchmen. Like many nineteenth-century narratives, Daudet's novel recounts the social education and progressive disillusionment of its protagonist. What is new, however, is that the disjunction between rhetoric and reality, ideology and policy that the hero discovers is one that pertains in the realm of *colonial* relations. By the mid-1880s, when Guy de Maupassant published his travel narrative *Au Soleil* (*To the Sun*; 1884), matters had evolved still further; unlike any of his literary predecessors, Maupassant saw fit to provide in his account of a journey through Algeria both an extended meditation on the French colonial venture and a concrete analysis of the merits and deficiencies of its system of regional government.

In this chapter, I focus less on the direct geopolitical impact of the selectiveness of Orientalist representation in the earlier part of the century than on the meaning of this excerption within the sphere of culture. I situate the prevalent aestheticization of the Orient in the context of a wider contemporary drive to divorce artistic creation from political and social questions and to emphasize in their stead the formal qualities of the work of art. In retracing this process, which I will call the "modernist turn" in Orientalism, I focus on the long and varied career of Théophile Gautier. Gautier's writing is undeniably less subtle than that of other early modernists—Baudelaire, Flaubert, and Nerval—whose texts persistently suspend the questions of linguistic reference that Gauthier's too readily resolve. However, what concerns me here is less the textual complexity of incipient modernism than the emergence of rhetorical links among the Orient, the feminine, and nonmimetic language that would absorb avant-garde writers, painters, and composers well into first decade of the twentieth century, and this beginning is most clearly legible in the work of Gautier. Through readings of two of Gautier's most celebrated Oriental fictions, I show how the modernist attempt to represent the autonomy of the linguistic sign dovetails with a fetishistic and dehistoricized representation of the "wholeness" or self-sufficiency of "Oriental woman." Maintaining my practice of double reading, I also show

how this project ultimately founders, generating ambivalence in relation to the closure of the linguistic system, but also in relation to the political containment of woman and the Orient.

ART FOR ART AND THE TRANSCENDENCE OF HISTORY

Although theoretical studies of nineteenth-century Orientalism have often neglected Théophile Gautier, the apologist of "art for art's sake" played a central role in the historical evolution of Orientalist literature and painting. Peter Brooks, in *Body Work*, aptly calls Gautier the "journeyman of romantic genres" (259), but he could equally be called the journeyman of Orientalist genres, for his interest in the Orient expressed itself in every literary form from journalism to poetry, travel writing to the novel. In addition to writing extensively about the Orient himself, Gautier, who by his middle years had become an important resource for younger writers, aggressively promoted the Orientalism of his contemporaries, including the painters Alexandre Decamps, Prosper Marilhat, and Jean-Léon Gérôme, the composer Félicien David, and the writer Gustave Flaubert.[4] Gautier's real importance, however, derives from the fact that his writing provides one of the first and most influential illustrations of the shift toward a modernist aesthetic of Orientalism which occurred over the latter half of the nineteenth century, as a result of which the Orient—and more particularly the Oriental woman— ceased being simply the object of artistic representations and became instead a figure for the self-reflexivity of art.

Like most of the midcentury avant-garde—Flaubert, Baudelaire, the Goncourt brothers—Gautier bemoaned the political duplicity of his age and the emerging hegemony of bourgeois liberal capitalism consolidated in the aftermath of the 1830 revolution and reinforced after the events of 1848. A particular object of hostility was what Gautier, along with other disaffected intellectuals, perceived as the all-pervasive and uncritical ideology of utility and progress. While the majority of their contemporaries were hailing the technological advances of the century as unquestionable signs of progress, the literary avant-garde bemoaned the industrial disfigurement of France and the sacrifice of beauty to the exigencies of social utility. Gautier himself is perhaps best known as the exponent of an aesthetic doctrine expressive of this disaffection, the credo of "art for art's sake" that holds that art exists not as a vehicle for the expression of political beliefs or as a social vision, but rather for the sole purpose of creating beauty. As early as 1835, in the preface to his novel *Mademoiselle de Maupin*, we find him declaring categorically that "Nothing is truly beautiful unless it is absolutely useless" (23). But utility is rejected not only as a watchword of the middle class, but also because it is perceived as a symptom of human need, which Gautier describes as ignoble and disgusting. Need is the opposite of art, which should not be dependent on anything beyond itself, but rather should manifest the self-sufficiency of perfect form.[5]

Bereft of power and disabused of their political aspirations, many mid-century writers abandoned the political engagement that had characterized early romanticism and turned their attention instead to the formal qualities of art. Perhaps inevitably, this withdrawal from the political arena was theorized in terms of a rhetoric of transcendence: although the artist had abandoned the stage of history, he would achieve immortality through literary creation. As Gautier writes in "L'Art" ("Art"), the final poem of his most celebrated collection of poetry, the *Émaux et camées* (*Enamels and Cameos*) of 1852, "Everything passes. Art alone endures forever" (149). The last two stanzas of this poem hammer this message home, conveying the idea that because art alone is eternal, the poet should devote his life to "sculpting" verses from the resistant matter of language:

> The gods themselves die
> But sovereign verse
> Remains
> Stronger than bronze
>
> Sculpt, chisel, plane
> But let your wavering dream
> Be fixed
> In the enduring stone (*Émaux et camées*, 150)

The representation of poems as "enamels" and "cameos"—hard, highly polished ornamental surfaces—translates a belief that to endure, art must be durable, and indeed, congealed, perfect, solid, and unchanging. To preserve itself against the forces of time, poetry must protect its own integrity by excluding historical forces that threaten to render it different to itself, to disseminate its core of meaning. It seems not implausible to argue that this fixation on the static quality of form reflects the fact that avant-garde writers experienced in relation to modernity something akin to an identity crisis: unable and perhaps unwilling to participate directly in the making of history, they advocated a self-referential model of writing that appeared to exclude the uncontrollable forces of historical change.

ORIENTAL NOSTALGIA AND THE COLONIAL MISSION

One of several "manifestos" that Gautier wrote for the "art for art" movement is the poem entitled "Preface," which opens *Émaux et camées*. In this poem, Gautier explains his withdrawal from political reality in the wake of the 1848 revolution by comparing himself to Goethe, who immersed himself in the "Oriental meter" of Hafiz rather than heeding the roaring canons of the Napoleonic wars. This comparison locates in Oriental culture the possibility of an escape from political reality and identifies the Orient with the repetitious meter of poetic form, rather than with a linear or progressive historical evolution. As Ross Chambers writes of this poem, "the Orient is constructed both as the absence of history and as an aestheticizing culture, thus producing a model of poetry as pure codification" (*Writing of Melancholy*, 46). A more pointed way of putting this would be to say that in "Preface," the Orient becomes the vehicle for a meditation on literary form that obscures the historical changes occurring in both Europe and the Orient.

Given this dynamic, we should not be surprised that Gautier's most profound fascination was not with the contemporary Orient—which he visited on several occasions and about which he published a series of fragmentary travel narratives—but with the culture of ancient Egypt.[6] This fascination, with its emphasis on the distant past, was in fact quite consonant with the intellectual preoccupations of the age. The science of Egyptology grew rapidly after the Expédition d'Égypte of 1798. In 1822, the young François Champollion deciphered the hieroglyphics of the Rosetta stone before the

Académie des Inscriptions in Paris. In 1827, the Museé du Louvre in Paris opened its first Egyptian collection. And in 1836, one of the two obelisks of Luxor, a gift from the viceroy of Egypt to the July Monarchy, was erected in the Place de la Concorde.[7] As the example of Gautier illustrates, one of the consequences of this flourishing of Egyptology was that, at least on the French side, the relationship between Egypt and France was predominantly experienced as a relationship between ancient and modern worlds.

Gautier traced his personal obsession with Egypt to the Salon of 1834, when at age twenty-three he first saw Prosper Marilhat's painting *La Place de l'Esbekieh au Caire* (*Esbekieh Square in Cairo*). In several short texts written at different times in his life, Gautier tried to convey the overwhelming impact this painting had on him. In a retrospective piece on Marilhat published in the heat of the 1848 Revolution, at the very moment when the populist revolt was beginning to disintegrate and the forces of order were gaining the upper hand, he writes that "the sight of this painting made me ill, and inspired in me a *nostalgia* for the Orient in which I had never set foot. I thought that I had discovered my true homeland, and when I turned my eyes away from this dazzling painting, I felt as if I were in exile" (*Revue des deux mondes*, July 1, 1848). In condensed fashion, this cry of cultural alienation effects a transfer of Gautier's feelings toward the political transformation of France while naturalizing the act of appropriation by which Egypt is claimed as the true homeland of art—a place that Gautier had not yet visited but which aroused in him feelings of "nostalgia," a term that implies that this authentic homeland is irrevocably lost, that "the Orient" now exists only in the past tense.

Gautier's nostalgia for an authentic Orient did not, however, inspire a course of active resistance to Western imperialism. It did not even lead him to forego participation in colonial politics. During the period of economic distress that followed the 1848 revolution, he petitioned (unsuccessfully) for a concession near the Algerian town of Philippeville. In his Salon of 1859, he praised steam power—which he had consistently berated as the very emblem of industrial transformation—on the grounds that it facilitates the artist's quest for a refuge in the Orient, apparently impervious to the contradictions inherent to this position ("Exposition de 1859," *Le Moniteur universel*, May 28, 1859; reproduced in *Voyage en Algérie*, 191–97). And in 1862, when he was invited by the Blidah Railway Company to attend the opening of the first Algerian railway, and 1869, when he reported on the opening of the Suez Canal for the *Journal officiel,* he took up the pen as a virtual *porte-parole* for French colonial ventures. Thus, of the opening of the Algiers–Blidah railway, he writes, "this is the start of a network that will soon stretch throughout the territory of our beautiful colony. . . . A future full of promise is opening for African France ['La France africaine']" (*Le Moniteur universel,* August 24, 1864, reproduced in *Voyage en Algérie,* 106–7), assimilating the colonial rhetoric of "the greater France" to a degree that seems extraordinary when we reflect that it required endorsement of two processes that Gautier purported to deplore: industrial development and the Westernization of the Orient.[8] As a result, although I would concur with the claim, formulated in somewhat different terms by both Ross Chambers (*The Writing of Melancholy*) and Chris Bongie (*Exotic Memories,* 10), that nineteenth-century writers took refuge in Oriental exoticism from both domestic and colonial politics, this analysis paints only a partial picture. A more complex model is required to explain the mechanism by which Gautier and other contemporaries were able to advocate colonial expansion while concurrently recoiling before the loss of authentic traditions.

The best recent critical thinking on Orientalism and oppositionality has drawn on the Foucauldian-inspired model developed by Richard Terdiman. As previously noted, Terdiman, in *Discourse/Counter-Discourse,* argues that the contestatory counterdiscourses of midcentury intellectuals were ineluctably reenveloped by the "dominant discourse" that they sought to subvert.[9] As one illustration of this process, he cites the fact that although Flaubert traveled to the Orient to escape the hegemony of bourgeois values and media capitalism in France, the critical goals of his voyage were undermined, both because of the physical domination of the East that made his travels possible and because of his own uncritical use of a rhetoric of appropriation in writing about the Oriental other.

Although I find this conceptualization of nineteenth-century Orientalism highly persuasive, I nonetheless feel that it does not adequately convey the degree of writers' *overt* complicity with colonial policy—the degree to which, far from taking an oppositional stance toward colonial ideology, writers, including Flaubert and Gautier, explicitly and actively endorsed colonial expansion.[10] Before looking in more detail at the oeuvre of Gautier, I would like to illustrate my point by briefly reconsidering the case that Terdiman analyzes: that of Gustave Flaubert.

Before Flaubert set out for the Orient, he received (at the behest of his traveling companion, Maxime Du Camp) a "mission" from the Ministry of Agriculture that furnished letters of introduction to the French commercial and diplomatic representatives residing in the region, although it did not provide financial assistance. Unlike Du Camp, who characteristically devoted a great deal of time and energy to the accomplishment of his mission (to photograph the leading monuments of Egypt from perspectives stipulated by the Académie des Inscriptions et des Belles-Lettres), Flaubert made light of his mission and made no attempt to fulfill it. He did not, however, explicitly critique the principle behind such missions—although they obviously contributed to the consolidation of French knowledge of, and power over, the Orient (Flaubert's mission was to collect statistics on the harvests and production and consumption of grain in the various regions he visited)—nor did he discard the letters of introduction provided to him. In fact, he seems to have thoroughly enjoyed his visits to the various local agents of French commerce and diplomacy. In laying out Flaubert's antihegemonic position, Terdiman cites the writer's violent reaction to the stupidity ("bêtise") of previous European travelers, epitomized by the fact that many of them immortalized their insignificance by inscribing their names on the leading monuments of Oriental antiquity. Writing as a sort of "lone Jeremiah," Flaubert contrasts himself with a certain "Thompson of Sunderland" who had carved his name on Pompey's column, exemplifying the appropriative stupidity of the dominant European discourse on the Orient (*Discourse/Counter-Discourse*, 44). What this stark opposition between a Thompson and a Flaubert obscures, however, is the existence of a series of intermediary positions, including those of French Orientalists and archaeologists whose intentions were no less appropriative, but who did not draw the same scorn.[11] In other words, although Flaubert deplored the most glaring illustrations of Western appropriative stupidity, he did not actually deny the validity of Orientalism or of the colonial project per se.

In a parallel, although more extreme, fashion, Gautier both valorized the Orient as an unsullied utopia, a refuge from the banal modernity of con-

temporary France, and accepted—even endorsed—the ideological and material exploitation of the Orient.[12] I say apparent paradox because, as I have
previously argued in relation to Nerval, the expectation that domestic and
colonial politics coincide reflects the values of contemporary liberalism
rather than the political outlook of mid-nineteenth-century France, a period
in which support for colonial expansion was drawn largely from the left-
wing opposition. Rather than analyzing Gautier's Orientalism in terms of a
dialogue or tension between oppositionality and dominant discourse, I
therefore want to emphasize the coexistence of ostensibly opposed strands of
thinking. To articulate this structure of ambivalence, I will draw on the conceptual resources offered by the psychoanalytic concept of fetishism—not, I
must emphasize, because I think that the politics of Orientalism can be
reduced to a psychosexual malaise, but rather because this politics is elucidated when it is situated within the broader problematic of the construction
of personal and cultural identities. The suggestion that the Western fascination with the Orient is fetishistic in nature is one that has been mooted by
Homi K. Bhabha but never applied in sustained fashion to a corpus of cultural representations; this application is what I now propose to attempt.[13]

The concept of fetishism, an ethnographic category used by European
travelers since the seventeenth century to describe the overvalorization of
ritual objects in "primitive" cultures, was coopted by Sigmund Freud to
describe and explain certain psychosexual abnormalities. Exploiting the
established exchange between racial and sexual categories, in his essay
"Fetishism," Freud invested the ethnographic concept with psychosexual
meaning. The basic argument of the essay is that when the little boy discovers that his mother lacks a penis, he experiences castration anxiety, a feeling
whose underlying origin is a narcissistic preoccupation with the wholeness of
his own body. The discovery of "maternal castration" may be so traumatic
that the memory of the event is displaced onto a fetish object—often shoes
or a piece of underclothing—that is in turn overvalued because it represents
a symbolic substitute for the imagined maternal penis.

Freud's theory of fetishistic substitution is not particularly valuable as an
account of the genesis of sexual identity (in this capacity, it is must be said
to incorporate uncritically a number of misogynistic assumptions about the
deficiencies of female anatomy); however, it does elucidate an important site

of epistemological and linguistic complexity in the sense that by his behavior, the fetishist does not simply affirm or deny feminine difference—the "castration of woman"—but rather hesitates between positions of affirmation and denial. As a result, although fetishism arises out of a desire for the wholeness of identity and the elimination of difference, it effectively problematizes the very notion of a whole body or integral identity, thereby enacting a cleavage of the subject in its relation to the other.

When I suggest that the structure of fetishism corresponds to that of mid-century Orientalist representation, what I mean is that the crisis of social and political identity that afflicted the literary avant-garde generated anxiety about the diverse identities of "others," notably women and Orientals. In response to this anxiety, the Orient was invested with powers that, from the European standpoint, it really did not possess. The overvaluation of selected aspects of Oriental culture thus became a mechanism by which creative artists expressed their disillusionment with French society, but it also fulfilled the subsidiary function of turning the East into a colorful plaything, thereby affirming its political "castration."

Let us consider the following passage, which is taken from a review that Gautier wrote of Félicien David's symphony *Le Désert* (*The Desert*, 1845), and which has sometimes been read as an expression of anxiety about cultural difference:

> What a strange thing! We think that we have conquered Algiers, but it
> is Algiers that has conquered us. Our women are already wearing multi-
> colored scarves, threaded with gold, that were once worn by the slaves
> of the harem, while our young men have taken to wearing the camel-hair
> burnous. . . . [. . . .]
>
> If things continue at this rate in but a short time France will be Mo-
> hammedan, and we will see the white domes of mosques rise above our
> cities. . . . We would like to live to see that day, because frankly, we prefer
> Oriental fashions to English ones. ("Concert de Félicien David," *La Presse*,
> January 6, 1845, reproduced in *Voyage en Égypte*, 98)

On a first reading, this text appears to give voice to the paranoia of the colonizer, persuaded that as a result of cultural miscegenation, the domes of mosques will soon dominate the Paris skyline. This anxiety is, however, tempered by Gautier's ironic tone. Unlike many French citizens in our own times—with the journalists at *L'Express* and *Figaro Magazine* included (see Introduction, 28–31)—the author does not seem seriously worried that Parisians will convert en masse to Islam. On the other hand, when we reflect that Gautier's flippant claim that he would prefer to be Oriental is made in reference to the French conquest of Algeria, the Orient seems to be being reduced to a mere fashion or fetish, signaling, perhaps, the underlying presence of real anxiety. What this passage ultimately conveys, I think, is the convoluted desire that Europe be Orientalized as a result of its own Europeanization of the Orient. In this regard, it constitutes an exemplary statement of midcentury ambivalence toward colonial expansion, for it encapsulates an extremely widespread tension between the desire to escape the banality of the familiar and the wish to facilitate this escape by consolidating Europe's foothold in the Orient.

FEMININE FIGURES OF LANGUAGE

The ambivalence toward Oriental difference that we have begun to identify among writers of the midcentury is paralleled by and intertwined with an ambivalence toward the alterity of the feminine whose roots lie, in part, in the literary tradition. The early romantics often imagined the love object as a corpse: a woman lost forever and incapable of assuaging the poet's (therefore) endless desire. But by midcentury, the romantic expression of vulnerability was being attacked by a younger generation of writers, including most prominently Gautier and Baudelaire, who asserted that formal perfection rather than the release of emotion is the essential object of literary creation. Correspondingly, Gautier, and the group of his followers who in the 1860s constituted themselves as the Parnassian movement, represented the object of desire not as a dead woman but as a statue, a figure for the perfection and self-absorption of the work of art. In Gautier's Orientalist works, this rigid and impassive figure is "translated" into the form of the female mummy, a figure not only of art's self-reflexivity, but also of its capacity to transcend history.

If avant-garde writers from Gautier to Mallarmé deployed feminine figures to represent the autonomy of art, it was largely because they started from the premise that woman is absolutely determined by biology—"woman is *natural*, that is to say, abominable," as Baudelaire famously wrote; "Woman is hungry and she wants to eat. Thirsty, and she wants to drink. She is in heat and she wants to be fucked" (*Mon coeur mis à nu [My heart laid bare]*, *Oeuvres complètes*, 1:1272). The transformation of woman's brute materiality and physical neediness into the cold perfection of the work of art offered incomparable evidence of the artist's ability to transcend nature and to reconstruct his own version of reality in language. Pursuing this logic, it seems plausible to argue, as Charles Bernheimer has done, that the disgust inspired by the imperfection of the female body translates anxiety about feminine difference or female sexuality, and that the use of idealized feminine figures to represent artistic creation masks an attempt to control this difference by displacing the reproductive capacity of women onto the creative genius of the male artist.[14] If we apply this interpretation to Gautier's Oriental fictions, it can be argued that women are killed off and then resuscitated so that they can become idealized figures of a creativity that is not only male, but also Western.

Many of the most celebrated French figures of the autonomy of art are in fact not only feminine, but also Oriental; in addition to Gautier's mummies, one could cite Flaubert's Salammbô and Hérodias, Moreau's and Wilde's portraits of Salome (Wilde's *Salome* was originally written in French), and Mallarmé's Hérodiade. Although this cluster of narcissistic and intimidating women reflects the intertextuality of avant-garde art, their Oriental identity also underscores the fact that it is the perceived alterity, and inferiority, of the female other that underlies the displacement of referential onto figural representation.

This displacement may be qualified as fetishistic in the sense that the avant-garde's preoccupation with the perfection of woman and the plenitude of the artistic sign betrays anxiety, not only about women's appetites and desires, but also about the openness of language. In other words, it constitutes an attempt to neutralize the dangerous possibility that language does not correspond to itself without residue—that it does not constitute a closed totality, whether that of reference (the totality of signs represents the totality of things in the world) or that of figure (signs refer only to themselves in a closed system). In what follows, I examine, along the lines that I have established, two of Gautier's best known Oriental fictions, both set in ancient Egypt. Through these readings, I demonstrate that both narratives are structured around a persistent tension between the attempt to represent the perfection of Oriental woman and the absolute autonomy of the literary sign, and a recognition of the impossibility of achieving (formal) closure. That is to say, I argue that these texts manifest ambivalence, both in relation to the integrity of the work of art and in relation to the question of feminine desire.

THE MUMMY'S FOOT

Gautier's short story *Le Pied de momie* (*The Mummy's Foot*) first appeared in 1840 in the *Musée des familles*, a periodical publication devoted to fiction. It was inspired by a "scholarly" anecdote that Gautier had come across while researching another Oriental tale, *Une nuit de Cléopâtre* (*One of Cleopatra's Nights*; 1838): in Dominique Vivant Denon's *Voyage dans la Basse et la Haute-Égypte pendant les campagnes du Général Bonaparte* (*Voyage to Lower and Upper Egypt*; 1802), the Egyptologist and one-time libertine novelist recounts that while excavating an Egyptian burial chamber, he discovered the mummified foot of a young woman that he stole in an act of "amorous larceny" and preserved as a lucky omen or fetish (2:278). The name "Hermonthis," which Gautier gave in his story to the owner of this foot, also had an Egyptological source: it is cited in François Champollion's *Lettres écrites d'Égypte et de Nubie en 1828 et 1829* (*Letters from Egypt and Nubia in 1828 and 1829*; 1833) as the name of a town in the vicinity of Thebes. Since at the beginning of *Une nuit de Cléopâtre* the queen is represented returning in her barge from a religious rite at "Hermonthis," this substitution of place for woman's name cannot simply be attributed to ill-informed exoticism: Gautier knew what Hermonthis was and elected to identify the woman with the polis in a manner characteristic of the Orientalist exchange between colonizable territory and a female body susceptible to "amorous larceny." *Le Pied de momie* operates, in fact, as a fictionalized account of this kind of larceny, a meditation on France's eroticized appropriation of the Oriental patrimony. However fantastic the events related in the narrative may appear, they are in this respect anchored in a concrete historical and commercial reality that is acknowledged from the very beginning of the story when the narrator, a Parisian dandy, wanders into a boutique filled with Oriental curiosities and emerges with the charming foot of a female mummy that he intends to use as a paperweight (247).

From the outset, this idiosyncratic purchase is associated not with work, productivity, or utility, but with the Bohemian lifestyle of an artist at leisure to browse through shops on the lookout for inessential collectibles. The narrator ironically reflects that such shops usually contain more inauthentic than authentic objets d'art, and he speculates that the most ancient items on display are the dust and the cobwebs (247). Surprisingly, however, he discovers amid the artificial exotica "an authentic foot" (250). Our apprehension that some form of foot fetishism is at work in this narrative is reinforced by the anxiety generated in the otherwise nonchalant consumer by the "patriarchal" shop owner (248), a disturbing father figure who, in a manner resonant of the Freudian oedipal scenario, follows the young man through the boutique, silently menacing castration by beating down "the hazardous sweep" of his tails and surveying his elbows with "the anxious attention of an antiquarian and a usurer" (248). He is eager to sell the narrator a lethal weapon such as a sword or a dagger—either by way of a threat of castration or because he means to imply that the young man is in need of such a phallic object—but the customer protests that he has quite enough weapons of carnage at home, and that what he really needs is a paperweight. He is hesitating between a porcelain dragon and a small Mexican fetish when he spots the foot.

It is obviously possible to read in this scenario a confirmation of the psychoanalytic theory of foot fetishism, because the foot appears to be purchased to assuage the narrator's fear of castration. This apparent consonance is, however, less a proof of the validity of Freud's theory than a testimony to the affinity between psychoanalytic theory and nineteenth-century fiction. If psychoanalysis is able to bring the explanatory power of a set of master narratives to bear on themes that are recurrent in the novel and short story, it is in part because it shares many of the preoccupations of the contemporary fiction. In this vein, Freud's claim that foot fetishism arises from a traumatized response to the discovery of female "castration" may in fact be read as an *overt* expression of the anxiety about female sexuality that is *latent* in the fetishistic representations of nineteenth-century fiction. As we will observe, Gautier's story seems to hover around the recognition that the overvalorization of the female foot has less to do with castration than with the will to control woman's desire by immobilizing it. In this respect, it anticipates feminist thinking on foot fetishism, which—beginning with Julia Kristeva's analysis in *Des Chinoises* (*On Chinese Women*) of foot binding in Chinese culture—has approached foot fetishism as a sociopolitical symptom, a product of the drive to restrict women's participation in public life.[15]

Having brought the foot home and set it atop a pile of papers, the dandy is awoken in the night by a disturbing noise emanating from his desk; he discovers that the paperweight has taken on a life of its own and that it is dancing on his papers (254). With ironic understatement, he coolly explains that he was rather annoyed by this unexpected mobility but mollified when Princess Hermonthis herself—rigid, swathed in bandages, and quite as fetishistic as her foot—emerges from behind a fold in the curtains. As the narrator surmises, the princess hopes to make herself whole again by seizing the missing foot. The foot, however, conscious that it has been bought and sold, refuses to comply. Because Hermonthis is unable to buy it back—her jewelry has also been stolen, an allusion to the history of tomb robbing and its licit form, archaeology—the narrator intervenes and agrees to return it. With all the bad faith of gallantry, man agrees to restore to woman what was already hers.

In a parody of bourgeois family life, Hermonthis proceeds to bring the narrator home to meet her father. Delighted by the restoration of his daughter's wholeness, Pharaoh Xixouthros extends his scepter, symbol of phallic power, and invites the Frenchman to name his reward. The young man boldly asks for the princess's hand in exchange for the foot, but the father rejects his suit on the grounds that, unlike the ancient Egyptians, modern Europeans simply do not know how to preserve themselves. Playing on the semantic overlap between duration and durability, he tells the Frenchman that "we must give our daughters husbands who will endure ['durent']. You no longer know how to preserve yourselves. . . . Behold, my flesh is as hard ['dure'] as basalt, my bones are bars of steel." He proceeds to invite him to test this rigid durability with a handshake: "'See how vigorous I am, and how strong my arms are,' he said, shaking my hand in the English fashion and nearly severing my fingers" (261). With this gesture, Xixouthros implicitly contrasts his own solidity and implied sexual vigor with the narrator's lack of staying power while simultaneously threatening him with both physical and symbolic castration. The anxiety is in fact so strong that the narrator is awakened.[16]

The possession of the foot, or of a castrated female figure, seems to give the narrator renewed confidence, assuaging the castration anxiety, or crisis of identity, that he experiences in relation to the bourgeois order of work and utility. This compensatory scenario, however, entails the complete repression of the princess's needs and desires: Hermonthis never voices either a wish or a disinclination to be united with the narrator and seems intent only on pleasing the two men who want to make her whole (wholeness and desire are, of course, incompatible, because desire always betrays an incompletion or lack that marks the openness of self to other). The play of compensation and repression that unfolds here betrays the structure of France's relationship to the Orient as well as the complexities of man's relation to woman. These two dimensions are intertwined because in this narrative, as in many Orientalist texts, possession of the Orient is represented as the possession of a female body, an exchange underscored by the fact that Hermonthis herself is named after a place: to own Hermonthis is, quite literally, to own a piece of Egypt. Although as I argue in my Introduction it is dangerous to generalize about Europe's relationship to the Orient on the basis of literary texts, Gautier's narrative would seem in this instance to translate a key dimension of the geopolitics of contemporary Egyptology: much like Pharaoh Xixouthros, the Egyptian viceroy Mehemet-Ali allowed France to "fetishize" ancient Egyptian culture, to reconstitute its wholeness through the practice of archaeology. This permission was consecrated by his gift to France of the obelisk of Luxor, a phallic symbol of mastery "erected" in the Place de la Concorde in 1836, just four years before the publication of Gautier's story.[17] The official motive for this gift was the pro-European viceroy's wish to acknowledge François Champollion's achievement in using the Rosetta stone to decipher Egyptian hieroglyphics. In other words, the obelisk was offered as a reward to the French for having reconstituted the fragmented body of Egyptian history. As in Gautier's tale, this exchange between the Ottoman–Egyptian ruling elite and the European imperial power involved the thorough suppression of the potential wishes of a third, less powerful party—the majority of contemporary Egyptians whose wishes were eclipsed by the concern with resuscitating and reconstituting past glory.

The anxiety expressed in *Le Pied de momie* is not simply anxiety about either cultural or sexual identity; it is also, as the narrator's decision to buy a paperweight rather than a sword testifies, anxiety about textuality.[18] On returning home with his acquisition, the narrator immediately places it on top of "a pile of papers scribbled over with verses, an undecipherable mosaic of crossings-out: articles begun but never finished, letters forgotten and posted in the desk-drawer" (252). Like the foot itself, the narrator's work is fragmentary, consisting of texts begun but never completed, letters written but never mailed, such that there is absolutely nothing to assure the survival of these fragments or the posterity of their author.

The presence of the foot seems to reassure the would-be author; after securing his stack of papers, he goes out, feeling very pleased with himself—indeed, priding himself on possessing what others lack—because he is conscious that in representing a decorative object as an essential item, he is inverting the values and priorities of bourgeois society ("The proper occupation of every sensible man seemed to me to consist of having a mummy's foot on his desk" [252]). We must, however, ask whether the dandy, whose sense of social superiority derives from his overvalorization of a degraded object, a woman's bound foot, an Oriental knickknack, in fact "possesses" the foot or whether he is "possessed" by it, and because his creative prowess and social independence seem to be boosted by the possession of this reified figure of femininity, we must ask whether this female figure is in fact successfully coopted as an emblem of male, literary virtuosity or whether, by contrast, the alterity of the Oriental, female other exceeds this attempt at aesthetic instrumentalization.

To reward the narrator for making her whole, Hermonthis gives him a figure of Isis, mythological muse of wholeness, that she has worn as a necklace. When he awakens at the end of the story, he finds this same figure on top of his papers.[19] This final appearance of Isis in the guise of a paperweight suggests that the two female figures—the foot and the statuette—have enabled the author to fashion a story, or a form of completion, from disparate textual fragments.[20] In other words, the figure of Isis in this scene can be read as an emblem of the self-reflexive process by which the text recounts its own genesis. The production of a finished work counteracts the anxiety generated by Pharaoh's warning that unlike ancient Egyptian civilization, contemporary European civilization simply won't endure. To the extent that the story gives the appearance of being equivalent to itself, it presents to its future readers a structure as pristine and impenetrable as Egyptian sculpture.

Fetishism and the aesthetic ideology of art for art are structurally linked in that the substitution involved in fetishism is a substitution for something that was never there in the first place: the fetish creates the "original" that it replaces (the maternal phallus) in the same way that the Parnassian poem attempts to construct its own referents. In rhetorical terms, this substitution for an absent original can be identified as a catachresis—the figure that has been called the trope of tropes because it illuminates the fact that meaning is constructed within language, rather than between linguistic signs and a set of exterior, extralinguistic referents. The absence of such an original referent is felt throughout the story in a confusion that shakes the mimetic order such that it quickly becomes impossible to distinguish between original and copy, literal and figural. The princess's foot at first appears to be made of bronze, but it turns out to be both a real foot and a genuine antique; it is nonetheless described throughout the narrative as if it were a sculpture, as shiny and as polished as agate, tinted with the warm rust tones of a Florentine bronze. This indeterminacy ultimately extends to the body as a whole, for the body qua mummy consists of successive layers of "text"— bandages covered in hieroglyphs—with no determinate boundary between flesh and clothing. The foot itself is correspondingly represented as a piece of clothing, a slipper that can be adjusted at will (257). The narrator's final request for the princess's hand in exchange for her foot simply confirms the exchange between literal and figural meanings operative throughout the text.

The foot's status as an intermediary between literal and figural domains is signaled from the very beginning of the story when the narrator notices among the fake antiques "a Louis XV duchess nonchalantly stretching its (her) feet under a massive Louis XIII table" (248). By this turn of phrase, as Franc Schuerewegen notes, the metaphorical *duchesse* (a kind of chair), is brought to life, transformed into a real duchess whose feet dangle beneath a table, an act of literalization by which the catachrestic foot ceases to be conventional and draws the reader's attention toward the intralinguistic construction of meaning.

As this rhetorical conversion illustrates, the hesitation between literal and figural meaning is at the core of another suspended opposition: the opposition between the supernatural and the real that is the defining characteristic of fantastic literature.[21] If numerous midcentury writers, including Gautier, Nerval, Prosper Mérimée, and Charles Nodier, favored the fantastic as a genre, it was not only due to the tremendous influence of Edgar Allen Poe on the French writers of this period, but also because the fantastic was an ideal medium for covert political writing.

In his seminal work on the fantastic, *Introduction à la littérature fantastique*, Tzvetan Todorov points to two distinct registers in which this mode abetted politically transgressive writing. Fantastic literature could break social taboos by representing "perverse" desires such as necrophilia and incest in a way that realist literature could not, and it was also subversive by reason of its propensity to suspend the opposition between reference and figure. This capacity was significant in the context of mid-nineteenth-century France because maintaining the boundary between literal and figural meaning seems to have been one of the primary concerns of the censorship implemented under both the July Monarchy and the Second Empire.[22] In a political atmosphere in which the desire for transparency reflected the will to control, avant-garde writing was subversive because it blurred the distinction between fact and figure; and the fantastic mode offered a particularly fertile terrain for this surreptitious transgression of boundaries.[23]

As Todorov suggests, the hesitation between the figural and the literal, the supernatural and the real, is typically resolved at the end of the fantastic narrative either by the affirmation of the laws of nature or by the revelation that a supernatural world does in fact exist (Todorov calls these two solutions the "strange" and the "marvelous" in *Introduction à la littérature fantastique* [82]). Gautier's story affirms the "marvelous," for although the narrator awakens from his dream, the figure of Isis remains as evidence of the supernatural events of the previous night. The discovery of this figure not only affirms the existence of a supernatural reality, but also marks the triumph of "figural" over literal language, the successful replacement of the banal referentiality of contemporary social and political thought with an Orientalist reverie.

However, in interpreting this ending, I think that we must attend not only to this suggestive closing figure, but also to the narrative unfolding of the tale, which actually recounts not a successful process of appropriation, but rather the narrator's loss of Princess Hermonthis and the exotic world that she embodies. This abrupt return to the "real" world suggests that the fantasy of the Orient as a pure space of literary invention cannot be maintained, that the Orient and woman are not pure figures devoid of reference to things beyond the text. If the ending is read in this way, Princess Hermonthis, figure for the plenitude of the artistic sign, must be said to escape the grasp of the artist rather than to solidify his creative vision.

What, then, of the figure of Isis that Hermonthis leaves behind and that seems to confirm that the Oriental woman has successfully been transformed into a text? Significantly, when it is invoked at the end of the story, the figure of Isis is called not a "figure" but a "figurine," an antique-store trinket that seems to deride the narrator's desire to turn the Oriental woman into a frozen figure of language. Given that the loss of "Hermonthis" is also the loss of Egypt, the ending of the story seems to foretell presciently what perhaps could always have been foretold: that Europe would not forever succeed in freezing Egypt in the image of its own prehistory and that modern Egypt would ultimately shake off the imperial hegemony of Europe.

'THE ROMANCE OF THE MUMMY' OR THE MUMMY'S ROMANCE

The ambivalence manifested in the denouement of *Le Pied de momie* may offer one explanation of why, seventeen years later, Gautier returned to the subject of the female mummy to tell her story in the more complete form of a novel, *Le Roman de la momie*, serialized in *Le Moniteur universel*, March–May 1857. Because this narrative enjoys a central place in a literary tradition in which Oriental women are represented as narcissistic figures,[24] symbols for the self-reflexivity and plenitude of art, I want once again to raise the question whether, in this follow-up text, the Oriental woman is simply coopted as a symbol for the creative genius of the male artist, or whether feminine desire is in some sense acknowledged and given play in the narrative. The genitive construction of the title in fact seems to inscribe this dilemma: has the mummy been transformed into a *roman*, or does the *novel* recount the mummy's romance?

The text is divided into two parts, the prologue and the romance proper, although an untitled and undifferentiated epilogue to the main text suggests a tripartite structure. The prologue tells of an archaeological expedition undertaken by a German Egyptologist, Dr. Rumphius, and his aristocratic patron Lord Evandale, the quintessential English dandy. In an unopened tomb of the Valley of the Kings, the two men unexpectedly discover a female mummy. This anomalous body is accompanied by a papyrus scroll that recounts the body's history, and it is this story that forms the substance of *Le Roman de la momie* (*The Romance of the Mummy*). The "epilogue" brings the reader back to the present day and relates that Lord Evandale decides to keep the mummy at his country seat rather than donating it to the British Museum, as he had originally intended. Absorbed by his passion for the dead woman, he remains coldly indifferent to the young women of his day and never marries. The formal structure of the work therefore seems to mirror its subject: the prologue and epilogue contain the mummy's tale in much the same way that the tomb cradles the mummy. Moreover, the different sections of the text appear to echo each other,[25] creating the impression of a *mise-en-abime*, both among the various parts of the story and between the story that is told and the formal configuration of the narrative. In this regard, the novel gives the appearance of closing narcissistically on itself, presenting the reader with a perfect and impenetrable facade.

This does not, however, mean, as Nathalie David-Weill suggests, that the novel presents the reader with a "refusal of historical facts" or with the "construction of an independent reality," "an Orientalist reverie as defined by Edward Said"—an interpretation that reduces the novel to a doctrinal statement in favor of "art for art" (*Rêve de pierre*, 19). On the contrary, what the frame narrative offers is a condensed account of European relations with Egypt in the mid–nineteenth century, a story that articulates the uneasy relationship between Orientalist reverie and colonial reality by showing that the reverie is contingent upon the material encroachments of European imperialism. In this regard, *Le Roman de la momie* transposes the ambivalence that is a central feature of mid-nineteenth-century Orientalism: the Orient is fetishized as an ideal "elsewhere" unsullied by the bourgeois commercialism and industrial disfigurement of Europe, yet at the same time, colonial expansion is represented as the means by which this exotic "elsewhere" is attained.

Like historical archaeologists from François Champollion to Howard Carter, what Rumphius and Evandale hope to find in the Valley of the Kings is a tomb that has remained inviolate. To achieve their objective, they retain the services of a Greek scout named Argyropoulos, who makes his living by selling fragments of Oriental heritage to wealthy foreigners. In his employ are a group of Egyptian peasants who presumably draw little profit from the exchange of Egyptian artifacts. Interestingly, whereas the majority of Western representations emphasize Oriental indolence and erase the material conditions of production, Gautier lingers over the description of their labor, drawing the reader's attention to the iniquitous economic and racial hierarchy between the imperial power and the indigenous workforce. This minute attention to the material relations among European patrons, Greek intermediary, and Egyptian laborers does not, however, produce an entirely transparent representation of the material processes of colonial reality, for what is thoroughly obscured in this narrative is the strong *French* presence in Egypt in the mid–nineteenth century. Throughout this period, French and English scientists, military officers, and administrators vied for influence, establishing themselves as "advisers" to the pro-Western viceroys, Mehemet-Ali and his anglophile successor, Abbas Pacha. Since the days of the *Description de l'Égypte*, French scholars had played a particularly active role in the field of archaeology. Given the critical picture of European archaeology painted in this novel—the name Evandale, for example, may be read as "est vandale" ("is a vandal")—it seems plausible to argue that Gautier wished, either consciously or on a subliminal level, to exculpate France so as to maintain a delicate balancing act between advocating French colonialism and deploring European encroachments into the Orient.

The travelers are led to a narrow gorge in which Argyropoulos locates a tomb so well concealed that it has escaped the attention of robbers and vandals. Out of deference, Evandale is offered the "virginity" of the tomb (72), which he enters, although not without reticence about "violating" this closed space. This penetration, emblematic of the penetration of the secrets of the Orient as a whole, is represented as a reversal of the flow of history, a return to the *archae*, or origin of time. The valley in which the tomb has been cut is itself said to resemble the residue of an originary cosmic catastrophe, and Gautier's use of catachrestic expressions such as "entrails," "flanks," and "mouths" to describe the desiccated gorge intimates that the catastrophe in question is none other than the origin of language. The reader's sense that the party is pursuing the origin of language is intensified by the fact that its advance through the labyrinthine tomb to the sarcophagus that lies within is represented as a process of sign reading: Argyropoulos painstakingly interprets for his companions both the signs presented by the formation of the rock and the hieroglyphic carvings that cover the walls.

Evandale and Rumphius believe that they have attained the elusive origin when they at last discover the sarcophagus. Yet a further surprise awaits them at this juncture because as they raise its lid to observe the body/truth that it conceals, they discover not the mummy of a powerful pharaoh, but that of a woman. "A woman, a woman," Rumphius cries in astonishment (46), as he recognizes the sex of the mummy.[26] His surprise registers the fact that, far from attaining the truth or point of origin that they had hoped to reach, the party has encountered a "foreign body" that, Rumphius surmises, must have been "substituted" for the body of a pharaoh. For the scholar in particular, the discovery of a female body in the Valley of the Kings represents a considerable anomaly: "This upsets all my notions and all my theories; it overturns the most carefully built systems on the subject of Egyptian burial rites" (80). The discovery of this body, buried in the tomb of a pharaoh, in fact upsets not only the archaeological systems and theories of European scholars, but also the political hierarchy of the sexes, for Rumphius's claim that "women, in the Orient, have always been considered inferior to men" (46) exemplifies the process by which gender inequality in Europe has been—and still commonly is—neutralized through favorable comparison with gender relations in the Orient.

As mere substitute the body remains figural, a metaphor that diverts the Europeans away from the literal origin, and whose metaphoricity must be decoded if this final meaning is at last to be determined. To this end, Evandale commands the Egyptian workers to remove the sarcophagus to his barge so that Rumphius can set about penetrating its secret. Once on the barge, the two Europeans slowly undress the mummy, which is described as though it were their infant: "Rumphius lifted the mummy from its casing . . . and began to unwrap it with the gentleness and skill of a mother exposing the limbs of her infant" (87). The mummy is in fact repeatedly represented as a baby, a trope that captures the archaeological inversion of history but also suggests that in taking possession of the mummy—itself a self-reflexive figure of language—the two men have successfully usurped feminine reproductive capacity. The dream of archaeology coincides here with the modernist aesthetic: having represented the Orient/woman as a lifeless body, the European men demonstrate their creative power by breathing life into the corpse. Unsurprisingly, the mummy is brought to life as an idealized representation from which all trace of the imperfect "natural" body has been expunged; its pose is said to resemble that of the Venus di Medici, and its skin, polished like marble, displays the gold and amber tones of a Florentine bronze.

But the body reserves yet another surprise for the two Europeans, for pinned against its side they find a papyrus scroll. Rumphius, who assumes that this text contains the funeral ritual, is once again astounded when he realizes that it narrates the life, rather than the death, of the mummified woman. The mummy thus continues to obstruct narrative closure by posing a new enigma, and the prologue ends on the question of whether, by translating the hieroglyphic scroll, Rumphius will succeed in uncovering and possessing the secret of woman/language. The reader is informed that after three years' work, the doctor does produce a translation, although certain "damaged parts" ("endroits altérés") and passages that contain "unknown signs" ("signes inconnus") escape his erudition (94).

The romance proper opens with a prolonged descriptive passage. By use of a narrative technique that confirms Edward Said's characterization of Orientalist representation as a movement from the outside in, the narrative first surveys the city of Thebes, then zooms in on the house of Tahoser, daughter of the high priest Pétamounoph, and finally penetrates the house and provides ekphrastic descriptions of Tahoser and her serving women. Characteristically, these idealized women are portrayed as works of art: gold and pink tones "color" Tahoser's face like paint on a canvas; her nose is said to consist of a "straight line," and her rounded chin shines like "polished ivory" (102). But having lingered over Tahoser's physical perfections as though she were a statue, the narrator brings her to life by indicating that far from being narcissistically absorbed in her own beauty, Tahoser is suffering from unrequited love for Poëri, a Jewish captive employed as the overseer of Pharaoh's farms and estates.

Much like Evandale, Tahoser desires the "other." Unmoved by the physical perfection of Egyptian men, she succumbs to Poëri's aquiline nose, olive skin, and blue eyes, a preference that reflects the strong undercurrent of racial thought in this novel and that gives voice to an established Orientalist tradition that Islamic women prefer fair-skinned European men.[27] The pairing later in the novel of Tahoser and Ra'hel, Poëri's Jewish fiancée, in fact draws heavily not only on the erotic stereotypes of Orientalism, but also on contemporary racial discourse. Just as eighteenth-century writers fantasized about the despot's prerogative to choose among women of various colors, so Gautier dwells on the exquisite contrast formed by the svelte Tahoser, said to embody the "purest Egyptian type," and the more matronly Ra'hel, said to represent the "Israelite ideal" (222).[28] In his description of these women, Gautier seems to take up the mandate that he had himself proffered in the Salons of the 1840s and 1850s, where he argued that the strongest hope for the revival of French painting was the ethnographic depiction of the whole range of human types, a mandate most enthusiastically embraced by Jean-Léon Gérôme, whose career Gautier had helped to launch with an enthusiastic article in *La Presse* and who remained a friend and protégé.

Gérôme's Orientalist canvases, like Gautier's Orientalist writing, employ an aesthetic of contrast in which striking variations in color and form are underpinned by ideas of racial difference. His neoclassical style and preference for "timeless" Oriental subjects such as the Turkish baths suggest an aesthetic transcendence of historical forces that parallels Gautier's own preoccupation with the splendors of ancient Egypt. However, in Gérôme, as in Gautier, Orientalist representation combines Parnassian ahistoricism and predilection for the perfection of classical sculpture with contemporary racial concerns.[29] For example, in Gérôme's *Bain maure* (*Moorish Bath*; 1870; Figure 12), the figure of the black attendant performs an aesthetic function, throwing into relief the luminous whiteness of the bather, but this aesthetic contrast is also invested with the social idea that the black figure is destined to play the secondary role of highlighting and serving the white woman. The racial overtones of this aesthetics of contrast emerge forcefully in Gautier's blazon of Tahoser, which negotiates the difficult relationship between Egyptian and African racial "types." Tahoser's lips are said to be only "only a little full," and she is described as beautiful "despite her imperceptibly African profile," while her complexion is rendered as an "ardent pallor" (102).[30] As in many exotic representations, alterity was (is) tailored to conform to a European standard that could not (cannot) accommodate the beauty of African bodies.

Tahoser's wishes in regard to Poëri are on the point of being fulfilled (Ra'hel generously offers to include her in an enticing ménage à trois), when the novel abruptly shifts gear by invoking the biblical story of Pharaoh's confrontation with Moses.[31] The decision to stage this symbolic encounter in the context of an historical romance would seem to be a rather surprising one, and it calls for some interpretation. I suggest that this confrontation—which is represented as the struggle between an imperial power and an enslaved people, and on a secondary level as a conflict between a culture that seeks immortality in the durability of plastic form and the people of the book—acts as a testing ground on which Gautier's ambivalence in relation to both European imperialism and his own artistic ideals is explored.

When we first encounter Pharaoh, he is returning triumphant from an imperial war at the head of a long procession of Ethiopian slaves. More statue than man, he is physically perfect and thoroughly self-absorbed. In his person, the contemporary discourse of dandyism is combined with the precepts of Oriental despotism. Pharaoh is portrayed as a ruler consumed by his own voluntarism, impervious to the world around him and in particular to the feminine other.[32] This demeanor changes when he catches his first glimpse of Tahoser. Experiencing at first an almost imperceptible sense of longing, he is progressively drawn from his self-absorption toward the open state of desire. As he admits to Tahoser, from the moment he first saw her, he no longer felt whole: "an unknown feeling entered my soul . . . I desired something; I understood that I am not everything." Although he initially claims that whether or not Tahoser returns his love is a matter of indifference (241), he ultimately expresses the hope that she will reciprocate his feelings

Figure 12. Jean-Léon Gérôme, *Bain maure* (*Moorish Bath*; 1870). Oil on canvas. Courtesy Museum of Fine Arts, Boston. Reproduced with permission. © 2000 Museum of Fine Arts, Boston. All rights reserved.

and speaks of his desire to make her his equal (250). Whereas he formerly practiced polygamy and treated women as slaves—exploiting the established exchange between categories of gender and of ethnicity, he says that he perceived women as members of another *race*—Pharaoh's acknowledgment of Tahoser's desire leads him to propose a monogamous and equal relationship.

Pharaoh's transformation from statue or divinity to human being is also represented as a fall into language. After he delivers a long speech in which he tells Tahoser that although he was once a god, she has turned him into a man, the narrator observes that "Never had Pharaoh uttered so long a speech. Habitually, a word, a gesture, a blink of the eye sufficed to convey his will . . . the execution followed the thought as thunder follows lightning" (240). As in the *Lettres persanes*, the Oriental despot is forced by a woman to modify his conception of language and to come to terms with the deferral of gratification that is built into the differential structure of the linguistic sign.[33] In Pharaoh's case, this lesson takes on a universal significance because the conflict between Egyptians and Jews is represented as the conflict between sculpture and writing, or between the desire to freeze the present moment for all eternity and acknowledgment of the temporal motion of history. Needless to say, Egypt loses this battle: because he is drowned pursuing the tribes of Israel across the Red Sea, Pharaoh's body is never buried in the elaborate tomb that had been prepared to preserve it, unaltered, for all eternity.

After Pharaoh's death, Tahoser takes his place on the throne of Egypt. As Claudie Bernard remarks, the details of her reign are remarkably sparse: the narrator states only that "Tahoser waited in vain for Pharaoh and reigned over Egypt, and after a short time she died" ("Démomification et Remomification," 465). This rather vague account of her reign and her death leaves open the central question as to whether, at the end of her life, Tahoser pined for Poëri or for Pharaoh. Although initially indifferent to Pharaoh's attentions, she is moved by his transformation from god to man and, given the obstacles involved in her love for Poëri, would certainly prefer to love him. The lack of narrative resolution of this question perhaps suggests that it is Tahoser's desire, and not its object, that is of real importance, and indeed her story ends on the suspended question of feminine desire: "Was it Pharaoh or Poëri that she regretted? Kakevou the scribe does not tell us, and Doctor Rumphius, who translated the hieroglyphs . . . did not venture to settle the question" (279). Because in at least one regard Tahoser remains as enigmatic at the end of the text as she was at its beginning, it must be judged that Rumphius fails to render the text/body in a decisive and complete manner and that the "foreign body" unearthed by the two Europeans retains its aura of untranslatable otherness.

The ending of *Le Roman de la momie* manifests a high degree of ambivalence that works on several different, although interrelated, levels. The first point to be made about this ambivalence concerns the text's articulation of feminine desire. Although the narrative framing of Tahoser's story suggests the containment of her desire within the tomb or within the *mise-en-abime* structure of the work of art, the question of desire nonetheless seems to be suspended in a way that obstructs the closure of the text around the body of the Oriental woman. On the other hand, although Tahoser's desire is acknowledged by Pharaoh—who ties it to her right to equality and political power—this recognition is partially neutralized by her untimely death. It would seem, therefore, that although the novel is able to represent Tahoser's desire, it cannot fully accommodate it.[34]

A parallel ambivalence can be discerned in regard to the European suppression of, or indifference to, the desires of contemporary Egypt. In this case, ambivalence arises from the fact that in this novel, nineteenth-century Europe is identified with both Egyptian captors and Jewish slaves. The stakes of this double identification are inscribed in a striking ethnographic mural that hangs in Pharaoh's palace and that shows "the nations of the four corners of the world . . . with their particular physiognomies and costumes" (236). This frieze—which exemplifies the kind of painting advocated by Gautier and practiced by Gérôme—places the Egyptians at the fore and Europeans, "the least civilized of all," at the end (237). The eventual downfall of Pharaoh at the hands of a captive people (to say nothing of the subsequent rise of Europe) demonstrates the arrogance of the Egyptian frieze and confirms the identification of modern Europeans with Jewish captives. To the extent that Europeans are identified with the Jews, they are represented triumphing over "Oriental despotism"—a common justification for colonial intervention in Oriental affairs.[35] On the other hand, given the imperialist aspirations and ethnographic interests of nineteenth-century Europe—interests exemplified by the novel's own aestheticized racial discourse—Europeans are also implicitly identified with the Egyptian masters. To the extent that Europe is identified with Egypt, its imperialist aspirations are exposed as vain manifestations of arrogance, doomed to succumb to the forces of history, or to the feminized Oriental other that it attempts to subjugate.

Finally, the ending of the *Le Roman de la momie* manifests considerable ambivalence in relation to the structure of language. Throughout this book, I have argued that in Orientalist texts, the quest to *know* the absolute other, Oriental woman, generates awareness that knowledge is destabilized from within by the language in which it is articulated, such that Oriental women function as figures of the alterity of language. In the case of early modernism, the situation is more complex because artists self-consciously sought to divorce sign from referent and used Oriental woman as a figure for this separation. As deconstructive theory has amply demonstrated, the attempt to represent language as a closed system that the writer can observe or represent from a position of external mastery is doomed to failure. However, it can be argued that precisely *because* the aesthetic program of modernism fails, the figure of Oriental woman does indeed encapsulate the irreducible alterity of language. Gautier's relationship to this failure was perhaps not one of pure unconsciousness, because what the narrative of *Le Roman de la momie* appears to recount is the vulnerability of its own aesthetic doctrine. That is to say, the structural similarity between Gautier's aesthetic ideals and the Egyptian faith in the durability of plastic form must be seen tacitly to acknowledge the epistemological vulnerability of art for art's sake as a theory of literary creation.

THE RETURN OF THE MUMMY

At the beginning of this chapter, we saw how Gautier's fiction helped to create the cultural conditions for an historical event—the undressing of the mummy of Nes-Khons at the Exposition universelle of 1867—an unveiling charged with all of the ambivalence in relation to the Orient and woman that fills the novel itself. In closing, I want to examine a subsequent performance of unveiling, an act that in narrative terms parallels those that I have described, yet that expresses a markedly different set of cultural and sexual attitudes.

As if to demonstrate that no unveiling is ever final, no knowledge ever complete, in 1907, some fifty years after the publication of Gautier's novel, the vaudeville actress and future writer Colette performed at the Moulin Rouge a sketch called "Rêve d'Égypte" ("Dream of Egypt") in which she played the role of a mummy brought back to life by an Egyptologist. The sketch consisted of a striptease in which the mummy's bandages were gradually unwound until the actress was naked on the music-hall stage, at which point, filled with gratitude for her resuscitation, she enthusiastically kissed the Oriental scholar, played by a woman in drag, her real-life lover, Missy de Belbeuf. The public was purportedly shocked by this display of female nudity and lesbian eroticism, the spectacle was closed down, and the affair was reported in the newspapers as the "Scandal of the Moulin Rouge."

If Colette's performance had the power to "surprise," indeed to shock, it was, I think, not only because it violated taboos surrounding the exposure of the female sex and the display of lesbian sensuality—although these were certainly powerful taboos, even on the vaudeville stage—but also because the unveiling subverted the meaning of a powerful modernist image. The selection of the mummy as theme reflected, after all, a continuing fascination with ancient Egypt in both high and popular culture—Oscar Wilde's *Salome* was written in French in 1896, Richard Strauss's opera of the same title was performed in Paris in 1905, and several recent modernist operas had adapted Flaubert's *Salammbô* to the stage.[36] But whereas the unveilings depicted in avant-garde art reveal only more representation, Colette's performance could be characterized as the "return of the real." The "real" in this context was shocking both because no one expected to see it, and, one suspects, because the artistic abstraction of the female body had always masked not only a fear of female sexuality, but also anxiety about women's desire and women's agency. The modernist striptease had always been orchestrated by male writers; by contrast—with some caveats as to the role of the predominantly male theatrical establishment in the staging of this undressing—I think it is possible to assert that Colette removed her own clothing in a transgressive act of artistic self-fashioning. The point that I want to make about this act is not that Colette's body represented an "absolute" real, a fundamental truth concealed as a result of misogynistic abstraction—a claim that would contradict all I have said in these pages about the irreducibility of representation and the impossibility of a definitive unveiling—but rather that her nudity constituted a "relative" real that subversively deconstructed the frozen abstraction into which the body of Oriental woman had fallen.

Above all, what Colette's provocative sketch undertook was a Nietzschean parody of the seriousness with which male philosophers, psychoanalysts, and artists have sought to unveil "woman," "the Orient," or, in a more profound sense, "truth" itself. To parody the will to truth and the drive to unveil is not, of course, tantamount to overcoming it. Rather, what Colette, like Nietzsche, really accomplished was to demonstrate the resilience of this paradigm—to illustrate the almost insurmountable difficulty of dispensing with the idea of a hidden or veiled truth existing just beyond our reach, but also, at the same time, to show that this is precisely an irreducible epistemological paradigm, and as such, it carries within itself a positive potential for *another* unveiling, an unveiling from a different perspective of a different set of truths.

Conclusion

Mummies returned again in the summer of 1999, stalking across the screens of U.S. multiplexes in Universal Studios's $80 million blockbuster, *The Mummy*. Billed as a remake of the 1932 movie of the same title, in certain ways this high-spirited adventure seems closer to the Orientalist reverie of Théophile Gautier than to the classic zombie movie. The chronology of *The Mummy*, like that of Gautier's novel, is split between the era of European colonialism and the Egypt of antiquity; the film, like the novel, presents us with a lavish reconstruction of Thebes, circa 1200 B.C.; and although the producers of *The Mummy* certainly did not devote to this computer-generated tableau the scholarly care and attention of a Gautier or Feydeau, they clearly did seek some guidance from professional Egyptologists.

The Thebes of *The Mummy* is a steamy place. Its high priest, Imhotep, keeper of the dead, is carrying on an illicit affair with Anck-sa-namun, the favorite mistress of Seti I. When the pharaoh discovers their liaison, the lovers kill him, only to find themselves pursued and apprehended by his loyal guards. Anck-sa-namun takes her own life, but her lover suffers at the hands of Pharaoh's factotums a fate worse than death: he is buried alive in a sarcophagus crawling with "flesh-eating scarabs." We are told that, were Imhotep ever to rise from the dead, he would be "a walking sickness," a plague on humanity equipped with a superhuman capacity to wreak whatever destruction he saw fit.

With the mummy safely entombed, the scene shifts to Cairo in the 1920s, the high period of European archaeology. In sketching this era, the film draws heavily on colonial stereotypes of Arabs, repeatedly depicted as

slovenly, rapacious, and disorganized. Amid this Oriental mayhem, a mot-
ley group of Westerners descends upon Hamunaptra, fabled City of the
Dead and burial site of the eponymous mummy. As they advance toward the
tomb, they are repeatedly set upon by a cohort of black-robed warriors
whose mission is to keep the mummy entombed. The members of this
desert caste represent a clear threat to the lives of the Western "heroes," and
we are at first inclined to see them as the bad guys; however, when the short-
sighted Westerners finally dig up the mummy and unleash its curse, we see
them rather as guardians of cultural tradition, vital impediments to the
unbridled pursuit of historical knowledge and material gain.

The immense popularity of this ripping yarn would perhaps be less surprising in France, where Oriental exoticism has continued to exercise a
strong hold on the cultural imaginary and where the critical message of
Edward Said's *Orientalism* has never been fully absorbed. In the United
States, on the other hand, fantasies involving deserts and archaeologists,
mummies and their tombs, have never held as much sway. However, the
recent success of films such as *The Mummy* and *The English Patient*—
another epic set in the Middle East and featuring a central mummified
figure—suggests a new receptiveness to Orientalist reverie in the North
American cultural arena.

Although one would certainly not want to make too much of *The
Mummy*, whose predominant tone is that of tongue-in-cheek, it seems plausible to ascribe this surge in interest to geopolitical factors, and in particular
to American anxieties in the wake of the Gulf War, about Arab-sponsored
terrorism. A rather curious episode in the film lends support to this hypothesis. Unleashed along with the mummy are (inexplicably) the ten plagues of
Egypt: swarms of locusts fill the air, boils beset the natives, and we see images
of bolts of fire raining down from the heavens on an Egyptian city in a manner reminiscent of CNN's coverage of U.S. missile attacks on Baghdad. In a
subsequent scene, brainwashed masses chanting the mummy's name and
brandishing flaming torches march on the hotel where the Europeans are
gathered, once again recalling media coverage of anti-Western demonstrators
in Iran, Iraq, and other parts of the Arab world.

In a broader sense, it is clearly plausible to advance the notion that, as
world superpower, the United States has assumed the colonial mantle once

worn by Western Europe and inherited along with it the anxieties of empire. Following its colonial precursors, it also appears to have identified ancient Egypt, the world's first self-conscious superpower and a civilization preoccupied with its own immortality, as a terrain on which its own aspirations and anxieties can be measured. If we still want to unwrap the mummy, it is because it is bound in highly charged emotions concerning the mortality and afterlife of empires. Since the beginning of the nineteenth century, these feelings have oscillated between the West's sense that it has outdistanced in scientific and technological achievement all other civilizations, past and present, and the opposing fear that these cultures, embalmed in their own traditions, might yet rise again and demonstrate the fragility of this dominance. But the perennial fear of the mummy's curse is perhaps not merely a symptom of cultural anxiety. It may also be read as a faint sign of recognition that the belief systems and burial rites of other cultures deserve respect and ought not to be sacrificed unquestioningly to the demands of progress.

The displacement of American anxieties regarding Islamic terrorism and the fragility of geopolitical power onto the fantastical terrain of a film such as *The Mummy* illustrates both the enduring power and the broad cultural scope of Orientalist discourse. Western perceptions of the Middle East, perhaps to a greater degree than any other part of the world, continue to be shaped by ethnocentric stereotypes cemented in the colonial age. In consequence, we find ourselves confronted with representations such as the prevalent media depiction of Saddam Hussein as "Oriental despot" that are almost impossible to evaluate because they are so saturated with cultural history. As I have stated, I believe that what will improve this predicament is not an attempt to progress "beyond Orientalism," but rather an effort to modify historically determined representations from within. With this objective in view, the refinement of historical and rhetorical consciousness emerges as the key task before us. Given all this, a film such as *The Mummy* represents something of a paradox, for while it demonstrates, rather dismally, that intercultural relations remain fraught with the attitudes and beliefs of the colonial past, it also suggests the historical perspective within which these relations should be examined. As such—like other recent returns to the terrain of Orientalism—it demands the kind of double reading that is advocated throughout this book.

Notes

Introduction

1. For a critique of the use of the category of "Third World woman" in Western feminism, see Chandra Talpade Mohanty, "Under Western Eyes." On the homogenizing category "Middle Eastern woman," see Marnia Lazreg, "Feminism and Difference," 88.

2. On the range of concepts of alterity ascribed to women in psychoanalytic theory, see Sarah Kofman, *The Enigma of Woman*, 82–84.

3. Anne McClintock, *Imperial Leather*, 5.

4. See, for example, Lisa Lowe, *Critical Terrains*; Alain Buisine, *L'Orient voilé*; Ali Behdad, *Belated Travelers*; Dennis Porter, *Haunted Journeys*; Syrine Chafic Hout, *Viewing Europe from the Outside*; and two collections of essays, *Europe and Its Others*, edited by Francis Barker, Peter Hulme, Margaret Iverson, and Diana Loxley, and *L'Exotisme*, edited by Alain Buisine, Norbert Dodille, and Claude Duchet.

5. Several studies have, however, dealt with issues closely related to my topic. Alain Grosrichard's *La Structure du sérail* explores representations of Oriental despotism, polygamy, and the harem in classical French literature; Julia Douthwaite's *Exotic Women*, also about seventeenth- and eighteenth-century French literature, addresses the representation of exotic, rather than specifically "Oriental," heroines; and McClintock's *Imperial Leather*, which deals primarily with the British context, explores the relationship between colonial history and popular culture, focusing on issues of race and gender.

6. Flaubert's niece Caroline Franklin-Grout published the first edition of his travel notes in 1910 (Conard edition), omitting many passages that she felt would be damaging to his reputation. For a contemporary edition, see *Voyage en Égypte*, edited by Pierre-Marc de Biasi.

7. Symptomatically, in the economy of Flaubert's letter, the negation of Kuchiouk's subjectivity fails to be entirely successful, for several paragraphs later, he returns to the question of her desire and observes that whereas he and Colet are thinking of her, she does not think of them; she has forgotten the "famous traveler," disclosing the pitifully small place he really occupies in the world. This textual return, which mirrors Flaubert's physical return during the voyage itself to spend a second night with Kuchiouk, inscribes a tension characteristic of Orientalist representation between the wish to erase the subjectivity of the Oriental woman and the desire to be desired by her.

8. See Suzanne Rodin Pucci, "Veiled Figures of Writing," also discussed below, Chapter 2.

9. These analyses are obviously informed by psychoanalytic theory, which more than any other discourse has made the limits of the body the prototype for all other psychological and cultural boundaries. For example, the reactions elicited by the foreign body can be approached as the social equivalents of such psychic processes as phobia and fetishism, introjection (the neurotic's incorporation of objects or individuals perceived as sources of pleasure into his or her own ego), and projection (the paranoiac expels displeasing objects or ideas from the self and identifies them with the world). On these concepts, see J. Laplanche and J. B. Pontalis, *Le Vocabulaire de la psychanalyse*, 209–10, 343–50.

10. On this point, see Michèle Duchet, *Anthropologie et Histoire*, 9.

11. In *The Oriental Renaissance*, Raymond Schwab maintains that from the eighteenth century on, Europe drew on the Orient in the same way that, during the Renaissance, it had drawn on ancient Greece and Rome. Although this claim accurately represents the scope and importance of Orientalism, it erases the very different political circumstances of the two movements.

12. See Michel Foucault, *History of Sexuality*, 1:87. Foucault's critique of the conventional view of power as coercion derives directly from Nietzsche's representation of power as a primal force, a constituent of all organic life and therefore a creative as well as a potentially repressive force.

13. For a recent attempt to relate Foucault's account of the technologies of the self to the history of colonialism, see Ann Laura Stoler, *Race and the Education of Desire*.

14. See Schwab, *Oriental Renaissance*, 1. The word "Orient" first appeared in French circa 1080; the term "Oriental" dates to circa 1160; and the term "Levant," which also draws on the solar model, to 1260. These dates appear significant because they roughly coincide with the age of European Crusades to

the Holy Land, inaugurated by Pope Urban II in 1095 and brought to a close in 1291. However, I would note that over the same period, cultural exchange between Islamic and Christian worlds flourished in the Moorish kingdom of Al-Andalus and spilled over into the south of present-day France. The terms "Orientalist" ("Orientaliste"; 1799) and "Orientalism" ("Orientalisme"; 1830) are, by contrast, relatively recent. They express self-conscious awareness of a new level of European engagement with the Orient and therefore suggest an historical break rather than an unbroken continuity of interest or hegemony.

15. On the romantic tradition of the "Westering" of world spirit, see Edward Said, "Orientalism Reconsidered," 1:17.

16. On this point, see Aijaz Ahmad's far-reaching critique of Said's *Orientalism* in *In Theory*, 183.

17. On the myth of Westerness, see Maria-Rosa Menocal, *The Arabic Role*.

18. See Homi K. Bhabha, "Signs Taken for Wonders," 172–77.

19. My concern here is not to question that the works of these authors manifest a complex textuality which in and of itself counters the state's desire for transparency and unambiguous meaning; rather, I want to suggest that writers' self-conscious opposition to the bourgeois culture and political duplicity of the Second Empire did not necessarily entail a contestation of French colonial expansion, and that in some cases (notably that of Nerval), their active *advocacy* of colonial expansion could be read as a form of counterdiscourse.

20. Peru was popularized in Marin le Roy, Sieur de Gomberville's *Polexandre* (1641); Voltaire's *Alzire ou les Américains* (1736); Françoise de Graffigny's *Lettres d'une Péruvienne* (1747); and Jean-François Marmontel's *Les Incas ou la déstruction de l'empire du Pérou* (1777), among other works.

21. Voltaire addresses the history of French colonial establishments in the New World in two chapters of the *Essai sur les moeurs*; a number of travel narratives, including Charlevoix's *Histoire de la Nouvelle France* (1744), also represent the colonies, and several of these are cited in the Abbé Prévost's popular *Histoire générale des voyages* (1746–1789). Prévost's *Le Pour et le contre* (1734–1740) also examines the colonies, reporting the speech of the Jamaican *marron* (maroon) Moses Sam, and his novel *Manon Lescaut* (1733) offers a brief representation of colonial Louisiana.

22. See Robert Aldrich, *Greater France*, 14.

23. See David Brion Davis, *Problem of Slavery*, 118.

24. In book XIV, chapter IV, of *De l'Esprit des lois*, Montesquieu briefly mentions that Louis XIII is purported to have accepted slavery in his colonies on the

grounds that it promoted the conversion of Africans to Catholicism. Writing as a *porte-parole* of the Enlightenment, Montesquieu dismisses such religious justifications of slavery.

25. In *Le Siècle de Louis XIV* and the *Précis du siècle de Louis XV* (*Outline for the Century of Louis XV*), Voltaire briefly touches on the history of Anglo-French conflict in the New World, but he never does more than evoke the existence of the French colonies. In the *Essai sur les moeurs*, he devotes two chapters (CLI–CLII) to French colonies in the New World, condemning the employment of African slaves. However, it is interesting to note that the more popular, pathos-laden representation of a mutilated slave in *Candide* alludes to the sugar plantations of Surinam, a Dutch, rather than a French, colony.

26. In *Discours sur l'origine et les fondements de l'inégalité* (*Discourse on the Origin and Foundations of Inequality*, 1755), Rousseau addresses the primitive social organization of savages, evoking in passing primitive peoples' desire for liberty when faced with the threat of enslavement by Europeans; however, this general condemnation of slavery never generates a specific condemnation of French participation in the Atlantic slave trade. This pattern is repeated in *Du Contrat social* (*On the Social Contract*, 1762), which, despite the fact that it opens with the use of slavery as a metaphor for the absence of political liberty, never directly addresses the experience of servitude in the colonies.

27. The article "Esclavage" ("Slavery") by the Chevalier de Jaucourt presents a vehement condemnation of servitude in Roman and feudal times, yet it does not address the contemporary context. By contrast, the following article, "Esclave" ("Slave"), refers to the *Code Noir*—the corpus of laws that since 1685 had governed the treatment of slaves in French colonies—yet does so in dispassionate, nonjudgmental terms. The article "Noirs" ("Blacks") by the philosopher-naturalist Georges Buffon, offers anecdotal evidence of the bad character of black Africans, illustrating the underlying current of racist thought that made it possible not to empathize with the plight of slaves. (It should be noted that several articles in the *Supplement* to the *Encyclopédie* published in 1777 do undertake to represent slavery and the colonies.) On the ambivalence or indifference of the *lumières*, see Louis Sala-Molins, *Le Code Noir ou le calvaire de Canaan*, 255–56.

28. Slavery was restored by Napoléon in 1802 and only definitively abolished in 1848.

29. See Reinhart Koselleck, *Critique and Crisis*. Koselleck would perhaps deny that political theorists ever renounced the utopian dichotomy between

morality and power that evolved during the Enlightenment. However, it seems to me that at least in the case of colonial practice, we can discern a shift toward acknowledgment of and commentary on French foreign policy.

30. Colonial expansion into the Orient began with the Expédition d'Égypte of 1798. Although the *grande armée* led by the young Napoléon Bonaparte only temporarily succeeded in overthrowing the Ottoman regime, this incursion marked the beginning of a period in which France and Britain played active roles in Egyptian affairs. Although Egypt never became a French possession and only formally became an English protectorate in 1914, it is clearly necessary to regard the European powers' presence there as an instance of colonial intervention. From the early nineteenth century on, France also posed as the protector of the Maronite Christian minority of Syria-Lebanon. In 1914, it was granted a mandate over the region that lasted until the mid-1940s. Finally, through the occupation of Algiers and Oran in 1830, the French colonial arena was formally extended from the *vieilles colonies* to North Africa.

31. Gustave Flaubert and his traveling companion Maxime Du Camp received missions from the Ministry of Agriculture and the Ministry of Public Education, respectively. Although Flaubert made fun of his mission and during his travels made no attempt whatsoever to gather information, he was nonetheless willing to reap the benefits of the letters of introduction with which he was supplied, and he offered no general condemnation of French colonial activity.

32. Notable exceptions were the painters Eugène Fromentin—who spent extended periods in Algeria and consecrated two books to his experience, *Un Été dans le Sahara* (1857) and *Une année dans le Sahel* (1859)—and Théodore Chassériau, who visited Algeria in 1846; Théophile Gautier, who traveled to Algeria in 1845 and again in 1862 to cover the opening of the Algiers-to-Blidah railway and wrote a series of journal articles subsequently collected, first in *Loin de Paris* (1865) and more recently in *Voyage en Algérie*; and Guy de Maupassant, who visited the region in 1881 at a time when travel to Algeria was becoming more common and who published several short stories and a longer narrative, *Au Soleil* (1884), that were based on his experience.

33. Although Du Camp had already visited North Africa and Turkey by the time he embarked for Egypt with Flaubert, he did not feel that he had set foot in the Orient.

34. Although this model runs counter to Foucault's emphasis on interpreting what is given in discourse rather than excavating the buried truths of history, it nonetheless retains the objectives of the interpretative practice he calls geneal-

ogy: the identification of historical discontinuities or shifts in meaning to demonstrate the limited historical necessity of our cultural heritage, and thereby to effect change in the present. On the political objectives of genealogy, see Foucault's essay "What is Enlightenment?"

35. James Mackenzie (*Orientalism: History, Theory and the Arts*) argues that if Orientalist paintings are currently selling well in the Gulf States and if Arabs find that these images adequately represent their history, then it is inappropriate for Westerners to brand them politically incorrect. Although I feel some sympathy for Mackenzie's desire to reassert the aesthetic interest of Orientalist painting, I would also suggest that his arguments against political critique fail to consider such basic issues as the potential impact of nostalgia or what Homi K. Bhabha calls "colonial mimicry" on an elite class of Middle Eastern consumers (see Bhabha, "Of Mimicry and Man").

36. Buisine's dismissal of Said (*L'Orient voilé*) means, in my view, that his otherwise persuasive readings of the West's fascination with the "veiled Orient" are undercut by his failure to look at political as well as epistemological factors that contribute to the European sense of "exclusion."

37. The year 1998 marked the two hundredth anniversary of the Expédition d'Égypte, an anniversary celebrated by a major exhibition at the Petit Palais; the publication of several new books on the legacy of Bonaparte and the founding of the Institut d'Égypte; and a number of radio broadcasts. What was singularly absent from this celebration, however, was sustained political debate. In place of this, French scholars voiced surprise when their Egyptian counterparts declined to celebrate the "*Année France-Égypte*" or to consecrate 1798 as a key date in their history.

38. Porter, *Haunted Journeys: Desire and Transgression in European Travel Writing*, following Roland Barthes, *Leçon inaugurale*.

39. In the final chapter of *Haunted Journeys*, Porter discusses Barthes's *Empire of Signs* as a model of antihegemonic writing on the Orient, a writing that celebrates "the emancipatory play of a written word that has bracketed its referent" and whose "anti-representationalist aesthetic" undermines the paternalistic writing of the occident (288–89). Barthes's tactic is to offer, in lieu of the conventional "description" of Japan, an unmediated presentation of disparate symbols of Japanese culture. The force of this confrontation with an alien signifying system is undeniable, but I think it should be emphasized that it is a force that consists precisely in the *destabilization* of a powerful *established* discourse.

40. Enlightenment writers notably challenged the monarchy's use of mythological figures to represent its power.

41. See Ludmilla Jordanova, *Sexual Visions*, 87. The statue at the medical faculty in fact bore the inscription "Nature unveiling herself before Science."

42. See, for example, Heidegger's late essay, "Aletheia (Heraclitus, Fragment B16)." Heidegger's essential point is that the veiling and unveiling movement of truth constitutes an integral part of the way in which entities are brought to presence.

43. As Marnia Lazreg observes in "Feminism and Difference" (85), Islamic women writers have in many instances accepted the defining status of the veil. For example, the prominent Moroccan feminist Fatema Mernissi entitled her book on the everyday reality of Maghrebian women *Beyond the Veil*, a title that implies that sociological analysis will expose truths veiled by male and/or Western ideology. See also Noria Allami, *Voilées, dévoilées*.

44. Schwab, *The Oriental Renaissance*; Pierre Martino, *L'Orient dans la littérature française au 17è et au 18è siècle*; Marie-Louise Dufrenoy, *L'Orient romanesque en France*.

45. See, for example, Marie Catherine Desjardins (Madame de Villedieu), *Alcidamie* (Paris, 1661), *Mémoires du sérail*, and *Nouvelles afriquaines*, the latter two first published in Paris in 1670–1671 under the name of M. Deschamps and republished in *Oeuvres de Mme. de Villedieu* (Paris, 1702).

46. Madeleine-Angélique Poisson de Gomez, *Anecdotes, ou Histoire secrète de la maison ottomane* (1722); Gomez, *Histoire d'Osman, premier du nom, XIXème empereur des Turcs, et de l'impératrice Aphendina Ashada* (1734); Madame de Puisieux, *L'Histoire des amours de Sapho de Mytilène* (1743).

47. Belgiojoso, an Italian expatriate exiled from France as a result of her opposition to Louis-Napoléon, took up residence in Turkey, 1850–1855. On the basis of her experience, she published *Scènes de la vie turque* (1858), as well as a collection of Oriental tales entitled *Emina* (1856).

Chapter 1

1. On Michel Foucault's characterization of discursive formations, see my Introduction, 12.

2. Anquetil-Duperron belonged to the first generation of professional Orientalists who sought to replace the theory that all Oriental nations suffered under despotic rule with a more variegated account of Oriental government.

3. See Françoise Weill, "Montesquieu et le depotisme," 192. Montesquieu himself declined D'Alembert's invitation to write the article, stating that he had said all that he had to say on the subject of despotism.

4. Although the word "culture" did not gain its contemporary meaning until

later in the century, Montesquieu's use of the term *esprit,* like Voltaire's use of the term *moeurs* ("mores" or "customs") prepared the way for the birth of an idea of culture. See Voltaire, *Essai sur les moeurs et l'esprit des nations* (1756).

5. Paul Vernière has identified 213 citations referring to "exotic" locations in *De l'Esprit des lois,* 51 of which refer to Turkey or Persia. The most commonly cited sources for the Orient are the seventeenth- or early eighteenth-century travelers Chardin, Bernier, Hyde, Rycaut, and Tavernier. See Vernière, *Montesquieu et l'Esprit des lois,* 45–46.

6. As I have stated, I do not wish to assert that there were absolutely no representations of French colonial practice—Voltaire addresses the history of French colonial establishments in the New World in two chapters of his *Essai sur les moeurs,* and a number of travel narratives, including Charlevoix's *Histoire de la Nouvelle France (History of New France;* 1744), also offer descriptions of the colonies, and several of these are cited in Abbé Prévost's popular *Histoire générale des voyages* (1746–1789)—but rather to suggest that these representations never attained either the prevalence or the discursive uniformity of Enlightenment writing on the Orient.

7. See, for example, Lisa Lowe, *Critical Terrains,* 52.

8. On the mechanism of displacement, see Sigmund Freud, *Interpretation of Dreams,* chap. 5.

9. The same pattern can be observed in the Chevalier de Jaucourt's article on slavery in the *Encyclopédie.* Basing his critical account of slavery on Montesquieu's, Jaucourt cites Roman and feudal laws but makes no reference to the contemporary context. By contrast, in the article "Esclave" ("Slave"), Jaucourt provides a detailed account of the *Code Noir,* yet makes no critical comments in relation to it.

10. To cite but one example, in his *Essai sur le caractère, les moeurs, et l'esprit des femmes dans les différents siècles* (1772), Antoine Léonard Thomas repeatedly describes Oriental domestic arrangements as either "domestic servitude" or "domestic slavery" ("servitude domestique" or "esclavage domestique"). See *Qu'est-ce qu'une femme?,* edited by Elisabeth Badinter, 52, 84.

11. On this continuing perception of Islam, see Marnia Lazreg, "Feminism and Difference," 88.

12. The claim that the *thèse nobiliaire* played a significant role in the French obsession with Oriental despotism is supported by the fact that the adjective "despotic" was first applied to the monarchy during the *Fronde.* The substantive "despotism," which replaced the more unwieldy term "despoticity" ("despotic-

ité"), first appeared in a dictionary in 1721, the year in which Montesquieu's *Lettres persanes* were published. For a more complete etymology of these terms, see Alain Grosrichard, *La Structure du sérail*, 8–26. Montesquieu's insistence that monarchies must respect the rights and privileges of the nobility is often cited as evidence that his critique of absolutism is a product of his social class. Despite the force of this argument, it should be noted that *De l'Esprit des lois* is also famous for its recognition of the advantages of the separation of powers guaranteed by the English constitution, a political argument that has little to do with the defense of hereditary rights.

13. Vernière rightly avers that with the depiction of despotism, Montesquieu's purportedly empirical reflection leaves the world of history and enters that of myth. The image of despotism that he paints is not that of a culture or a nation, but that of Kafka's castle, "in which the absurd fights against the horrifying" (*Montesquieu et l'Esprit des lois*, 104).

14. Thomas Laqueur shows that the appearance of the two-sex model cannot be directly attributed to specific advances in medical knowledge. On the contrary, it would seem that cultural forces shaped the evolution of scientific argument and experiment.

15. In 1672, Dutch physiologist Reinier de Graaf discovered the ovarian follicle; earlier, in 1651, the English medical scientist Robert Harvey had claimed that human life originates in eggs.

16. On the science of human reproduction in the late seventeenth century and the eighteenth century, see Jacques Roger, *Buffon*, 166–84, and Marie-Hélène Huet, *Monstrous Imagination*, 36–45.

17. The system of cultural representation that Joan Landes describes can be connected to the biomedical rethinking of sexual difference discussed above.

18. See Keith Michael Baker, "Defining the Public Sphere in Eighteenth-Century France," 200–201; Lawrence Klein, "Gender and the Public/Private Distinction in the Eighteenth Century"; Dena Goodman, "Public Sphere and Private Life"; and Suzanne Desan, "'War between Brothers and Sisters.'"

19. Michèle Crampe-Casnabet, "Saisie dans les oeuvres philosophiques": "Montesquieu, always under the veil of the Oriental woman, affirms that such duties are so cumbersome that women must devote all their time to them: whence the great efficacy of the enclosure of women in the seraglio" (3:342).

20. If Montesquieu places considerable emphasis on fashion, both in the *Lettres persanes* and in *De l'Esprit des lois*, it is in part because he perceives fashion as an instrument of social change. This perception, shared by many eighteenth-

century writers, is expressed in the common condemnation of the fashionable and female-dominated salon as a place in which social distinctions are set aside and intellectual exchange among members of different classes encouraged.

21. On the parallel between these two passages, see also Marie-Claire Vallois, "Rêverie Orientale et géopolitique du corps féminin chez Montesquieu." Vallois approaches the model of the "family within the family" as a manifestation of the emergent two-sex model of sexual difference and therefore as a response to the threat of social and sexual inversion contained in the metaphor of the "state within the state."

22. For a generalized discussion of women's alienation from the body politic, see Denis Kandiyoti, "The Nation and Its Discontents."

23. Joan Landes (*Women and the Public Sphere*) tends to overemphasize Montesquieu's affinity for republicanism, neglecting the many passages in which monarchy is represented as the only viable method of governing modern nation-states.

24. Montesquieu states this explicitly in the *Lettres persanes* (letter CXXXIX) and in the *Traité sur les devoirs* of 1725.

25. See, for example, Voltaire's *Dialogues entre A.B.C.*, first conversation, 323. Voltaire's rejection of Montesquieu's representation of Oriental despotism is in large part a reflection of his different perspective on domestic politics. Where Montesquieu essentially opposed the absolutist tendencies of the Bourbon monarchy and advocated respect for the nobility, Voltaire, perhaps because he was born a roturier, broadly speaking favored enlightened absolutism and the abrogation of the feudal privileges of the aristocracy.

26. See Carol Blum, "Une Controverse nataliste en France au XVIIIème siècle."

27. This passage may be compared to Rousseau's claim in book V of *Émile* (1760) that if the limitless appetite of women in warm climates went unchecked, it would surely cause the death of men unable to defend themselves against it. The result of this catastrophe would be depopulation: "the human race would perish by the very means established to conserve it" (467).

28. From the first chapters of *De l'Esprit des lois*, the size of a state is linked to its form of government: Montesquieu claims that republics must remain relatively small, while despotic states are usually vast empires: "a great empire requires a despotic authority in he who governs it" (575). If despotism is represented as the least effective form of government, it is in part because it prevails where territories are too vast to be successfully administered.

29. *Considerations on the Wealth of Spain*, believed to date to 1724, remained

unpublished until much of its argument was incorporated into books XXI and XXII of *De l'Esprit des lois*.

Chapter 2

1. On the argument that cultural identity is often as much the product as the cause of the experience of diversity, see Homi K. Bhabha, "Signs Taken for Wonders," 175.

2. Charles-Louis de Secondat, Baron de la Brède et de Montesquieu, *Lettres persanes*, in *Oeuvres complètes*, ed. Roger Caillois, vol. 1. All references are to this edition.

3. See Joan Landes, *Women and the Public Sphere*, 37. Neither *De l'Esprit des lois* nor the *Lettres persanes* explicitly advocates the model of gender relations that is most often associated with Rousseau; rather, this ideal emerges from the contrast between despotic and monarchic models, as well from Montesquieu's scattered praise for what Landes calls a chastened, republican ideal of womanhood.

4. On narrative and textual functions, see Ross Chambers, *Room for Maneuver*, 13, and Susan Suleiman, *Authoritarian Fictions*, 199–238.

5. Many travel narratives were accompanied by plates whose principal function was to illustrate the typical costumes of the region. In 1715, upon his return from Constantinople, M. de Ferriol, ambassador to the Sublime Porte from 1699–1712, arranged for the publication of a set of a hundred plates. These are based on original drawings by Jean-Baptiste Vanmour, who accompanied Ferriol on his embassy. The extreme popularity of these plates illustrates the process by which desire for Oriental women was displaced onto their costume.

6. It has been argued that the hermetic veiling of Persian women described by a number of contemporary travelers is one reason that Montesquieu decided to write about Persia, rather than the more popular Turkey.

7. See Josué Harari's account (*Scenarios of the Imaginary*, 83) of the fantasmatic relationship between the absent Usbek and his wives, amply illustrated in letter III, in which Usbek's body and person are literally venerated by his wives.

8. In the *Turkish Embassy Letters*, Lady Mary Wortley Montagu concurs that the women form a circle around the sultan and that he chooses one of them, but she aggressively refutes the claim that he throws a handkerchief to indicate his preference (116).

9. The Beaumont drawings first appeared in the edition of the *Lettres persanes* published in 1869 in Paris by Louis Lacour under the auspices of the Académie des Bibliophiles. They were subsequently reproduced in a number of

French, English, and American editions printed between the 1880s and the early 1900s. Other libertine novels reedited in this period with erotic illustrations include Crébillon-fils's *Le Sopha*, La Morlière's *Angola*, and Duclos's *Histoire de Mme. De Luz*, all ornamented with drawings by E. P. Milio in the series entitled "Conteurs du dix-huitième siècle."

10. On surrogate voyeurs in Orientalist painting, see Marilyn R. Brown, "The Harem Dehistoricized."

11. On the representationality of the nude, see Eugénie Lemoine-Luccioni, *La Robe*, 23–38.

12. *Arsace et Isménie* was published in 1783 by Montesquieu's son, but it was probably written in the 1740s. In his notes, Roger Caillois argues that it was written earlier, in the 1730s, and that it was initially incorporated in another unpublished Oriental tale (*Histoire véritable*), but Montesquieu's correspondence suggests that it was in fact written in Madrid in 1742. See Montesquieu's *Oeuvres complètes*, 1:1611. In a letter written shortly before his death, Montesquieu says he that he never published the story because he felt that the representation of triumphant conjugal love in an Oriental setting would appear unbelievable to a French public versed in the literature of despotism and polygamy. Oddly, but revealingly, he claims that such a depiction would be "too far from *our* customs" to be believable (letter to Abbé Vuasco, late 1754, *Oeuvres complètes de Montesquieu*, 3:1527; my italics).

13. See the Introduction, 28, on the conceptualization of truth as correspondence or *adequatio*.

14. A set of illustrations by Le Barbier, engraved by Noël Le Mire, first appeared in an edition of *Arsace et Isménie* published in 1794 in conjunction with *Le Temple de Gnide*. These illustrations were subsequently reproduced in several French and English editions.

15. For example, Bouyn's Roxelane, the Roxane of Racine's *Bajazet* (1672) and Defoe's *Roxana, or the Fortunate Mistress* (1724), are all loosely based on Khürrem, the Circassian slave whom Sultan Soleiman I married in an unexpected break with tradition.

16. See, for example, Heidegger's essay, "Aletheia (Heraclitus, Fragment B16)," 102–23.

17. For example, in letter CXVI, Usbek discusses the prohibition of divorce in Christian countries, and in letter CXIV, he questions the utility of polygamy, suggesting that it is a cause of sterility and depopulation.

18. Rica observes ironically that from an Islamic perspective, it makes sense

to deny women the right to read the Scriptures. Because they do not enter paradise, they do not need to read the text that points the way there (letter XXIV).

19. On the pure sign as the instrument of the despot's power, see Alain Grosrichard, *La Structure du sérail*, 81–86.

20. Michel Baudier, *Histoire générale du sérail et de la cour du Grand Seigneur, Empereur des turcs*, 14; Du Vignau, Sieur des Joanots, *État présent de la puissance ottomane*, 84; Jean de Thévenot, *Voyages de M. de Thévenot, tant en Europe qu'en Asie et en Afrique*, chap. 35; Jean Chardin, *Voyages de M. le Chevalier Chardin en Perse*, 2:261.

21. See, for example, Daniel Pipes, *In the Path of God*.

22. In the *Interpretation of Dreams* (1900), Freud recounts the anecdote of a man who, upon returning a broken kettle that he has borrowed, offers several contradictory excuses, including that the kettle was already broken when he borrowed it and that he never borrowed it at all. See *Interpretation of Dreams*, 4:119–20.

23. Moreover, whereas Roxane's rebellious writing is partly motivated by her love for a man other than Usbek, Graffigny (*Lettres d'une Péruvienne*) firmly separates women's writing from the force of erotic desire.

24. On these references, see my essay "'Langage inconnu': Montesquieu, Graffigny and the Writing of Exile."

25. François Poulain de la Barre's *De l'égalité des deux sexes* (1673) represents the inequality of the sexes as a function of social forces rather than as a fact of nature.

26. This point is clarified in letter XX, in which Usbek cautions Zachi that although she is as beautiful as Roxane, Roxane surpasses her in modesty and virtue, implying, of course, that it is for this reason that he prefers Roxane.

27. These letters are dated between the moon of Rhegeb, 1717, and the moon of Rebiab, 1720, whereas the last critical letter is dated the moon of Rhamazan, 1720—in other words, if we follow Montesquieu's calendar, it was written after the letter penned by Roxane that ends the novel.

28. On the dual meaning of the term *pharmakon*, see Jacques Derrida, "Plato's Pharmacy."

29. On language as the unknown within knowledge, see Barbara Johnson, *Critical Difference*, xii.

30. In *Some Reflections*, Montesquieu comments on the publication, in the wake of the *Lettres persanes*, of several "charming works" (he seems to be thinking in particular of the *Lettres d'une Péruvienne*) and asserts the merit of the novel as a philosophical genre. As Janet Altman suggests in "A Woman's Place in

the Enlightenment Sun," the immense success of Graffigny's novel seems to have persuaded Montesquieu to publish this short text, lending legitimacy to the novel, for in his original preface, he distances himself from what he clearly perceives as a frivolous genre (272).

Chapter 3

1. The 1740s saw both the final flourish of rococo art and the apogee of Oriental exoticism: more Oriental fictions were published in this decade than at any other moment. The merger of the rococo aesthetic and exoticism produced the *conte oriental* as a hybrid genre combining properties of the philosophical tale, the fairy tale, and the social satire characteristic of the worldly novel. Several novellas of the 1740s, including Charles de la Morlière's *Angola* (1746), Claude Henri de Voisenon's *Le Sultan Misapouf et la Princesse Grisemine* (1746), Charles Duclos's *Acajou et Zirphile; conte* (1744), the Comte de Caylus's *Nocrion, conte allobroge* (1747), and, of course, Diderot's *Les Bijoux indiscrets* (1748) and Crébillon-fils's *Le Sopha* (1742) illustrate this genre.

2. Crébillon's other libertine texts include *L'Écumoire* (*The Skimmer;* 1733), *Atalzaïde* (1745), and *Les Amours de Zéokinizul, roi des Kofirans* (*The Loves of Zéokinizul, King of the French;* 1746). This last tale represents an exception to my overall argument that exotic contexts amount to something more than an allegory of French society, for as the title, an anagram for "Louis Quinze, roi des français," suggests, the novel follows closely the intrigues of the French court in the early years of Louis XV.

3. *Le Sopha* can perhaps be viewed as a parody of the many French "sequels" to the *Thousand and One Nights* published in the first half of the century. Christiane Mervaud has made the interesting suggestion that the tale is deliberately presented as an insufficient version of the Oriental classic, lacking its charm. This would suggest that Crébillon intended an affirmation of the Oriental archetype and a critique of its European imitators. See Mervaud, "La Narration interrompue," 183–95.

4. In his *Pensées*, Montesquieu similarly observes that "A woman is required to please as though she has created herself" (no. 1247) and that "Women are false. This arises from their dependency: the greater the dependency, the greater the falseness" (no. 1254) (*Oeuvres complètes*, 998).

5. Philip Stewart (following Georges May) argues that female characters in the libertine novel should not be seen as the unwitting victims of men's sexual aggression because male and female roles are parallel—reversible but for the fact that men play an active and women a passive part. Although I would agree that

it is a mistake to view these women as mere victims, I believe it is also important to take into account the extent to which gender identity entails social performance or role playing. See Stewart, *Le Masque et la Parole*, 33.

6. The fact that Crébillon contrasts these two terms illustrates his view of *libertinage* as a constraining social system rather than as an economy of unbridled desire.

7. The displacement of desire from woman to apartment suggests the close association established in the eighteenth-century novel between intimate spaces and the female body. As the hero of Vivant Denon's *Point de lendemain* confesses, "it was no longer Mme. de T . . . that I desired . . . it was her *cabinet*" (Dominique Vivant Denon, *Point de lendemain*, 92). In Jean-Jacques Rousseau's *Julie*, Saint-Preux similarly exclaims, "Oh Julie! it [your *cabinet*] is full of you, and the flame of my desires spreads over every trace of your presence. . . . An almost imperceptible perfume . . . is exuded from every corner of the room" (Rousseau, *Oeuvres complètes*, 146–47).

8. As Jean Baudrillard asserts, "man never comes so close to being the master of a secret seraglio as when he is surrounded by [domestic] objects" (*System of Objects*, 88).

9. Several other authors, including Laus de Boissy and Mérard de Saint-Juste, also wrote plays about *petites maisons* in this period. Hénault's reference to a house in town ("une maison de ville") points to the fact that *petites maisons* were generally situated on the outskirts of Paris.

10. The historical relationship between these two novels is unclear. Although *Le Canapé couleur de feu* seems to have been published a year before Crébillon's novel, *Le Sopha* is known to have circulated in manuscript form for several years.

11. Thus, for example, in the fifth episode of the novel, two virtuous and abstemious characters called Almaïde and Moclès decide to test their virtue through temptation. Needless to say, they soon succumb to desire. Because the narrator is not released from his spell, it must be supposed that one or both lovers was concealing a sexual history, but the liar (or liars) is so credible that it is impossible to identify the culprit.

12. The libertine seducer can be compared with the Moslem man who (according to Montesquieu's Usbek) has sacrificed his virility by surrounding himself with too many women.

13. Impotence or anxiety over sexual performance is a recurrent theme of the Oriental tales of the period. In *Nocrion, conte allobroge* (1747), attributed to the Comte de Caylus, a young prince, worn out by sex, has lost his ability to "laugh" and will only be cured when a virgin tells him a story that is sufficiently enter-

taining. In *L'Écumoire* (1733), another novel by Crébillon, Tanzaï, prince of Chéchianée, and his wife Néadarné find it impossible to lose their virginity to each other as a result of successive enchantments.

14. According to Viktor Link ("The Reception of Crébillon-fils's *The Sofa* in England"), there were as many as eighteen English editions between 1742 and 1801. Pastiches included *The Adventures of a Sofa* (serialized 1783–1791) and *The History and Adventures of a Bedstead* (1784). There were also numerous stories in which heroes were turned into lapdogs, cats, and shillings.

15. On talking objects in English novels as manifestations of anxiety about the circulation of the written word in print culture, see Christopher Flint, "Speaking Objects."

16. Although the *canapé* seems first to have appeared in the 1650s, in 1690 Antoine Furetière's *Dictionnaire universel* still represents the word as a new addition to the language. The *canapé*, like the Turkish *divan*, at first consisted of a mattress draped with fabric, but it was soon Europeanized through the addition of a wooden frame.

17. Defining the word *fauteuil* in the *Dictionnaire universel*, Furetière states that in general, "one offers the armchair to persons of quality as the most honorable seat." He also claims that women often fight each other to secure this honor.

18. The word *tabouret* also has an Oriental root; it derives from the Arabic word *tabour/tambour*, imported into France in the sixteenth century.

19. I am using artists' engravings to illustrate the different types of chair because they show minute formal variations more clearly than photographs of actual pieces. But it should be noted, first, that these drawings portray "fantasy" models so ornate that they would have been unrealizable in practice, and second, that they appear in collections published between the 1760s and 1780s, somewhat after the age of *Le Sopha* and the height of the rococo. Portfolios of drawings by prominent Parisian furniture designers such as André Roubo, Jean-Charles Delafosse, and Pierre Ranson were widely available. They were intended for perusal by furniture makers as well as people of taste who took an active interest in the decoration of their homes.

20. This was the period of *turqueries*, in which all things Turkish were in vogue.

21. Distinctions among these various chairs were not absolute, as eighteenth-century furniture makers often admitted.

22. There were several different kinds of *duchesse*, including the *duchesse*

brisée, which is divided into two or three sections, and the *duchesse en bateau*, a one-piece chair in which the foot as well as the head is raised, creating the form of a gondola.

23. In the 1770s, an enlarged *bergère* intended for two sitters—the forerunner of today's loveseat—was ascribed the more elevated title of *marquise*.

24. On hoopskirts and their influence on furniture, see Guillaume Janneau, *Historique du meuble*, 46. Both recessed arms and hoopskirts went out of fashion in the 1780s. This does not necessarily mean (as Janneau assumes) that the change in female fashions occasioned the change in furniture. Like the realignment of arms and legs, the vogue for simpler, more natural feminine attire was attuned to the neoclassical and antirococo aesthetic of the period.

25. André Roubo also ties the tendency toward lower backs to the fashion (among both sexes) for pomaded and powdered hair (*L'Art du menuisier en meubles*, 614).

26. There has recently been some controversy surrounding the use of the word *salonnière* to designate a woman who hosted a salon during the eighteenth century. This debate arises because the word was not employed in the eighteenth century—it seems to be a coinage of the latter part of the nineteenth century— and because some scholars do not consider it authentically French. I have elected to retain the term *salonnière* because it acknowledges the role of an important set of actors in the Enlightenment whose contribution was not fully recognized, or named, by their contemporaries, and because at this juncture, the meaning of the word is clear and unlikely to be misunderstood by either anglophone or francophone scholars.

27. In his *Dictionnaire universel*—a good index of contemporary attitudes— Furetière emphasizes this point, defining the *canapé* as "a kind of very long chair on which two people may sit in complete comfort."

28. See on this point Katie Scott, *Rococo Interior*, 107. Scott cites Jean-François de Troy's much interpreted painting *Lectures de Molière* as an illustration of this merging of identities.

29. Valmont's desire for the Présidente de Tourvel is heightened when he sees her reclining on a chaise longue. Despite the inconvenient presence of her circle of intimates, the scene turns into a seduction scene between the two protagonists: "I went down to the drawing-room and discovered my lovely-one reclining delightfully relaxed on a chaise-longue. This sight excited me and brought a glint into my eyes" (Choderlos de Laclos, *Dangerous Liaisons*, 146). Later in the novel, when describing his final assault on the Présidente, he writes: "I was care-

fully reconnoitering the terrain and straight away selected the field for a successful operation. I could have chosen a more comfortable one because she even had an ottoman in her room" (278).

30. Stanislas de Boufflers, "La Bergère," 91–92 (spelling modernized):

Dans de riches appartements
On a vingt meubles différents
Un seul m'est nécessaire.
Mieux qu'avec un sofa doré
Mon petit réduit est paré
D'une simple bergère.

L'étoffe en est d'un blanc satin
Elle a la fleur du matin
La fraîcheur printanière.
Le lustre en est aussi parfait
Que le même jour que j'ai fait
L'essai de ma bergère.

Dans des contours bien arrondis
Entre deux coussins rebondis
Mon bonheur se resserre
J'aime à m'y sentir à l'étroit
Et chaudement, quand il fait froid
Je suis dans ma bergère.

Le jour, la nuit, sans embarras
Joyeux, je goûte dans ses bras
Un repos salutaire.
Avec délice je m'étends:
Ah! quel plaisir quand je me sens
Au fond de ma bergère!

Je n'en sors qu'avec des regrets
Souvent j'y rentre, et j'y voudrais
Rester ma vie entière.
Je lui sais plus d'un amateur,
Mais c'est moi seul qui par bonheur
Me sers de ma bergère.

31. Marx originally defined commodity fetishism as what occurs when the exchange value of products is perceived as an objective value, rather than as the

expression of labor. See Karl Marx, *Capital*, 1:71–83. Jean Baudrillard, among others, has argued persuasively against the claim that labor is the "true" referent of value on the grounds that this claim simply reinscribes capitalism's preoccupation with production. Baudrillard also questions the validity of the concept of use value, and, translating commodity fetishism into the terms of structural linguistics, calls into question the idea of an underlying referent that supports the system of exchange.

32. Roubo is particularly scathing about the use of the names *paphose* and *turqoise*.

33. Much like Jacques Lacan, Baudrillard, in *The System of Objects*, argues that desire is endless because it is grounded in absence or lack and in the barred access to possession that arises from the institution of the sign.

34. In *Crébillon-fils: Techniques of the Novel*, Peter Conroy argues that the sofa is a "non-human witness" (144). Although it is clear that the narrative voices a fantasmatic fear of being spied on by one's own material possessions, this episode suggests that Crébillon actually viewed the sofa as the material envelope of a human soul.

35. The hero of this tale is also given a magic ring with the power to elicit speech from a woman's genitals. The source of this topos is Garin's thirteenth-century fabliau, *Le Chevalier qui fit les cons parler* (*The Knight Who Made Cunts Speak*).

36. Diderot seems nonetheless to have felt rather ambivalent about his venture into the territory of the erotic novel. When imprisoned in 1749 (for the *Lettre sur les avengles* [*Letter on the Blind*; 1749]) he agreed to denounce *Les Bijoux indiscrets* as a youthful indiscretion. His friend and editor Naigeon later claimed Diderot had said he would sacrifice a finger if he could take the novel back. However, the fact that Diderot added three new episodes to the novel between 1770 and 1775 suggests that Naigeon may have been more anxious than the author himself about the novel's place in the Diderot canon. Diderot's daughter, Mme. de Vandeul, claimed that her father wrote the novel in two weeks, both to win a kind of bet and to raise money for his mistress, Mme. de Puisieux. On Diderot, Naigeon, and *Les Bijoux indiscrets*, see André Billy, *Oeuvres de Diderot*, 1375–1376, and Laurent Versini, *Diderot, Oeuvres*, 3:21–22.

37. The novel in fact reads as fictional rehearsal of the theme of the pursuit of truth that runs through many of Diderot's early writings, notably the *Pensées philosophiques* (1746) and *L'Oiseau blanc, conte bleu* (1747), a tale that served as a preliminary to *Les Bijoux indiscrets*.

38. See, for example, James Creech, *Diderot: Thresholds of Representation*,

chap. 2; Jane Gallop, "Snatches of Conversation"; and Thomas Kavanagh, "Language as Deception or the *Indiscreet Jewels*."

39. On this point, see Christie V. MacDonald, "Robe."

40. Franco Venturi claims that in this episode, experience is portrayed as a return to the philosophical goals of Plato and Socrates. Although this interpretation seems plausible, particularly given the use of the verbs *s'éclairer* and *s'améliorer* ("to enlighten" and "to improve oneself") to describe the thought of the ancients, it is important to note the apparent separation in the narrative between the violent arrival of Experience and Mangogul's conversation with Plato, a separation that suggests that Diderot does not consider empiricism and classical thought to be in complete harmony (*Jeunesse de Diderot*, 132).

41. This remark appears in the *Lettre à Mlle de La Chaux* appended to most critical editions of the *Lettre*. See *Oeuvres complètes* (Le Club Français du Livre edition), 2:575.

42. This story recalls the plot of Crébillon's *L'Écumoire*, in which Prince Tanzaï and his wife Néadarné suffer a similar fate.

43. The episode entitled "Of the travelers" is chapter XXVIII in the Naigeon edition of 1798, the first edition to incorporate the new chapters.

44. Sarah Bartmann, known as the "Hottentot Venus," was transported to Europe from the Cape of Good Hope in 1810. Distinguished by her prominent buttocks, she was exhibited in France and England as a medical specimen and for the purposes of popular entertainment. After her premature death, she was found to bear also the "Hottentot apron," the hypertrophy of the labia minorae that European travelers had observed among women of the Cape. On the shameful story of Sarah Bartmann, see Tracy Denean Sharpley-Whiting, *Black Venus*, 16–31.

45. A concept broached by Julien Offray de La Mettrie in his *L'Homme machine* (*Machine-Man*; 1748).

46. Mirzoza radicalizes the sultan's own materialism by refusing to accord priority to either the head or the sex on the basis of received opinion.

47. After this first allusion, the narrator makes numerous references to the "auteur africain" (African author) and on one occasion claims to be translating his journal, a claim that suggests that he is in fact the translator (141).

48. In a number of cases, Mangogul finds himself simply unable to translate the speech of a jewel. Such is the case of Sphéroïde l'aplatie, whose jewel speaks an abstract, geometrical language, and that of Girgiro l'entortillé, whose jewel speaks Crébillonese (127–30). The discourse of Callipigia's jewel is not reported—a lacuna in the text suggests that the author may have intentionally

omitted it (136–37), whereas the "traveling jewel" ("bijou voyageur") of Cypria speaks Latin, English, and a mix of French and Spanish—languages that Mangogul cannot understand (166–69).

49. The overlap between libertine exoticism and scientific taxonomy is illustrated in the following passage, taken from a text of the same period, Pierre de Maupertuis's *Vénus physique suivi de la Lettre sur le progrès des sciences* (*Physical Venus*; 1745). Reflecting on the first experiments in the genetic engineering of animals, Maupertuis asks himself, "Why do blasé sultans in harems that contain only women of all the known *species* not make themselves new *species*? If, like them, I were limited to the pleasures offered by a face or a figure, I would soon have recourse to these varieties" (134; my italics).

50. For example, the popular *libelle* (lampoon), *Les Fastes de Louis XV* (1782) portrayed the monarch as a dissolute harem master squandering the material resources of the nation, yet weakly subservient to a still more despotic and dissolute Mme. Du Barry.

51. On this topic, see Pamela Cheek, "Prostitutes of 'Political Institution.'"

52. As Marnia Lazreg argues in her fine article, "Feminism and Difference," 96.

Chapter 4

1. At this time, slavery was still legal in the French Atlantic colonies, although the reports of European travelers to the Orient characteristically depict it as an Oriental institution, either condemning it, or (as in the case of Nerval) explaining it and justifying its social utility.

2. Gérard de Nerval, *Voyage en Orient*, ed. Michel Jeanneret; all further references are to this edition and supplied parenthetically in the text.

3. This shift from fantasy to fact was prepared in the latter part of the eighteenth century by the emergence of "scientific Orientalism," the scholarly examination of Oriental languages, religion, and civilization pioneered by Abraham-Hyacinthe Anquetil-Duperron, Silvestre de Sacy, Claude-Étienne Savary, and Constantin de Volney.

4. Nerval and Fonfrède took photographic equipment with them, but they were unable to use it because the chemicals necessary to the development process deteriorated in the Egyptian sun. Later travelers enjoyed the advantage of being able to renew their supplies in Egypt. From the early 1840s on, the Académie des Inscriptions et des Belles Lettres awarded cultural missions to travelers who agreed to photograph the leading monuments of the Near and Middle East from a range of preordained perspectives, a task dutifully fulfilled by, among others, Flaubert's traveling companion, Maxime Du Camp.

5. Nerval left Marseilles on January 1, 1843, and returned on December 5. The textual *Voyage en Orient* links this journey to a stay in Vienna that in reality occurred two years earlier, in the winter of 1839-1840, and suggests that the author traveled over land from central Europe, rather than as he actually did, by sea.

6. This tradition would include works such as Princess Cristina Belgiojoso's *Emina* (1856), a collection of Oriental tales, and her *Scènes de la vie turque* (*Scenes of Turkish Life*; 1858), a collection of articles first published in the journal the *Revue des deux mondes*.

7. This view of Nerval gained currency in the 1950s and 1960s, largely due to the influence of Jean Richer.

8. For a detailed account of French mercantile and diplomatic practices in the Levant in this period, see Albert Vandal, *Une Ambassade française en Orient sous Louis XV*.

9. Nerval had a lifelong fascination with Freemasonry that comes to the fore in *Les Illuminés* (1852), a collection of semifictional biographies of prominent Freemasons and Utopian Socialists. In one section of the text, he discusses the efforts of the Knights Templar to forge an alliance between their beliefs and those of the Syrian population. See Nerval's *Oeuvres complètes*, 2:1173.

10. France finally broke from this treaty in the 1860s in response to a series of massacres of Maronite Christians.

11. In the same year, France undertook an expedition to reinstate French sovereignty in Madagascar.

12. This text is thought to have been written jointly by Nerval, Arsène Houssaye, and Edmond Tessier.

13. On the nonrepresentation of black Africans in European literature, see Christopher L. Miller, *Blank Darkness*. It is true that not all eighteenth- and nineteenth-century European representations of Africans or peoples of African descent were overtly negative. One could cite figures such as Aphra Behn's Oronooko or Saint-Lambert's Ziméo as evidence of an alternative tradition that ennobles blacks. However, it is often the case that in these counterimages, the black hero is subtly Europeanized or differentiated from the less civilized, less attractive mass of his or her people.

14. In his introduction to the Richelieu edition of the *Voyage en Orient*, Gilbert Rouger suggests that if Nerval's account of his stay in Lebanon is more highly fictionalized than any other episode, it is because Nerval experienced a renewed bout of mental illness during his stay there. The story of the mad caliph Hakem, Nerval's claim to have departed suddenly because of a "fever," and the

absence of any letters documenting the period lend support to this hypothesis. See the introduction to *Voyage en Orient*, 1:15–89.

Chapter 5

1. For example, when he discusses Ingres in his review of the Exposition Universelle of 1855, Baudelaire notes the "rarefied air" and "laboratory atmosphere" of Ingres's Oriental canvases and comments on his tendency to correct nature in his drawings. See Charles Baudelaire, *Oeuvres complètes*, 2:585–87.

2. On the projection of French colonial violence as Oriental cruelty, see Linda Nochlin, "Imaginary Orient," 52.

3. For a good account of the lack of unified national policy on and widespread public indifference to colonialism in this period, see Raoul Girardet, *L'Idée coloniale en France de 1871 à 1962*, 4–18.

4. In the Salons of 1846, 1849, and 1859, Gautier advocates travel to the Orient as the most promising prospect for a renewal of French art.

5. This aesthetic was interwoven with another midcentury ideal: that of dandyism. The dandy was defined by Baudelaire and Barbey d'Aurevilly as a superior individual capable of fashioning himself as though he were a work of art. This meant, among other things, suppressing impulses associated with need that rendered him dependent on objects and persons beyond his control. Thus, in his *Du Dandyisme et de George Brummel* (*Of Dandyism and of George Brummel*; 1845), Jules Barbey D'Aurevilly asserts that the dandy should not love, because to love is to become a slave to something beyond oneself.

6. Gautier traveled to Algeria in 1845 and 1862; the texts relating to these voyages are now collected in the *Voyage en Algérie*. He visited Constantinople in 1852 and wrote a series of articles for *La Presse* gathered in the volume *Constantinople* (1853). He visited Egypt in 1869 when he covered the opening of the Suez Canal for the *Journal officiel*, producing the texts now gathered in the *Voyage en Égypte*.

7. Although French forces were expelled from Egypt by the British in 1801, the scientists and historians whom Bonaparte had brought with him remained, and their research ultimately generated the monumental *Description de l'Égypte* (France), published in twenty-three volumes between 1809 and 1828.

8. These tensions inevitably come to the fore in Gautier's travel writing. His 1845 voyage to Algeria was partially financed by the publisher Hetzel, for whom he had agreed to produce a "voyage pittoresque" (picturesque voyage) to be illustrated by artists commissioned by the editor. Not only did Gautier not complete this text—his collected articles on Algeria were first published by Michel Lévy in

1865—but as Denise Brahimi has observed in her introduction to the *Voyage en Algérie*, his encounter with Algeria gave rise to a writing "in black and white," far removed from the publisher's demand for "local color" (10). Rather than producing the picturesque Orient that readers expected to discover, Gautier portrays a fragmented world in which the "authentic" Algeria, the Algeria that has not been transformed by the French colonial presence, reveals itself only in brief bursts or exposures. Gautier's writing on Turkey in *Constantinople* manifests greater narrative continuity, but it is characterized by remarkable coldness and distance. In marked contrast to Nerval's travel writing, which as we have observed is filled with dialogues that convey the author's syncretistic attitudes, Gautier's deploys a lonely "I"—or rather "we," because his travel narratives are written in the first person plural of the official critic—whose self-positioning outside of Oriental culture is suggestive of the increasingly polarized relations between East and West. Gautier in fact repeatedly invokes the Eastern question, bemoaning the *Tanzimat*, or program of reform undertaken by Sultan Mahmoud (1807–1839) and his successor, Abdul-Medjid (1839–1861), on the grounds that this liberalization entails the Europeanization of Turkey. Needless to say, he is only able to understand these reforms as the negative consequences of Westernization: it is part of the hegemonic apparatus to assume that historical change could not emanate from the Orient itself.

9. See also Ali Behdad, *Belated Travelers*, who applies the model of discourse/counterdiscourse to a range of nineteenth-century travel narratives.

10. I say "overt complicity" because I would follow Ross Chambers in drawing a distinction between the conscious attitudes attributed to writers such as Flaubert, Nerval, and Gautier and the "oppositional" effects that can be ascribed to their texts. See Ross Chambers, *Room for Maneuver*, 1–14.

11. Making perhaps a jibe at Du Camp, Flaubert makes fun of the ordinary tourist who, just because he has visited the Orient once, considers himself an Orientalist; he does not, however, question the scientific project of Orientalism in and of itself.

12. Gautier's ambivalence in fact exceeds the issue of Orientalism. Although he was one of the leaders of a literary movement that considered its aims to be oppositional, he made his living writing for the leading commercial newspapers of the day. Toward the end of his life, he became the literary critic of the *Moniteur universel*, one of the organs of the Second Empire, and was awarded the post of librarian to Princess Mathilde, such that he enjoyed a quasi-official status in relation to the regime.

13. See Homi K. Bhabha, "Difference, Discrimination and the Problem of Colonialism."

14. On this point, see Charles Bernheimer, *Figures of Ill Repute*, 272–73.

15. See also Lisa Lowe's critique of Kristeva's own exoticism in this text, *Critical Terrains*, 140–52. More recently, Naomi Schor and Emily Apter have sought to introduce into the debate on fetishism a different strand of feminist thinking by exploring the possibility of female fetishism. See Naomi Schor, *Breaking the Chain*; and Emily Apter, *Feminizing the Fetish*.

16. The fear articulated in this ending can be traced to the narrator's wish to overstep the boundaries imposed by the symbolic "law of the father," both by appropriating the daughter for himself and by flaunting the order of life and death and the social taboo against necrophilia.

17. In 1851, Gautier published in *La Presse* a poem entitled "Nostalgies d'Obélisques" ("The Nostalgia of Obelisks"), subsequently republished in *Émaux et camées*, in which the obelisk of Paris and the obelisk remaining in Luxor compare their respective fates; he also mentions the Paris obelisk in the preface to *Mademoiselle de Maupin* (1835), citing the need to borrow from ancient Egypt as evidence that humanity is not progressing.

18. See on this point Sima Godfrey, "Mummy Dearest," 307.

19. Earlier in the narrative, Xixouthros had warned him that because his society does not know how to preserve itself, after his death, not even Isis will be able to reassemble the disseminated fragments of his body (Gautier, *Le Pied de momie*, 261).

20. See on this point Franc Schuerewegen, "Histoires de pieds," 203.

21. See Tzvetan Todorov, *Introduction à la littérature fantastique*, 82.

22. For example, by the provisions of the Riancey amendment of 1850, journals were prohibited from publishing *romans feuilletons* (popular serialized novels) because they often carried politically subversive undertones; by contrast, historical prose, presumed to be unproblematically referential, was considered acceptable. These political measures were not a rejection of fiction writing per se, but rather an expression of anxiety about fiction's capacity to bear more than one meaning, to be ironic or allegorical.

23. Roger Caillois perfectly captures the transgressive potential of the fantastic when he writes that "The fantastic is always the rupture of established order; the eruption of the *inadmissible* in the unalterable *legality* of everyday life" (Roger Caillois, *Au coeur du fantastique*, 161; my italics).

24. Flaubert read Gautier's novel as he began working on *Salammbô* (1863);

in turn, *Salammbô* inspired Gustave Moreau's series of symbolist paintings of Salome (1873–1876), which are described in detail in Huysmans's *A Rebours* (*Against the Grain*; 1884), and which were one of the inspirations for Flaubert's *Hérodias* (1877). *Salammbô* is often cited as one of the sources for Mallarmé's *Hérodiade*, begun in 1864. Oscar Wilde brought Salome to the stage in 1896, and Richard Strauss wrote an opera based on the play in 1905.

25. For example, in the dedication, Gautier thanks his friend Ernest Feydeau, author of a monumental account of ancient burial practices—the *Histoire des usages funèbres et des sépultures des peuples anciens* (1856)—saying that "You have raised for me the veil of mysterious Isis and resuscitated the immensity of a lost civilization; the history is yours, the novel mine." This division of labor is reinscribed in the novel proper in the pairing of Rumphius and Evandale.

26. This story has an historical source in Champollion's *Lettres écrites d'É-gypte*, which allude to a tomb inscription indicating that a queen named "Thaoser" once reigned over Egypt (210).

27. For example, in *La Femme* (*Woman*), Jules Michelet asserts that African women love European men and in particular Frenchmen, and Nerval writes in the *Voyage en Orient* that "My European complexion may have some charm in this country. In France I would pass for a very ordinary cavalier, but in Cairo I become an amiable child of the North" (175).

28. In depicting Ra'hel and Tahoser, Gautier may have thought back to his *Voyage en Algérie*, since Ra'hel, with her athletic arms, recalls the description of a "belle juive" ("beautiful Jewess") that the author glimpses in Algiers, whereas Tahoser's portrait resembles that of the svelte young dancer named Ayscha whom he encounters in Constantine (39–40, 103).

29. Gautier's *Roman de la momie* appeared two years after Gobineau's infamous *Essai sur l'inégalité des races humaines* (*Essay on the Inequality of the Human Races*; 1853–1855). Although Gautier and Gobineau were not on good terms and Gautier's interest in race never amounted to systematized racism, the two writers shared with many of their contemporaries a strong interest in representing racial difference.

30. In *Le Pied de momie*, Gautier describes Hermonthis in a similar way, speaking of "the slightly African protuberance of her mouth" (255).

31. One source for this dimension of the novel was Rossini's opera *Möise et Pharaoh*, which Gautier had enthusiastically reviewed in 1852 (*La Presse*, November 8, 1852).

32. These traits are perfectly captured in *Rhamses in his Harem* (1885), an aca-

demic painting by Jules-Jean-Antoine Lecomte du Noüy. Noüy was a pupil of Gérôme who shared his teacher's interest in classical ethnography. He completed two paintings based on Gautier's novel, *Rhamses in His Harem* and *The Bearer of Bad News* (1872).

33. Much like Pharaoh, Usbek perceives his commands as "thunder that strikes in the midst of lightning and storms" (Montesquieu, *Lettres persanes*, letter CLIV).

34. On this issue, see Naomi Schor, *Breaking the Chain*, xi, 118–26. Schor considers this structure of recognition without accommodation of feminine desire to be typical of the nineteenth-century novel.

35. See, for example, Volney's *Voyage en Égypte et en Syrie*, a work read virtually as a guidebook during Bonaparte's Expédition d'Égypte and which argues for the overthrow of Ottoman tyranny in Egypt and its replacement with a "good European government."

36. For example, Ernest Reyer and Camille Du Locle's opera *Salammbô* (1892).

Works Cited

Ahmad, Aijaz. *In Theory: Classes, Nations, Literatures*. New York: Verso, 1992.

Aldrich, Robert. *Greater France: A History of French Overseas Expansion*. New York: Saint Martin's Press, 1996.

Allami, Noria. *Voilées, dévoilées: Être femme dans le monde arabe*. Paris: L'Harmattan, 1988.

Altman, Janet. "A Woman's Place in the Enlightenment Sun: The Case of Françoise de Graffigny." *Romance Quarterly* 38, no. 3 (August 1991): 261–72.

Anquetil-Duperron, Abraham-Hyacinthe. *Législation orientale*. Amsterdam: MM. Rey, 1778.

Apter, Emily. *Feminizing the Fetish: Psychoanalysis and Narrative Obsession in Turn-of-the-Century France*. Ithaca, N.Y.: Cornell University Press, 1991.

Badinter, Elisabeth, ed. *Qu'est-ce qu'une femme? Un débat/A. L. Thomas, Diderot, Madame d'Épinay*. Paris: P.O.L., 1989.

Baker, Keith Michael. "Defining the Public Sphere in Eighteenth-Century France: Variations on a Theme by Habermas." In *Habermas and the Public Sphere*, edited by Craig Calhoun, 181–211. Cambridge, Mass.: MIT Press, 1992.

Barbey D'Aurevilly, Jules. *Du Dandyisme et de George Brummel*. Caen, France: B. Mancel, 1845.

Barker, Francis, Peter Hulme, Margaret Iverson, and Diana Loxley, eds. *Europe and Its Others: Proceedings of the Essex Conference on the Sociology of Literature*. 2 vols. Colchester, UK: Essex University Press, 1985.

Barthes, Roland. *The Empire of Signs* [L'Empire des signes]. Translated by Richard Howard. New York: Hill and Wang, 1982.

———. *Leçon inaugurale de la chaire de sémiologie du Collège de France*. Paris: Seuil, 1978.

Bastide, Jean-François de. *La Petite maison*. Paris: Le Promeneur, 1993.

Baudelaire, Charles. *Oeuvres complètes*. 2 vols. Paris: Pléïade, 1975–1976.

Baudier, Michel. *Histoire générale du sérail et de la cour du Grand Seigneur, Empereur des turcs*. 2nd ed. Paris, 1623.

Baudrillard, Jean. *The System of Objects*. Translated by James Benedict. London: Verso, 1996.

Beaumarchais. *Le Mariage de Figaro*. Paris: Ruault, 1785.

Behdad, Ali. *Belated Travelers: Orientalism in the Age of Colonial Devolution*. Durham, N.C.: Duke University Press, 1994.

Behn, Aphra. *Oronooko, or, the Royal Slave*. London: Will Canning, 1688.

Belgiojoso, Cristina. *Emina*. Paris, 1856.

———. *Scènes de la vie turque*. Paris: M. Lévy Frères, 1858.

Bernard, Claudie. "Démomification et Remomification de l'histoire." *Poétique* 28:88 (November 1991): 463–86.

Bernheimer, Charles. *Figures of Ill Repute. Representing Prostitution in Nineteenth-Century France*. Cambridge, Mass.: Harvard University Press, 1989.

Bhabha, Homi K. "Difference, Discrimination and the Problem of Colonialism." In *The Politics of Theory*, edited by Francis Barker, vol. 1, 194–211. Colchester, UK: University of Essex Press, 1983.

———. "Of Mimicry and Man: The Ambivalence of Colonial Discourse." *October* 28 (spring 1984): 125–33.

———. "Signs Taken for Wonders." In *Race, Writing and Difference*, edited by Henry Louis Gates, Jr., 163–84. Chicago: University of Chicago Press, 1985.

Blum, Carol. "Une Controverse nataliste en France au XVIIIème siècle: La Polygamie." *Population* 1–2 (1998): 93–112.

Bongie, Chris. *Exotic Memories: Literature, Colonialism and the Fin de Siècle*. Stanford, Calif.: Stanford University Press, 1991.

Boufflers, Stanislas de. "La Bergère." In *Oeuvres choisies*, vol. 1. Paris: Librairie Ancienne et Moderne, 1827.

Braun, Theodore. "'La chaîne secrète': A Decade of Interpretations." *French Studies* 42, no. 3 (July 1988): 278–91.

Brooks, Peter. *Body Work*. Cambridge: Harvard University Press, 1993.

———. *The Novel of Worldliness*. Princeton, N.J.: Princeton University Press, 1969.

Brown, Marilyn R. "The Harem Dehistoricized: Ingres' Turkish Bath." *Arts Magazine* (summer 1987): 58–68.

Buisine, Alain. *L'Orient voilé*. Paris: Zulma, 1993.

————. "Voiles." In *L'Exotisme: Actes du Colloque de Saint Denis,* edited by Alain Buisine, Norbert Dodille, and Claude Duchet, 73–85. Paris: Didier-Érudition, 1988.

Buisine, Alain, Norbert Dodille, and Claude Duchet, eds. *L'Exotisme: Actes du Colloque de Saint Denis.* Paris: Didier-Érudition, 1988.

Butler, Judith. *Gender Trouble: Feminism and the Subversion of Identity.* New York: Routledge, 1990.

Caillières, François de. *Des mots à la mode et des nouvelles façons de parler.* Paris, 1692.

Caillois, Roger. *Au coeur du fantastique.* Paris: Gallimard, 1965.

Caylus, Comte de. *Nocrion, conte allobroge.* Paris, 1747.

Certeau, Michel de. *Heterologies: Discourse on the Other.* Translated by Brian Massumi. Minneapolis, Minn.: University of Minnesota Press, 1986.

Chambers, Ross. *Gérard de Nerval et la poétique du voyage.* Paris: J. Corti, 1969.

————. *Room for Maneuver: Reading (the) Oppositional (in) Narrative.* Chicago: University of Chicago Press, 1991.

————. *The Writing of Melancholy: Modes of Opposition in Early French Modernism.* Translated by Mary Seidman Trouille. Chicago: University of Chicago Press, 1993.

————. "1851, 2 December: Literature Deterritorialized." In *A New History of French Literature,* edited by Denis Hollier, 710–16. Cambridge: Harvard University Press, 1994.

Champollion, Jean-François. *Lettres écrites d'Égypte et de Nubie en 1828 et 1829.* Paris: F. Didot frères, 1833.

Chardin, Jean, Sir. *Voyages de M. le Chevalier Chardin en Perse.* Amsterdam, 1711.

Charlevoix, Pierre François Xavier de. *Histoire et description générale de la Nouvelle France.* Paris, 1744.

Chateaubriand, François René, Vicomte de. *Itinéraire de Paris à Jerusalem.* Paris: Le Normant, 1811.

Cheek, Pamela. "Prostitutes of 'Political Institution.'" *Eighteenth-Century Studies* 28, no. 2 (winter 1994–1995): 193–219.

Conroy, Peter. *Crébillon-fils: Techniques of the Novel. Studies on Voltaire and the Eighteenth Century.* Banbury: Voltaire Foundation, monograph 99, 1972.

Crampe-Casnabet, Michèle. "Saisie dans les oeuvres philosophiques." In *Histoire des femmes,* vol. 3, edited by Georges Duby and Michèle Perrot. Paris: Plon, 1991.

Crébillon, Claude Prosper Jolyot de. Atalzaïde. Paris, 1745.

———. *Les amours de Zéokinizul, roi des Kofirans.* Amsterdam: Michel, 1746.

———. *L'Écumoire: Histoire japonaise (The Skimmer).* Brussels: H. Kistemaeckers, 1733.

———. *Le Sopha.* 1742. Paris: Le Divan, 1930.

Creech, James. *Diderot: Thresholds of Representation.* Columbus: Ohio State University Press, 1986.

Creuzer, Georg Friedrich. *Symbolik und Mythologie der alten Volker besonders der Griechen.* Leipzig: K. W. Leske, 1810–1812.

Daudet, Alphonse. *Aventures prodigieuses de Tartarin de Tarascon.* 1872. Paris: E. Dentu, 1886.

David-Weill, Nathalie. *Rêve de pierre.* Geneva: Droz, 1989.

Davis, David Brion. *The Problem of Slavery in Western Culture.* New York: Oxford University Press, 1988.

Defoe, Daniel. *Roxana, or the Fortunate Mistress.* London: 1724.

Denon, Dominique Vivant. *Point de lendemain* (1777 version). Paris: Gallimard, 1995.

———. *Voyage dans la Basse et la Haute Égypte pendant les campagnes du Général Bonaparte.* 2 vols. Cairo: Institut Français d'Archéologie Orientale du Caire, 1989–1990.

Derrida, Jacques. "Plato's Pharmacy." In *Dissemination.* Translated by Barbara Johnson, 61–171. Chicago: University of Chicago Press, 1981.

Desan, Suzanne. "'War between Brothers and Sisters': Inheritance Law and Gender Politics in Revolutionary France." *French Historical Studies* 20, no. 4 (fall 1997): 597–634.

Dictionnaire de Trévoux (Dictionnaire universel du français et latin). 3 vols. Paris, 1704.

Diderot, Denis. *Les Bijoux indiscrets (The Indiscreet Jewels).* 1748. In *Oeuvres complètes,* vol. 3. Paris: Hermann, 1978.

———. "Hottentots." In *Encyclopédie, ou dictionnaire raisonné des sciences, des arts et des métiers,* edited by Denis Diderot and Jean Le Rond D'Alembert, 320–21. Paris: Briasson, 1751–1765.

———. *Lettre sur les sourds et muets.* 1751. In *Oeuvres complètes,* vol. 2.

———. *Le Neveu de Rameau.* 1762. In *Oeuvres complètes,* vol. 10.

———. *Oeuvres complètes.* Edited by Roger Lewinter and Yvon Belval. 15 vols. Paris: Le Club Français du Livre, 1969–1973.

———. *Diderot, Oeuvres.* Edited by Laurent Versini. 5 vols. Paris: Robert Laffont, 1994–1997.

———. *Oeuvres de Denis Diderot publiées sur les manuscrits de l'auteur par Jacques-André Naigeon*. 15 vols. Paris: Desray, 1798.

———. *Oevres de Diderot*. Edited by André Billy. 2 vols. Paris: Gallimard, Bibliothèque de la Pléïade, 1946.

———. *L'Oiseau blanc, conte bleu*. 1747. In *Oeuvres complètes*, vol. 1.

———. *Pensées philosophiques*. 1746. In *Oeuvres complètes*, vol. 1.

———. *Supplément au voyage de Bougainville*. 1772. In *Oeuvres complètes*, vol. 10.

Diderot, Denis, and Jean Le Rond D'Alembert, eds. *Encyclopédie, ou dictionnaire raisonné des sciences, des arts et des métiers*. Paris: Briasson, 1751–1765.

Dobie, Madeleine. "'Langage inconnu': Montesquieu, Graffigny and the Writing of Exile." *Romanic Review* 87, no. 2 (March 1996): 209–24.

Douthwaite, Julia. *Exotic Women: Literary Heroines and Cultural Strategies*. Philadelphia: University of Pennsylvania Press, 1992.

Duchet, Michèle. *Anthropologie et Histoire au siècle des lumières: Buffon, Voltaire, Rousseau, Helvétius, Diderot*. Paris: Maspéro, 1981.

Duckett, William A. *La Turquie pittoresque: Histoire, Moeurs, Description*. Paris: Victor Lecou, 1855.

Duclos, Charles. *Acajou et Zirphile; conte*. Paris, 1744.

———. *Les Confessions du Comte de****. 1742. Paris: Éditions de l'amateur, 1970.

Dufrenoy, Marie-Louise. *L'Orient romanesque en France, 1704–1789*. Montreal: Beauchemin, 1946.

Du Vignau, Sieur des Joanots. *État présent de la puissance ottomane*. Paris, 1687.

L'Express. November 17–23, 1994.

Fanon, Frantz. "Algeria Unveiled." In *A Dying Colonialism* (*L'An V de la révolution algérienne*). Translated by Haakon Chevalier, 35–67. New York: Grove Press, 1965.

Feydeau, Ernest. *Histoire des usages funèbres et des sépultures des peuples anciens*. Paris: Gide, 1856–1858.

Figaro Magazine. October 26, 1985.

Flaubert, Gustave. *Correspondence*. 4 vols. Paris: Pléïade, 1973.

———. *Hérodias*. In *Trois contes*. Paris: G. Charpentier, 1877.

———. *Salammbô*. Paris: M. Lévy, 1863.

———. *Voyage en Égypte*. 1850s/1910. Edited by Pierre-Marc de Biasi. Paris: Grasset, 1991.

Flint, Christopher. "Speaking Objects: The Circulation of Stories in Eighteenth-Century Prose Fiction." *PMLA* 113, no. 2 (March 1998): 212–26.

Fontenay, Elisabeth de. *Diderot, Reason and Resonance.* Translated by Jeffrey Mehlman. New York: J. Brazillier, 1982.

Foucault, Michel. *L'Archéologie du savoir.* Paris: Gallimard, 1969.

———. *The Archaeology of Knowledge.* Translated by A. M. Sheridan Smith. New York: Pantheon, 1972.

———. *Discipline and Punish: The Birth of the Prison.* Translated by Alan Sheridan. New York: Pantheon, 1977.

———. *The History of Sexuality.* Translated by Robert Hurley. 3 vols. New York: Random House, 1980.

———. *Surveiller et punir: naissance de la prison.* Paris: Gallimard, 1975.

———. "What Is Enlightenment?" In *The Foucault Reader,* edited by Paul Rabinow, 32–50. New York: Pantheon Books, 1984.

Fougeret de Montbrun. *Le Canapé couleur de feu.* Amsterdam: La Compagnie des Libraires, 1741.

France. Commission des Sciences et des Arts d'Égypte. *Description de l'Égypte, ou Recueil des observations et des recherches qui ont été faites en Égypte pendant l'expédition de l'armée française.* 23 vols. Paris: Imprimerie Impériale, 1809–1828.

Freud, Sigmund. "Fetishism." 1927. In *The Standard Edition of Freud's Complete Psychological Works,* vol. 21. Translated by James Strachey. London: Hogarth Press, 1953.

———. *The Interpretation of Dreams.* 1900. In *The Standard Edition of Freud's Complete Psychological Works,* vols. 4 and 5. Translated by James Strachey. London: Hogarth Press, 1953.

Fromentin, Eugène. *Un Été dans le Sahara.* Paris: M. Lévy Frères, 1857.

———. *Une année dans le Sahel.* Paris: M. Lévy, 1859.

Furetière, Antoine. *Dictionnaire universel.* La Haye: Arnout et Renier Leers, 1690.

Gallop, Jane. "Snatches of Conversation." In *Women and Language in Literature and Society,* edited by Ruth Barker, Sally McConnell-Ginet, and Nelly Furman, 274–83. New York: Praeger, 1980.

Gates, Henry Louis, Jr. "Writing 'Race' and the Difference It Makes." In *"Race," Writing and Difference,* edited by Henry Louis Gates, Jr., 1–19. Chicago: Chicago University Press, 1986.

Gautier, Théophile. *Constantinople.* Paris: M. Lévy, 1853.

———. *Émaux et camées.* 1852. Paris: Gallimard, 1981.

——. *Loin de Paris*. Paris: Michel Lévy, 1865.

——. *Mademoiselle de Maupin*. 1835. Paris: Garnier, 1955.

——. *Une nuit de Cléopâtre*. 1838. Paris: A. Ferroud, 1894.

——. *Le Pied de momie*. 1840. In *Contes et récits fantastiques*. Paris: Librairie générale française, 1990.

——. *Le Roman de la momie*. 1857. Paris: Gallimard, 1986.

——. *Voyage en Algérie*. Paris: Boîte à documents, 1989.

——. *Voyage en Égypte*. Paris: La Boîte à Documents, 1996.

Genlis, Stéphanie-Félicité de. *Manuel de la jeune femme: guide complet de la maîtresse de maison*. Paris: Charles-Bechet, 1829.

Girardet, Raoul. *L'Idée coloniale en France de 1871 à 1962*. Paris: Éditions de la Table Ronde, 1972.

Gobineau, Joseph-Arthur, Comte de. *Essai sur l'inégalité des races humaines*. Paris: Firmin-Didot, 1853–1855.

Godfrey, Sima. "Mummy Dearest: Cryptic Codes in Gautier's *Pied de momie*." *Romanic Review* 75, no. 3 (May 1984): 302–11.

Gomberville, Marin le Roy, Sieur de. *Polexandre*. Paris: A. Courbé, 1641.

Gomez, Madeleine-Angélique Poisson de. *Anecdotes, ou Histoire secrète de la maison ottomane*. Amsterdam, 1722.

——. *Histoire d'Osman, premier du nom, XIXème empereur des Turcs, et de l'impératrice Aphendina Ashada*. Paris: Prault, 1734.

Goodman, Dena. "Public Sphere and Private Life: Toward a Synthesis of Current Historical Approaches to the Ancien Régime." *History and Theory: Studies in the Philosophy of History* 31, no. 1 (1992): 1–20.

——. *The Republic of Letters: A Cultural History of the French Enlightenment*. Ithaca, N.Y.: Cornell University Press, 1994.

Graffigny, Françoise de. *Lettres d'une Péruvienne*. 1747. New York: Modern Language Association of America, 1993.

Grosrichard, Alain. *La Structure du sérail: La fiction du sérail dans l'occident classique*. Paris: Seuil, 1979.

Grotius, Hugo. *De jure bellis ac Pacis*, 1625.

Habermas, Jürgen. *The Structural Transformation of the Public Sphere: An Inquiry into a Category of Bourgeois Society*. Translated by Thomas Burger and Frederick Lawrence. Cambridge, Mass.: MIT Press, 1991.

Harari, Josué. *Scenarios of the Imaginary: Theorizing the French Enlightenment*. Ithaca, N.Y.: Cornell University Press, 1987.

Harbsmeier, Michael. "Early Travels to Europe: Some Remarks on the Magic of Writing." In *Europe and Its Others*, edited by Francis Barker et al., vol. 1, 72–88.

Heidegger, Martin. "Aletheia (Heraclitus, Fragment B16)." In *Early Greek Thinking*, translated by David Farrell Krell and Frank A. Capuzzi, 102–23. San Francisco: Harper and Row, 1984.

Hénault, Charles Jean François. *La Petite Maison*. Paris, 1769 (first performed privately, ca. 1740).

Hout, Syrine Chafic. *Viewing Europe from the Outside: Cultural Encounters and Critiques in the Eighteenth-Century Pseudo-Oriental Travelogue and the Nineteenth-Century 'Voyage en Orient.'* New York: Peter Lang, 1997.

Huet, Marie-Hélène. *Monstrous Imagination*. Cambridge: Harvard University Press, 1992.

Hunt, Lynn. *The Family Romance of the French Revolution*. Berkeley: University of California Press, 1993.

Huysmans, Joris-Karl. *A Rebours*. Paris: G. Charpentier, 1884.

Irigaray, Luce. *This Sex Which Is Not One. [Ce sexe qui n'en est pas un].* Translated by Catherine Porter and Carolyn Burke. Ithaca, New York: Cornell University Press, 1985.

Janneau, Guillaume. *Historique du meuble*. Paris: Éditions d'Art Charles Moreau, 1948.

Jaucourt, Louis de. "Despotisme" (Despotism); "Esclavage" (Slavery); "Esclave" (Slave). In *Encyclopédie, ou dictionnaire raisonné des sciences, des arts et des métiers*, edited by Denis Diderot and Jean Le Rond D'Alembert, 4: 886–889; 5: 934–39; 5: 939–43. Paris: Briasson, 1751–1765.

Johnson, Barbara. *The Critical Difference: Essays in the Contemporary Rhetoric of Reading*. Baltimore, Md.: Johns Hopkins University Press, 1980.

Jordanova, Ludmilla. *Sexual Visions: Images of Gender in Science and Medicine between the Eighteenth and Twentieth Centuries*. Madison: University of Wisconsin Press, 1989.

Kandiyoti, Deniz. "The Nation and Its Discontents." In *Colonial Discourse and Post-Colonial Theory*, edited by Laura Chrisman and Patrick Williams, 376–91. New York: Columbia University Press, 1994.

Kavanagh, Thomas. "Language as Deception or the *Indiscreet Jewels*." *Diderot Studies* 23 (1988): 101–13.

Klein, Lawrence. "Gender and the Public/Private Distinction in the Eighteenth Century: Some Questions about Evidence and Analytic Procedure." *Eighteenth-Century Studies* 29, no. 1 (fall 1995): 97–109.

Kofman, Sarah. *The Enigma of Woman: Women in Freud's Writings.* Translated by Catherine Porter. Ithaca, N.Y.: Cornell University Press, 1985.

Koselleck, Reinhart. *Critique and Crisis: Enlightenment and the Pathenogenesis of Modern Society.* Cambridge, Mass.: MIT Press, 1988.

Kristeva, Julia. *Des Chinoises.* Paris: Des Femmes, 1974.

Laclos, Choderlos de. *Dangerous Liaisons.* 1787. Translated by Douglas Parmée. New York: Oxford University Press, 1995.

La Fayette, Madame de. *Princesse de Clèves.* Paris: Claude Barbin, 1678.

La Mettrie, Julien Offray de. *L'Homme machine.* Leiden, France: Luzac fils, 1748.

Lamartine, Alphonse de. *Souvenirs, impressions, pensées et paysages pendant un Voyage en Orient, 1823–1833.* 1835. Paris: Nizet, 1849.

Landes, Joan. *Women and the Public Sphere in the Age of the French Revolution.* Ithaca, N.Y.: Cornell University Press, 1988.

Laplanche, J., and J. B. Pontalis. *Le Vocabulaire de la psychanalyse.* Paris: Presses Universitaires de France, 1967.

Laqueur, Thomas. *Making Sex: The Body and Gender from the Greeks to Freud.* Cambridge: Harvard University Press, 1990.

Lazreg, Marnia. "Feminism and Difference: The Perils of Writing as a Woman on Women in Algeria." *Feminist Studies* 14, no. 1 (spring 1988): 81–107.

Lemoine-Luccioni, Eugénie. *La Robe: Essai psychanalytique sur le vêtement.* Paris: Seuil, 1983.

Link, Viktor. "The Reception of Crébillon-fils's *The Sofa* in England: An Unnoticed Edition and Some Imitations." *Studies on Voltaire and the Eighteenth Century* 132 (1975): 192–203.

Lokke, Kari. *Gérard de Nerval: The Poet as Social Visionary.* Lexington, Ky.: French Forum, 1987.

Loti, Pierre. *Aziyadé.* Paris: Calmann-Lévy, 1879.

Lowe, Lisa. *Critical Terrains: British and French Orientalisms.* Ithaca, N.Y.: Cornell University Press, 1991.

MacDonald, Christie V. "Robe." *Stanford French Review* 8, nos. 2–3 (fall 1984): 167–74.

Mackenzie, James. *Orientalism: History, Theory and the Arts.* Manchester: Manchester University Press, 1995.

Mallarmé, Stéphane. "Ballets." In *Oeuvres complètes.* Paris: Pléiade, 1945.

———. *Hérodiade.* 1864–1898. In *Les Noces d'Hérodiade,* edited by Gardner Davies. Paris: Gallimard, 1959.

Marivaux, Pierre Carlet Chamblain de. *Le Paysan parvenu.* In *Romans de Marivaux.* Paris: Pléïade, 1949.

Marmontel, Jean-François. *Les Incas ou la déstruction de l'empire du Pérou.* Paris: C. Lacombe, 1777.

Martino, Pierre. *L'Orient dans la littérature française au 17è et au 18è siècle.* Geneva: Slatkine Reprints, 1970.

Marx, Karl. *Capital: A Critique of Political Economy.* Translated by Ben Fowkes. 3 vols. New York: Vintage, 1977.

Maupassant, Guy de. *Au Soleil.* Paris: Victor Harvard, 1884.

Maupertuis, Pierre de. *Dissertation physique à l'occasion du nègre blanc.* Leiden, 1744.

———. *Vénus physique suivi de la Lettre sur le progrès des sciences.* 1745. Paris: Aubier-Montaigne, 1980.

McClintock, Anne. *Imperial Leather: Race, Gender and Sexuality in the Colonial Context.* New York: Routledge, 1995.

Menocal, Maria-Rosa. *The Arabic Role in Medieval Literary History: A Forgotten Heritage.* Philadelphia: University of Pennsylvania Press, 1987.

Mercier, Louis-Sébastien. *L'An deux mille quatre cent quarante.* Amsterdam: E. Van Harrevelt, 1770.

Mernissi, Fatima. *Beyond the Veil: Male–Female Dynamics in a Modern Muslim Society.* Cambridge, Mass.: Schenkman, 1975.

Mervaud, Christiane. "La Narration interrompue dans *Le Sopha* de Crébillon." *Studies on Voltaire and the Eighteenth Century* 249 (1987): 183–95.

Michelet, Jules. *La Femme.* 1859. Paris: Flammarion, 1981.

Miller, Christopher L. *Blank Darkness: Africanist Discourse in French.* Chicago: University of Chicago Press, 1985.

Mirabeau, Victor de Riquetti, Marquis de. *L'Ami des hommes.* Avignon, France, 1756.

Mohanty, Chandra Talpade. "Under Western Eyes: Feminist Scholarship and Colonial Discourses." In *Third World Women and the Politics of Feminism*, edited by Chandra Mohanty, Ann Russo, and Lourdes Torres, 51–80. Bloomington: Indiana University Press, 1991.

Montagu, Mary Wortley. *The Letters of the Right Honourable Lady Mary Wortley Montagu: Written during Her Travels in Europe, Africa and Asia.* London: T. Becket, 1763. Reprinted as *The Complete Letters of Mary Wortley Montagu.* Oxford: Oxford University Press, 1965.

———. *Turkish Embassy Letters.* 1763. Athens: University of Georgia Press, 1993.

Montesquieu, Charles-Louis de Secondat, Baron de la Brède et de. *Considérations sur les richesses de l'Espagne* (*Considerations on the Wealth of Spain*). In *Oeuvres complètes*, vol. 2. Edited by Roger Caillois. Paris: Gallimard, 1951.

———. *De l'Esprit des lois.* 1748. In *Oeuvres complètes*, vol. 2.

———. *Lettres persanes.* 1721. In *Oeuvres complètes*, vol. 1.

———. *Lettres persanes.* Paris: Louis Lacour, 1869.

———. *Mes Pensées.* 1720–1755/1899–1901. In *Oeuvres complètes*, vol. 1.

———. *Oeuvres complètes.* Edited by Roger Caillois. 2 vols. Paris: Gallimard, Bibliothèque de la Pléiade, 1949–1951.

———. *Oeuvres complètes de Montesquieu.* Edited by André Masson. 3 vols. Paris: Nagel, 1950– .

———. *"Le Temple de Gnide" and "Arsace et Isménie."* Paris: Didot Jeune, 1794.

Morlière, Charles de la. *Angola.* Paris, 1746.

Nerval, Gérard de. *Angélique.* 1851 In *Les Filles de Feu: Nouvelles.* Paris: D. Giraud, 1854.

———. *Les Illuminés; récits et portraits.* Paris: V. Lecou, 1852.

———. *Oeuvres complètes.* 2 vols. Paris: Pléiade, 1952–1956.

———. *Sylvie.* 1853. In *Oeuvres complètes.* Paris: Pléiade, 1952–1956.

———. *Voyage en Orient.* 1851. Edited by Michel Jeanneret. 2 vols. Paris: Garnier-Flammarion, 1980.

———. *Voyage en Orient.* Edited by Gilbert Rouger. 4 vols. Paris: Éditions Richelieu, 1950.

Nietzsche, Friedrich. *Beyond Good and Evil.* 1886. Translated by Walter Kaufmann. New York: Vintage, 1966.

Nochlin, Linda. "The Imaginary Orient." *Art in America* 71 (May 1983): 118–31; 187–91.

Pipes, Daniel. *In the Path of God: Islam and Political Power.* New York: Basic Books, 1983.

Porter, Dennis. *Haunted Journeys: Desire and Transgression in European Travel Writing.* Princeton, N.J.: Princeton University Press, 1991.

Poulain de la Barre, François. *De l'égalité des deux sexes.* Paris: Jean Du Puis, 1673.

Pratt, Mary Louise. *Imperial Eyes: Travel Writing and Transculturation.* London: Routledge, 1992.

Prévost, Abbé. *Histoire générale des voyages.* Paris: Didot, 1746–1789.

———. *Manon Lescaut.* Rouen, 1733.

———. *Le Pour et le contre.* Paris: Didot, 1733–1740.

Pucci, Suzanne Rodin. "Letters from the Harem: Veiled Figures of Writing in Montesquieu's *Lettres persanes.*" In *Writing the Female Voice: Essays on Epistolary Literature*, edited by Elizabeth C. Goldsmith, 114–34. Boston: Northeastern University Press, 1989.

Puisieux, Mme de. *L'Histoire des amours de Sapho de Mytilène.* 1743.

Racine, Jean. *Bajazet.* Paris: 1672.

Raynal, Abbé Guillaume Thomas François, and Denis Diderot. *Histoire philosophique et politique du commerce et des établissements des Européens dans les deux Indes.* 6 vols. Amsterdam, 1770.

Regnard, Jean-François. *Le Distrait.* Paris, 1697.

Revue des deux mondes. Paris: July 1, 1848.

Roger, Jacques. *Buffon: Un philosophe au jardin du roi.* Paris: Fayard, 1989.

Roubo, André. *L'Art du menuisier en meubles.* 1769. Paris: 1772.

Rousseau, Jean-Jacques. *Discours sur l'origine et les fondements de l'inégalité.* Amsterdam: Michel Rey, 1755.

———. *Du Contrat social.* Amsterdam: MM Rey, 1762.

———. *Émile.* 1760. Paris: Garnier-Flammarion, 1966.

———. *Julie ou la Nouvelle Héloise,* 1761.

———. *Oeuvres complètes.* Paris: Pléiade, 1964.

———. *Politics and the Arts: Letter to d'Alembert on the Theatre.* 1758. Translated and edited by Allan Bloom. Ithaca, N.Y.: Cornell University Press, 1968.

———. *Rêveries du promeneur solitaire.* 1780. Paris: Garnier-Flammarion, 1964.

Rycaut, Paul. *Present State of the Ottoman Empire.* London: John Starkey and Henry Broome, 1668.

Sacy, Antoine Isaac, Baron Silvestre de. *Exposé de la religion des Druzes.* Paris: l'Imprimerie Royale, 1838.

Said, Edward. *Culture and Imperialism.* New York: Vintage, 1994.

———. *Orientalism.* New York: Pantheon, 1978.

———. "Orientalism Reconsidered." In *Europe and Its Others*, edited by Francis Barker et al., vol. 1, 14–27.

Saint-Lambert, Jean-François, Marquis de. *Ziméo.* 1769. In *Contes américains.* Exeter, UK: Exeter University Press, 1997.

Sala-Molins, Louis. *Le Code Noir ou le calvaire de Canaan.* Paris: Presses Universitaires de France, 1987.

Schaeffer, Gérald. *Le Voyage en Orient de Nerval. Étude des structures.* Neuchâtel: La Baconnière, 1967.

Schaub, Diana J. *Erotic Liberalism: Women and Revolution in Montesquieu's Persian Letters.* London: Rowman and Littlefield, 1995.

Schopenhauer, Arthur. *The World as Will and Representation*. 1819. Translated by E. F. J. Payne. New York: Dover, 1966.

Schor, Naomi. *Breaking the Chain: Women, Theory and French Realist Fiction*. New York: Columbia University Press, 1985.

Schuerewegen, Franc. "Histoires de pieds: Gautier, Lorrain et le fantastique." *Nineteenth-Century French Studies* 13, no. 4 (summer 1985): 200–210.

Schwab, Raymond. *The Oriental Renaissance: Europe's Rediscovery of India and the East*. Translated by Gene Patterson-Black and Victor Reinking. New York: Columbia University Press, 1984.

Scott, Katie. *The Rococo Interior*. New Haven, Conn.: Yale University Press, 1995.

Sharpley-Whiting, Tracy Denean. *Black Venus: Sexualized Savages, Primal Fears and Primitive Narratives in French*. Durham, N.C.: Duke University Press, 1999.

Starobinski, Jean. *Montesquieu par lui-même*. Paris: Seuil, 1953.

Stewart, Philip. *Le Masque et la Parole*. Paris: José Corti, 1973.

Stoler, Ann Laura. *Race and the Education of Desire: Foucault's History of Sexuality and the Colonial Order of Things*. Durham, N.C.: Duke University Press, 1995.

Suleiman, Susan. *Authoritarian Fictions: The Ideological Novel as a Literary Genre*. New York: Columbia University Press, 1983.

Terdiman, Richard. *Discourse/Counter-Discourse: The Theory and Practice of Symbolic Resistance in Nineteenth-Century France*. Ithaca, N.Y.: Cornell University Press, 1985.

Thévenot, Jean de. *Voyages de M. de Thévenot, tant en Europe qu'en Asie et en Afrique*. Paris: Charles Angot, 1689.

Thomas, Antoine Léonard. *Essai sur le caractère, les moeurs, et l'esprit des femmes dans les différents siècles*. Paris: Moutard, 1772.

Todorov, Tzvetan. *Introduction à la littérature fantastique*. Paris: Seuil, 1970.

———. *Nous et les autres, la réflexion française sur la diversité humaine*. Paris: Seuil, 1989.

———. *On Human Diversity: Nationalism, Racism and Exoticism in French Thought*. Translated by Catherine Porter. Cambridge, Mass.: Harvard University Press, 1997.

Vallois, Marie-Claire. "Rêverie Orientale et géopolitique du corps féminin chez Montesquieu." *Romance Quarterly* 38, no. 3 (1991): 363–71.

Vandal, Albert. *Une Ambassade française en Orient sous Louis XV*. Paris: Plon, 1887.

Vanmour, Jean-Baptiste. *Recueil de cent estampes représentant les différentes nations du Levant.* Paris: 1714.

Venturi, Franco. *Jeunesse de Diderot (1713–1753).* Translated by Juliette Bertrand. Geneva: Slatkine Reprints, 1967.

Vernière, Paul. *Montesquieu et l'Esprit des lois, ou la raison impure.* Paris: Société d'Édition d'Enseignement Supérieur, 1977.

Villedieu, Mme de. *Alcidamie.* Paris: C. Barbin, 1661.

———. *Mémoires du sérail* and *Nouvelles afriquaines* (1670–1671?). In *Oeuvres complètes,* vol. 6. Paris: Veuve Barbin, 1720.

Voisenon, Claude Henri de. *Le Sultan Misapouf et la Princesse Grisemine.* London, 1746.

Volney, Constantin-François de Chasseboeuf. *Voyage en Égypte et en Syrie.* 1787. In *Oeuvres complètes de Volney.* Paris: Firmin-Didot Frères, 1846.

Voltaire, François Marie Arouet de. *Alzire ou les Américains.* Amsterdam: E. Ledet, 1736.

———. *Candide ou l'Optimisme.* 1759.

———. *Dialogues entre A.B.C.* In *Oeuvres complètes de Voltaire.* Paris: Garnier, 1879.

———. *Essai sur les moeurs et l'esprit des nations et sur les principaux faits de l'histoire depuis Charlemagne jusqu'à Louis XIII.* Geneva, 1756.

———. *Précis du Siècle de Louis XIV.* Geneva, 1769.

———. *Le Siècle de Louis XIV.* Berlin: C. F. Henning, 1751.

Weill, Françoise. "Montesquieu et le despotisme." In *Actes du colloque de Montesquieu, Bordeaux 1955.* Bordeaux: Imprimeries Delmas, 1956.

Index

In this index *passim* is used for a cluster of references in close but not consecutive sequence.